B. B. Zayon

MIDNIGHT ECONOMIST

MIDNIGHT ECONOMIST

Choices, Prices, and Public Policy

WILLIAM R. ALLEN

Introduction by Milton Friedman

PLAYBOY PRESS

Library of Congress Cataloging in Publication Data

Allen, William Richard, 1924-
    Midnight economist.

    Radio and television commentaries broadcast
July 1979-Feb. 1981.
      1. Economics—Addresses, essays, lectures. I. Title.
HB171.A46   330   81-80405
ISBN 0-87223-699-4   AACR2

Designed by Tere LoPrete

CONTENTS

Mainly Macroeconomics: Income and
Monetary Analysis

Contents

Contents

INTRODUCTION

I have always been fascinated by what seems a puzzle about
economics. On the one side, the fundamental principles of
economics are elementary—simple common sense, seemingly
accessible to every intelligent person. On the other side,
many very intelligent persons fail to understand them and
err egregiously in applying them to specific problems.

Surely, it is the simplest common sense that a low price
for any product will encourage buyers and discourage sellers;
that a high price will discourage buyers and encourage sellers.
Whence then the indignation, the uproar, the charges of
fraud and villainy when the legal fixing of a *maximum* price
for rental quarters—that is, an artificially low price—produces more prospective buyers of rental space than prospective sellers? Or when the legal fixing of a *minimum* price for
an hour of unskilled labor—that is, an artificially high price
—produces fewer prospective buyers of that labor than
prospective sellers?

Economics, it seems, is more than obvious common sense.
It is also a way of reasoning, of thinking about problems.
Many are the occasions in which I have participated in dis-
cussions about policies involving economic issues in which
those participating have included economists of all shades of
political opinion together with noneconomists of all shades
of political opinion. Almost whatever the subject of discussion, the outcome after a brief interval is predictable. The
economists will be found aligned on one side of the subject—
the free enterprisers along with the central planners, the
Republicans along with the Democrats, libertarians, and
generally even the socialists—along with a few allies; the
bulk of the group—academics, businessmen, lawyers, you

name it—generally on the other. I have been amused to observe the same phenomenon, if in somewhat muted form, emerge even when the subject of discussion has been rather far removed from economics—foreign policy, or academic policy, for example.

Some people have a natural instinct for economics and the economic way of reasoning, and some people are completely lacking in such an instinct—just as some people have an aptitude for mathematics or an ear for music and other people do not. And just as a great man may lack an ear for music, so also he may lack a feeling for economics. My favorite example—for economics, not music—is Winston Churchill, surely one of the greatest men of our time or any time. Yet when it came to economics, he came a cropper every time he had occasion to get involved, whether before World War I when he played a leading role in the early development of the welfare state, between the wars when as chancellor of the Exchequer he decided to return the British currency to gold at the prewar parity, or after World War II when as prime minister he decided to retain a fixed exchange rate for the pound instead of permitting it to float.

A striking example on the opposite side—a noneconomist who had a real feel for economics—was Leo Szilard, a famous natural scientist who played a key role in persuading President Franklin Roosevelt to initiate the Manhattan Project to develop the atomic bomb. Leo, a colleague of mine at the University of Chicago, was always coming around, tapping me on the shoulder, and saying, "You know, I've been thinking about . . ." and out would come a sophisticated economic proposition, original with him though generally well known to professional economists. More surprising, it was usually correct—he was almost the only physical scientist, I may say, with whom I have had that experience.

While some people may be tone-deaf to economics and other people born economists, for most people economic reasoning is an acquired skill—and taste. That, at least, is the only way I have been able to justify spending the best years of my life trying to teach elementary common sense—often dressed up, it is true, in fancy mathematical clothes—to successive generations of students.

William Allen is a professional economist with a natural ear for economics. He reasons like an economist, eats, sleeps, and breathes economics, as a good economist should. But he has something else, a quality that is far rarer—the ability to explain his economic reasoning to others, in language they can understand, and in language that will intrigue and interest them. He has demonstrated his skill over the years in the classroom. He demonstrates it even more dramatically in the gems of radio and television commentaries reprinted in this book.

Bill's commentaries are not sugarcoated pills to be swallowed by the listener with no questions asked. They seldom tell the listener the answer. That is not Bill's aim. His genius is in bringing into the open the elementary principles involved in an issue so that his listener or reader will be induced to think about the problem on his own and to think about the economic principles in a different way. As the poet has it, "He that complies against his will is of his own opinion still." No one else can persuade us. We must persuade ourselves. But someone else can help us find the right way to think about a problem, to break it down, recognize the familiar ideas in an unfamiliar guise, enable us to make up our own minds.

That is what Bill Allen does over and over again in these commentaries. I marvel at his versatility, the wide range of problems and issues he covers, and even more at his skill at finding a fresh and arresting way to present each item. He is skillful at finding arresting turns of phrases precisely applicable to the particular issue he is dealing with.

Few people will be able to read—or read widely in—this

book without being both educated and entertained, without finding themselves questioning beliefs they have long taken for granted, and forming new beliefs. Best of all, some will even end up reasoning like economists.

MILTON FRIEDMAN

FOREWORD

The radio and television commentaries printed here were broadcast, on behalf of the International Institute for Economic Research, over a period of about a year and a half, from July 1979 into February 1981. Most of them were previously distributed by the Institute in three pamphlets and also in monthly flyers.

The audience demand for publication of these broadcasts could hardly have been vast (they were aired at midnight, and professionals in the electronic-media game have hinted to me that midnight is not generally considered "prime" time), and it is not my belief that inscribing these commentaries in stone is either a necessary or a sufficient condition for the salvation of Western civilization. Still, there is something of the ephemeral in broadcasting: The product is consumed—or otherwise disappears—in the moment of its creation. (One is reminded of an unfortunate distinction by the great Adam Smith between "productive" and "unproductive" labor. The former, in contrast to the latter, "fixes and realizes itself in some particular subject or vendible commodity which lasts for some time at least after that labor is past. It is, as it were, a certain quantity of labor stocked and stored up." Smith made no mention of broadcast commentators, but he included such as opera singers and teachers among laborers who, although useful, must be classified as unproductive.) Perhaps for a few, preservation of this selection of brief remarks in a form less permanent than stone but not as transitory as mere echoes will justify the investment.

These remarks are brief indeed: Each commentary was delivered in approximately three minutes. In their preparation, time for presentation was not the only constraint. The audience is diverse in various dimensions, and it includes few specialists in economics. It receives no prior announcement of topics, much less a reading assignment, and it is not to be later tested and graded on how well it has listened; it can only listen—and research into the psychology of learning indicates that we comprehend better through the eye than through the ear.

Still, the intent has been to provide to a lay audience capsules of reputable economics, useful applications of well-established, elemental analytics. The analysis itself, the substantive content, was to be dispassionate utilization of those fundamental concepts and techniques that economists have laboriously developed and quite generally adopted. The exposition, however, designed to catch the ear at midnight, may at times be rather more vigorous and colloquial than usually provided by an academic.

Actually, some of these commentaries have been broadcast at various hours, for they have been heard on several series. One is nationally syndicated by the Public Affairs Broadcast Group (P.O. Box 48911; Los Angeles, California 90048). Indeed, the president of PABG, Mark Bragg, was responsible for inflicting the initial presentation of a weekly, two-minute commentary on some 150 stations in January 1979. In July, the commentaries were lengthened to three minutes, and a separate one-minute weekly series was added to the PABG distribution, the two programs reaching a total of about 250 stations.

At the same time, the "Midnight Economist" broadcasts were begun on KBIG, the largest FM station in southern California (7755 Sunset Boulevard; Los Angeles 90046). (Although the Midnight Economist speaks every night, each commentary is repeated a second night, so some fifteen new pieces are presented during a month.) Beginning in August 1980, the commentaries have been presented five days a week, twice each day, on television channel 22, KWHY (5545 Sunset Boulevard; Los Angeles 90028). I am indebted for encouragement and professional guidance to Mark Bragg; to Phil Reed, director of news and public affairs, KBIG; and to Rodney Buchser, operations manager, KWHY.

The KBIG series, the Institute, and I have received awards—an Honor Certificate, a George Washington Honor Medal, and an Award for Excellence in Private Enterprise Education—from the Freedoms Foundation at Valley Forge.

Several of the scripts have been based on pamphlets distributed by the Institute. The pamphlet authors include: Francis A. Allen, Charles W. Baird, Peter T. Bauer, J. T. Bennett and M. H. Johnson, Tom Bethell, Harold Demsetz, Elliott M. Estes, Robert Hessen, M. C. Jensen and W. H. Meckling, Rachel McCulloch, Richard B. McKenzie, Allan H. Meltzer, William C. Mitchell, John H. Sheridan, Stephen F. Williams, and Walter B. Wriston.

Some help has been received in drafting of scripts. Indeed, very considerable assistance in recent months has come from William Dickneider. Other coauthors of one or more pieces are: Clive Bull, R. Scott Harris, Thomas W. Hazlett, Joseph Kalt, Linda Kleiger, and Vicki Lynn Ransom.

Beyond such immediate aid, there is the great body of thought and evidence accumulated from the efforts of many writers, past and contemporary. It is not feasible to note them all, but I have directly and consciously drawn heavily on some of the work of the following: Armen A. Alchian, Clark Lee Allen, Daniel Bell, Karl Brunner, James M. Buchanan, William P. Butz, Kenneth W. Clarkson, Marshall R. Colberg, Julie Da Vanzo, Martin Feldstein, Henry Ford II, Roger A. Freeman, David Friedman, Axel Leijonhufvud, the National Federation of Independent Business, Paul Craig Roberts, and Murray L. Weidenbaum.

The words of the "Midnight Economist" are (generally) mine. As any fellow professional in economics would recognize, the essentials of substance come entirely from the common heritage.

General Meditations

❧❧❧

ECONOMISTS AND
THEIR WORLD

How Come Economists Never Get Together with Themselves?

(July 1979)

Everyone knows that if all economists were placed end-to-end, they would reach . . . no conclusion—or at least not the *same conclusion*.

Does it matter what economists do and how well they do it? Well, the *subject* of economics matters. Economics deals with the most basic and pervasive issues of how society is organized and how individuals behave. We live in a world of scarcity and thus in a world of conflict and tears. We do well, therefore, to use our limited resources efficiently. Economists study the management of scarce resources.

Economics is a complex subject, and much is not yet understood. But ignorance does not distinguish economists uniquely. Nor are economists unique in disagreeing. Doctors, clergymen, Supreme Court justices, and gardeners, too, lack omniscience and have been known to quarrel.

The degree of disagreement among economists on fundamentals is often exaggerated. Still, the arguments can be disconcerting, for economics deals with very important matters. Since nearly all economists seek truth nearly all the time, how can they differ?

One explanation is incompetence. Some economists are simply not very good.

But dull-wittedness is not to be confused with *incomplete knowledge and imperfect analytic techniques*. The brightest of economists can be uncertain to some extent about the price and output effects of deregulating natural gas, or the employment and income-distribution effects of tariff policy.

Further, like real people, economists can offer conflicting prescriptions because of conflicting social and political orientations. Two economists may largely agree on some predicted effects of a welfare or regulatory program, but disagree on how big a cost is warranted to attain those effects.

Then there are those who are less concerned with either science or philosophy than with differentiating their personal product. It is an old marketing technique to attract attention by being simplistically outrageous. The economist, like the movie producer, who can be shockingly different or play to the populist gallery may thereby prosper.

By contrast, some scholars fear to a fault for their sober image and acceptability. They are too shy to advocate fluctuating exchange rates or extol the efficiency of Adam Smith's "invisible hand" of the market when the reigning establishment prefers to peg prices and impose controls.

There will be no excessive shyness—and, I hope, no excessive innocence—in this series of broadcasts. Upon occasion, we will even reach a conclusion.

Complexity and Profundity

(FEBRUARY 1980)

There are economic problems to be resolved. They include fundamental questions of social organization. How are we to approach the issues of economics? From what orientation? On what assumptions do we build our stance? What sorts of principles and criteria and standards can we call on in our analysis of a grubby world?

Some of us, with goodly heritage, believe that people, even if descended from the angels, are selfish, acquisitive, aggressive. We believe that, unlovely as people are in many respects, it is possible to have a viable society—indeed, an adaptable, innovative, flourishing society—which not only permits but requires a great and wide span of personal freedom. This is a creative freedom, drawing on and developing the ambitions and aspirations of individuals, thereby inducing socially fruitful use of human self-centeredness. This is a community of invention, investment, construction, and accumulation, for in such a society there are rewards for productivity.

The analytical and philosophical heritage on which this hopeful but realistic view of society is built dates back most directly to the eighteenth century and Adam Smith. Its closely allied and intertwined political counterpart is represented by Thomas Jefferson, a contemporary of Smith.

But there are many among us who disparage the tradition of individualism, personal liberty and accountability, and rewarded productivity. They scorn the notion of a market and social organization with inherent processes of equilibration and optimization, of a self-generating mechanism and procedure that will induce selfish people to act in a coordinated fashion of mutual advantage. They deny the essence of American history—and do not want it continued! Their notion of organization is mandates from on high. For them, there must be a visible, concrete central authority in charge through discretionary decree. Big Brother is to command us and direct us and constrain us.   ~ Orwell's opinion

Now, not everyone hungers to be commanded, directed, and constrained. But the Big Brotherites insist that an individualist society of personal decisionmaking, while it may have had some whimsical appeal to a certain sort of eighteenth-century philosopher, is not now operational. The world has become so big, so complex, so interdependent that such private-property, market-enterprise societies are quixotic.

So, we are told that big, important problems require complex, discretionary tactics of deliberate, centralized intervention, direction, and participation. The well-being of people is too important to leave to the people themselves.

There is no more pernicious doctrine. It is a monstrous myth that large problems require convoluted solutions or totalitarian decrees. Do not confuse complexity of argument and action with profundity. An issue can be big in various dimensions and still be dealt with best through impersonal rules and coherent institutional arrangements—evenhandedly formulated and applied, administered with little *ad hoc* discretion.

Freedom and efficiency are not separable. Nor are they luxuries to be fearfully and foolishly abandoned in a complex world.

Cynicism and Sense

(JUNE 1980)

One of the devices adopted in recent years to keep college customers sufficiently content to deter burning of the administration building is having them evaluate their teachers. In these little exercises in catharsis, a few of the young scholars have lamented my "cynicism."

According to one dictionary, to be cynical is to "doubt the worth of life," and a cynic is "inclined to believe that the motives for people's actions are insincere and selfish." Well, life *is* well filled with sound and fury, but I do not instruct my charges that it is only a tale told by an idiot, signifying nothing. And an economist has solid ground for believing that people are selfish, whatever the degree of their sincerity.

An economist, after all, analyzes a world of scarcity. Scarcity gives rise to economizing. Economizing entails making choices and bearing costs. This striving to make do is not only constrained by stingy nature but is a contest with other greedy people, who compete for goods which are too few to satisfy every want. All in all, there is reason for the economist to view the world and its occupants with a dour eye.

The pain and frustration inevitably visited upon the beleaguered economist is compounded by considering the quality of public economic policy. Income stabilization, regulation of business, domestic and foreign trade restriction, welfare—whatever broad area one investigates, government policy typically is made in a disjointed, if not incoherent, manner; it is often implemented capriciously by a largely unaccountable bureaucracy; and, in its repercussions, it commonly weakens and divides the community.

But some able economists find grounds for optimism. Certainly, progress has been made on the professional front. There are many particular questions—some of them important—for which economists do not yet have good answers. But in broad, elemental outline, as well as in many interesting details, the intellectual debate over the nature of the free society and its efficient economy is over. It has been won by the proponents of the private-property, open-enterprise, price-directed mode of social order. The bullyboys of both communism and fascism do not provide significant professional competition; as analysts, the commissars and their stooges have had their ears definitively pinned back.

Even in the arena of general opinion, where the sloganeering demagogue has always had enormous advantage in playing to the gallery, the battle has not always gone badly. In recent years, not only the bulk of economists but more and more members of Congress and editorial writers appreciate flexible exchange rates, emphasize proper monetary control, and comprehend some of the consequences of overregulation of business.

The question is, will enough understand enough before it is too late? The intellectual battle has been won. The battle of policymaking and policy implementation is still in doubt.

It will require a mighty effort to bring economic policy into conformance with the established principles of freedom and efficiency. If we stumble and drift much further toward tyranny and waste and weakness, we—with most of the rest of the world—will pass the point of no return.

Conservatism: Thought, Feeling, and Reaction
(OCTOBER 1980)

Is there a growing conservative mood? Are we experiencing a swing of the political pendulum back to the "right"? Many say so—including those who applaud the shift and those who are appalled by it.

If there is a growth of "conservatism," is it a change in genuine *thought* or in only superficial *feeling*? Is there any cerebral content involved, or is it solely a matter of vibrations? And of what does the shift of conclusion and opinion consist? What are the concrete manifestations and consequences?

Even generally to describe, much less rigorously to define, "conservatism"—or "liberalism," for that matter—is a considerable challenge. But presumably the key ingredients of the conception of conservatism include: severely limited and carefully contained government; rights to use of property which are privately held and exercised; a degree of individual autonomy and accountability which basically characterizes society; and a market in which producer entry and operational initiative is combined with a consumer sovereignty, all induced and guided by private calculations based on market-determined prices. Much of the essence of the notion of conservatism is captured by the expression "free men in free markets."

Is this the sort of thing most people have in mind as they observe the community becoming increasingly conservative? Surely not—at least, not in any elaborate and systematic thought process. If there is today a conservative shift, it is not likely to be mainly a consequence of philosophy and analysis—or a philosophy based on, and stemming from, analysis. Conservative and reactionary shifts presumably are no more intellectual phenomena than are the quite mindless liberal and radical shifts—even if conservatives may be relatively hardheaded in a grubby sort of way while liberals are too anxious to do good. *with your money*

No, if there is a conservative swing, it is hardly a product or reflection of high philosophy and elaborate analysis. Rather, it stems from a growing magnitude of people being jolly well fed up, *not* with decency and compassion but with ever-growing taxes and what they perceive to be ineffectual and silly government expenditures; with drowning in a cascade of paper work dumped on them by an intruding and officious bureaucracy; with centrally imposed quotas and procedures in hiring, firing, promoting, and admitting; with stultifying constraints, specifications, and requirements in an incomprehensible world of government regulation; in the substitution of ill-conceived social engineering for substantive progress in proper goals. In short, people are increasingly frustrated by broken promises and small (or perverse) payoffs from massive requisitions by Big Brother of the community's income.

It may be that people are eager not for *smaller* government but for *better* government. But over the past half-century we have persistently been plagued with the worst of worlds: Government has grown neither smaller nor better—instead, it keeps getting bigger and worse.

Practical Politics and the Economist

(DECEMBER 1980)

Save me from a certain kind of terribly shrewd, worldly-wise, self-styled practical person.

The "practical" person and I may be soul mates in general orientation. We may share an appreciation of the individualistic society, for both its philosophic attractiveness and the economic efficiency it engenders. But he is a "political" person. And he becomes impatient with the economic analyst, who, he feels, is too logically "pure," too dedicated to "intellectual integrity" and too little concerned with "political and social realities."

As one columnist has put it, "The conservative prescription . . . accords with both economic theory and economic experience, but does it accord with democratic political realities?" Another is sarcastic toward "conservatives who refuse to contaminate their lofty theories with a little political realism."

Well, I am all for realism, for genuine understanding of the real world, for deducing prescriptions for institutions and policies that will actually improve the lot of flesh-and-blood people. We individualists, after all, are interested in the activities and the well-being of the individual.

But it is not very helpful simply to exhort me, in my

capacity as an economist, to be "practical." *How* am I to take most effective account of "realities"? Just what is the economist to do, and how is he to do it, in considering problems with public policy implications?

There are several pertinent considerations.

First, appreciate the limits of anyone's expertise. By definition, no one can be a specialist in everything. The economist knows and can do some things relatively well. But typically, he is *not* an expert in politics.

Second, if the economist tries to play amateur politician, not only may he give bad political guidance, his *economics* may suffer. By trying extensively to intertwine considerations of political tactics with his rigorous analysis, the economics itself can be diverted, diluted, and compromised.

Third, while deductions of economics on a particular point may not be politically acceptable today, good analysis effectively presented has much staying power. It is not likely to win policy debates quickly in dramatic battle, but patient reiteration of truth can gradually gain the advantage. Many positions now widely supported were heresies twenty or thirty years ago.

Finally, a kind of division of labor is in order for economists. Fittingly, some are active in short-term policymaking, operating as seems best within given political and institutional constraints. But others usefully hew persistently to strict dictates of analysis, providing long-term perspective, dispassionate application of the best professional techniques, demonstrating the costs of policy deviations from the conclusions thus deduced.

In the short run, sometimes bad economics is good politics. But the economist of integrity is obliged, even in his discouragement, to continue to promote the best economics available. If he does not impatiently and inappropriately compromise, he will at least keep the faith—and occasionally he will eventually win a major political debate.

On Politely Sticking to One's Last

(DECEMBER 1980)

Nobel Prizes of 1980 were recently conferred. Such cere-
monies remind us of much of the best in the human mind
and spirit—the brilliance, the training, the perseverance
required for intellectual accomplishment at the highest levels.

Unhappily, we are reminded of more. An episode of a few
years ago made it distressingly clear that, even with those
who work so effectively in the research library and laboratory,
all is not gentility and sense.

In 1976, Milton Friedman received the Nobel Prize in
Economics. Nobel Prize committees do not always choose
so well. Indeed, this committee could not have chosen better.
Magnificent scholar and teacher, Friedman has elucidated
not only numerous aspects of formal economic analytics but
real workings of real economies and prerequisites of survival
of free societies.

Yet awarding of the prize was publicly denounced by a
few. Those few were *not* of the lunatic orangutan fringe.
They *must* have been honorable and able men: After all,
they themselves had received Nobels—in medicine and
chemistry.

According to the belligerent vilification—earlier begun by
others—Friedman was an enemy of liberty and advocate of
fascistic repression. It was charged that he had been an
adviser to the militarist government of Chile; had taught
Chilean graduate students attending his university; and,
through his direct advice to the government and his influence
on students who returned to Chile as government officials,
had wreaked economic havoc and political misery on the
people of Chile.

The charges were ludicrously and demonstrably false—

and demonstrations of falsity were, in fact, provided on several occasions by both Friedman and a colleague. But, in bravura displays of literal nonsense, the Nobel scientists retracted nothing and clung to their pose of superiority, not only in morality but in economic and social analyses.

Friedman set straight the factual record. In particular, he had never been an adviser to the government of Chile and had visited the country only once, for six days under private sponsorship to deliver university lectures. One of the lectures was entitled "The Fragility of Freedom."

Friedman also asked questions of those who had attacked him. Why their selective outrage? He had not been criticized for longer visits to Russia and Yugoslavia. Why their complaints over the economic policies of Chile when those policies were beneficial and better alternatives had not been offered? Is it not probable that reducing economic chaos will enhance, rather than reduce, movement toward freedom? Is it inadvisable to admit into our universities students from countries that have, or someday might have, repressive governments? Is it sinful for scholars to travel to and lecture in nations with unattractive governments? Do we uphold traditions of freedom by applying political tests in recognizing scientific achievement?

We have grown accustomed to Hollywood personalities and such lecturing the community on political theory, physics, and economics. But we should expect elite scholars to demonstrate civility while confining themselves professionally to their research specialties.

CAPITALISM AND CAPITALISTS

Capitalism and Its Spokesmen

(APRIL 1980)

Individualistic, private-property, free-market capitalism is not simply an economic arrangement. As Adam Smith and Karl Marx would agree, the property-market arrangement reflects, and provides the basis of, the entire society. Cultural, psychological, political, and economic attributes of the social order intertwine and mold each other. A community that tries to remain politically free while economically controlled by central authority is a house divided against itself and will perish.

Many in this warring world wish us ill. Some envy us, others fear us—although the envy is more easily explicable than the fear. Even in our own midst, there are those who long to experiment with five-year plans, communal direction of business firms, state dictation of prices and income distribution, and the order of the Gulag Archipelago. At least, they are attracted by the prospect of such a society if *they* can be the planners, commissars, and wardens—tyranny looks good to would-be tyrants.

Surely the great majority in this blessed Land of the Free want our heritage to persist. We did not *earn* our unique status in the world community, to be sure, for we were *born* free. But it is possible to learn well enough what we have inherited and what the alternatives to freedom are, to defend what we have, to reject the siren song of socialistic surrender.

But if the attractiveness of freedom, including the economic efficiency it conduces, is so great, why is the defense of freedom seemingly so hesitant, so apologetic, so inept? Perhaps the major beneficiaries of capitalism are not the most conspicuous spokesmen of capitalistic society.

The beneficiaries are the community at large, workaday people conducting their own affairs in accordance with their own aspirations, criteria, and capabilities, in a social and economic setting that provides something approaching maximum alternatives.

But who *speaks* for capitalism? While we individually gain from capitalism as consumers and as suppliers of our personal productive services, it would seem reasonable to ask business leaders to help articulate the advantages of capitalism. Some do—a few do so effectively. But most are silent and inactive in the defense of freedom. And many, even when professing love of liberty, find freedom often uncongenial and act in ways to subvert it. While espousing freedom, they seek tariffs, subsidies, and protective regulation; while voicing virtues of competition in the abstract for others, they desire monopoly in the concrete for themselves.

It may be an exaggeration to say that businessmen have a natural wish to destroy the open, competitive economy. Still, even collectivist economies must have managers. Those managers who are merely adequate in their politicized environment will be well rewarded. And the prospects of survival in collectivism may be more attractive to some than the difficulties of prospering in market competition.

We can hardly expect capitalism to survive *without* business people; but, evidently, we cannot rely heavily on the defense of capitalism *by* business people.

How Can We Best Survive in This Vale of Tears?

(AUGUST 1979)

There has long been a debate—largely unstructured and at a low level of analysis—concerning alternative societal arrangements and the economies on which they are based. Call it what you will—capitalism versus communism, individualism versus collectivism—the argumentation has inspired shrill recriminations and distractions more than comprehension and resolution of differences.

Occasionally, a calm voice attempts to inject a degree of reasonableness and candor into the dogfight. Recently, at the University of Chicago, Henry Ford II, chairman of the board of Ford Motor and a champion of capitalism, presented a lecture on "Where Capitalism Falls Short."

In part of his address, Mr. Ford acknowledged "inherent imperfections" of capitalism. In particular, "capitalism," he said, "is a revolutionary force." Indeed, it has been an agent of massive change. In its nature, it strongly tends "to uproot and overturn things."

Inevitably, there will be costs associated with wide and major changes, even as there are gains. Along with advancing technology, increasing wealth, and emergence of a middle class and liberal values under capitalism, there were "polluting smokestacks and urban slums." With broadening freedom and individualism over these past two centuries, there were physical and psychological dislocations and losses of traditions. While community poverty was strikingly relieved, the very freedom and adaptability engendered by the economic and political experiments of the Western world sometimes weakened the community itself, its roots, its orientation.

There have been major inconveniences, uncertainties, and costs accompanying the democratic capitalist revolution. Some of these costs stemmed from the very incentives and fluidity, the innovating dynamics and flexible adjustability, of the capitalist-market system. Different people can reasonably assign different weights to these costs and returns—and thus they can reasonably differ in their net assessments of capitalism.

But realize that to overturn modern capitalism—or modify and restructure it in fundamentals so as to leave it unrecognizable as "capitalism"—would *not* take us back to an earlier idyllic situation of simple, wholesome, just, and stable tranquillity. One reason is that such a condition never existed: The essence of history has been, and for most people of the world continues to be, soul-searing, body-racking poverty and political tyranny.

Even if a golden age for the mass of humanity had existed sometime at some place since the Garden of Eden, you can be sure that those who would subvert capitalism would not return us there. Capitalism, after all, does not prevail through most of the world today—and the current noncapitalist world, like the precapitalist world, hardly resembles "an idyllic situation."

Capitalistic Self-Defense: How Not to Survive

(AUGUST 1979)

Henry Ford II has spoken of where capitalism falls short.

Mr. Ford first considered "inherent weaknesses" of capitalism because it is "a revolutionary force." In the process of "uprooting and overturning things," there have been inevitable costs along with splendid accomplishments. In addition to "built-in shortcomings of the system," capitalism falls short, he feels, because of "the failure of businessmen to respond intelligently to their social and political environment."

Surely it is true that the business community has failed to take seriously important criticisms and recommendations—ignoring some legitimate challenges and replying ineptly to many of the illegitimate. Those who are efficient in producing goods quite typically demonstrate little skill or even interest in economic analysis, history, philosophy, and psychology. They meet consumerists, environmentalists, unionists, bureaucrats, and agitators on alien and uncongenial ground—and they commonly get their ears pinned back.

Not only do business people face formidable adversaries, there is weakness in their own ranks: Some fear or distrust the discipline of the market, and many have little appreciation of the essence of the system in which they work and the prerequisites of its survival.

In addition to indifference, indecision, and inadequate orientation, there are numerous tactical difficulties and deficiencies of capitalists in supporting capitalism.

One is the ineptitude often displayed in so-called economic education, including both in-plant programs and subsidization of outside programs. In-plant propaganda is sometimes silly to the point of having negative value; and some of the outside efforts actually give aid and comfort to the enemy.

Business failures in education are predictable. Confronted by a smothering mass of economic illiteracy, business people with few credentials in either economics or education can be expected to blow it.

Then there is the subtle problem of how to deal with critics who persist in comparing incomparables. Many a radical philosopher has effectively appealed to the gallery by comparing the beauties of a never-never utopia with grubby reality.

In the debates, basic notions are easily twisted and corrupted. The person in business may properly speak of motivating self-interest, equity, and clarity of ground rules; the critic and reformer replies in terms of envy, egalitarianism, and governmental controls.

Finally, even when the capitalist promotes capitalism with profundity, he is vulnerable to the charge of being a self-serving lobbyist. The case for capitalism can often be made more effectively by those who, with reason, appear to be relatively disinterested.

If the free and efficient society is to prevail, it is necessary for the business community to defend itself. But *self*-defense will not be sufficient. The people in business will have to obtain effectual support from others.

Let's You and Him Maybe Fight, Sort Of
(July 1979)

The battle for an efficient economy within a free society is being lost. The barbarian is at the gate. The barbarian is represented, in major part, by large, growing, and hyperactive government—government that increasingly strives not to make the market more efficient but to supersede the market; not to promote creation of wealth but to redistribute wealth; not to enhance the role of individual initiative and responsibility but to make people and their organizations subservient to Big Brother.

No one of us guards the gate alone. But the barbarian is *not* confronted by a well-led legion. The attack on freedom and efficiency and individualism has not inspired general and complementary defense. Not even the corporate world presents a unified, much less effective, front. Why not? There are several possible reasons, none very flattering.

First, some corporate officers do not *comprehend* that the

barbarian is really battering the gate—or do not believe that he constitutes a significant danger—despite the current massive governmental and radical attack on private rights to the use of property. Dilution, revocation, and abrogation of rights not only threaten the corporate structure but subvert the very essence of the free society.

Second, there are some who realize that the barbarian is at the gate—and who *welcome* him. Not everyone opposes price controls and pervasive regulation; not everyone applauds the mechanism of the free market and the consequences of free market activity. After all, allegedly, Mussolini made the trains run on time, and Jane Fonda assures us that Red China has no flies.

Third, some know that the barbarian is attacking, and they wish he would go away—but they fear he will win, and they do not want to antagonize him: Better to ride "the wave of the future," wherever it may take us, than to drown.

Fourth, there are those who, with purity of heart and simplicity of brain, oppose the barbarian but do so with awesome ineptitude, even to the extent of inadvertently subsidizing the enemy. Sophistication in economic analysis, persuasiveness in education, and shrewdness in identifying and supporting effective allies do not universally characterize inhabitants of the corporate boardroom.

Finally, we are blessed with *free riders*: They realize that the barbarian is pressuring the gate, they hope that he will be kept out, but—perhaps through sloth or pound-foolishness —they rely on others to do the bloody fighting.

Keeping the barbarian of Leviathan at bay will require more than the confusion, faintheartedness, and indecision that have characterized many of the supposed stalwarts of the community.

COMMUNISM AND
COMMUNISTS

Karl Marx, Reactionary

(JANUARY 1981)

A modern scholar highly appreciative of Karl Marx concluded that Marx was quite consistently wrong and misleading in his sweeping analyses—but he was so magnificently
wrong! And, as a contemporary economist has put it in
speaking of Marx, "To study the errors of a great, if wrong-
headed, mind is often more valuable than to skim the
platitudes of a small one."

It is commonly believed—both by those who applaud and
those who condemn what they sense to be Marxian doctrine
—first, that Marx was a completely independent innovator,
bursting into the nineteenth century with a wholly (and
devastatingly) original body of analysis, and, second,
that that analysis was progressive to the point of being
revolutionary.

In actuality, much of the great erudition of Marx con-
sisted of the best economic analytics of his day. He drew
fundamentally on "establishment" thought—the heritage of
Adam Smith and the rest of the classical school. And, in
adapting the conventional concepts and lines of thought to
his own purposes, the resulting Marxian doctrine, for all of
the revolutionary sloganeering associated with it, is essentially *reactionary*. That Marx was a premier reactionary is
a persuasive thesis of a commentator, Paul Craig Roberts.

Dr. Roberts speaks of the "private" individual, whose

existence in some places has distinguished some of modern times, especially in the last two centuries. The so-called private individual is very largely his own person, basically free of governmental constraints within general, clear, consistent, and stable ground rules. Obviously, the slave and the serf are not private individuals. Less obviously, the persistent and pervasive encroachment of government—with its controls and restrictions and stipulations, enforced by increasingly autonomous bureaucracy—dilutes our status as private individuals.

The essential ingredient, the foundation, of a society of private individuals is private property. When one can work and play at what one pleases, invest and sell as one pleases, and buy and consume as one pleases—negotiating and contracting in the market with other free men—one is a private individual. Without private property, we have only "the rulers and the ruled, lords and serfs."

Historically, as different groups—landowners, merchants, capitalists, laborers—attained specific property rights, they wished government to protect those rights, and they struggled with each other over control of government. Much of the message of Adam Smith was that powerful government was the common *enemy*, not the *protector*, of private individuals, who could best prosper together in the coordination of a free market.

But Marx feared individualization. "Man," he said, "originally appears as . . . a herd animal." And private property, by making people largely autonomous and individually accountable, unhappily "dissolves the herd."

Those who fear freedom, who seek relief from personal decisionmaking, who hunger for the specious security of the slave and the serf, find it attractive, while shouting slogans of revolution and freedom, to follow the reactionary Karl Marx back to the government-dominated herd.

Communism and Tyranny

(SEPTEMBER 1980)

A Hollywood personality, who apparently finds it highly satisfying to tutor the community in both physics and economics, has been quoted as saying: ". . . if you understood what communism was, you would hope, you would pray on your knees, that we could someday become Communists."

More recently and more sensibly, the captain of Australia's Olympic basketball team said in Moscow: "The best thing to do is to have people come here. There's no way they'd ever want to be Communists."

It is not difficult for an economist to find deficiencies and difficulties in *any* economic system, including the characteristically open-market, enterprise, private-property system of the free world. *Every* economy is an economy of *scarcity*— and thus an economy of frustration and conflict. Indeed, in the absence of scarcity, there would be no occasion to economize.

Growing economies, in particular, will have the untidiness of change and unpredictability, for growth entails invention, innovation, investment, and adaptation. Dynamic change, inspired and directed by preferences of millions of people in the marketplace, is inherently risky and will inevitably have some failures as well as successes, and there will be some injuries and losses along with a persistent trend of aggregate betterment. But most in this blessed land—uncorrupted by Hollywoodian absurdity—prefer expansive, promising freedom and its efficiency to the certain subservience and stagnation of tyrannical serfdom.

One of the ghastly aspects of Russian communism-in-action has just been documented. A privately prepared and privately circulated study of officially published Russian population data has analyzed how many Russians died unnaturally from 1927 to 1958, roughly corresponding to the period of Stalin's reprehensible rule. The study, by a Russian geophysicist, has reached the West and been summarized in the *Wall Street Journal*. The author has been arrested by the Russian secret police.

The study concludes that during the thirty-one-year period, there were between 43 and 52 million unnatural deaths. Some 30 million of them were during World War II—20 million in actual fighting, the rest from civilian deprivation and the rigors of Russian prisons. The remaining 13 to 22 million perished at other times, mainly prior to 1941, from deliberate slaughter, prison camp conditions, and massive government ineptitude.

Economic ineptitude is easily predictable in a totalitarian "command" society. So is insensitivity and fanaticism on the part of those few who have obtained vital power over the many. When government is not severely contained, when the range and extent of its authority is not bounded by private rights to use of property, impersonal mechanisms of the market, and individual commercial and intellectual initiative, then capricious, callous, and dastardly tyranny is not simply predictable—it is inevitable.

Thugs and Fanatics

(SEPTEMBER 1980)

In significant part, this is a world of unfair discrimination, cruel oppression, and stultifying tyranny. To some extent, discrimination, oppression, and tyranny are to be found in every community. But the extent is not evenly spread; nations differ greatly, fundamentally, in amount of inhumanity, in manifestations of injustice, and in processes of appeal.

What determines and distinguishes the few, beleaguered oases of civilized liberty in this global vale of tears? Private rights to use of property, broad personal autonomy, individual initiative and accountability, are, in their essence, barriers to domineering government. Dilution of such rights and suppression and diversion of such initiative, replacing the efficient, evenhanded processes of the market with the capricious, discriminatory machinations of the state, are the road to tyranny.

The deficiencies of totalitarian societies are so obvious, the failures are so readily explained, the resultant waste and oppression are so predictable—and the advantages of the alternative of freedom are so undeniable—that support of a Nazi Germany or a communistic Russia or China requires a perversity of well-nigh incredible magnitude. Yet, such perversity, such blinking at evidence and shunning of logic, does exist. It exists not only in confused minds of untutored Hollywood poseurs but in precious minds of intellectualoids overanxious to remake the nature of man.

I once engaged in debate on the issue of alternative social systems with another professor of economics. He had managed to be seduced into Maoism. One of his messages from the fantasyland of Mao pertained to order. He gave assurance that within a generation there would be no more greed in China, that competition would be replaced with spontaneous brotherhood and pure cooperation. Even now, he said, there was no problem of organization and order in China.

I replied that after 40 or 50 or 60 million potential dissidents had been knocked off—common estimates of the Chinese purges—the rest of the boys could be expected to fall into line. "Oh," he said, "not as many as *sixty* million were liquidated," suggesting that the number might be no more than, say, 59.9 million. "Besides," he added, "most of them were just landlords, anyway."

In mannerism, the Maoist professor is soft-spoken and reticent. But this gentleman-scholar was prepared fastidiously to sign the death warrants for any vast number of people in the interest of establishing his version of the good society.

The experience lends credence to the editorial view of the *Wall Street Journal*, which suggests that only two types of people can produce the horrors of twentieth-century repression and slaughter—"the stupid and callous or the intellectual and idealistic. The stupid, not to be moved by the suffering they caused; the intellectual, to rationalize it away."

Surely the more chilling and reprehensible of the two types is not the dull-witted thug but the genteel lieutenant of the devil.

The Good Life: A Future As Well As a Heritage?

(SEPTEMBER 1979)

It is difficult to make meaningful international comparisons of living standards. Even though they do it their own way, do the French live better than the Germans?

Indeed, *domestic* comparisons are hard enough, even without complications of converting data in one national currency into supposedly equivalent figures in another. Do people of California live better than those of New York? How about Los Angeles compared to San Francisco? Are we talking about *average* people in each of the areas? Or comparing people with *identical money incomes*, but faced by different prices, product availabilities, and climates, and with different tastes and traditions?

A useful way to compare how well people live is to note

approximate *worktimes* required for an average manufacturing employee to buy various commodities.

The average American worker can buy a liter of milk in Washington, D.C., for only seven minutes of worktime; in Moscow, the "work price" is eighteen minutes—over two and one-half times the American figure. For potatoes, the Russian "work price" is three times higher than the American; for eggs, ten times; for sugar, twelve. For a food basket, the ratio is three and one-half to one.

It is a similar story with other common items. A suit in Moscow is three and one-half times more expensive than in Washington; soap, four and one-half times; a refrigerator, five times; a television or a car, eight and one-half times. And, comrades, pantyhose, when available in Moscow, sell at a "work price" twenty times higher! What price communistic revolution?

There is reason to be gratified by such comparisons. We can reasonably infer from them some generalizations concerning alternative economic arrangements and methods. The economic facts of living hardly inspire a reasonable person to beg on bended knee for communism.

But gratification is not a basis for complacency. Indeed, there is reason to fear that the United States—truly the last, best hope of Earth—is losing the battle to prevail as a citadel of freedom and efficiency.

Big Brother, even in this Land of the Free, is already huge and steadily getting bigger. American productivity is barely rising, and the growth rate of gross national product has been falling. Increasingly, solutions offered to deal with our problems *reject* the presumptions, the institutions, and the processes that have vitally contributed to our strength and well-being, and, instead, tend to emulate the centralized and dictatorial characteristics of our sworn enemies.

Finally, note that even the relatively poor can amass fearsome power of the jungle by strategic allocation of resources. Russia devotes more than *twice* as big a proportion of its national output to the military budget as does the United States; in the last fifteen years, the Russian military budget, in real terms, has *doubled* while that of the United States has *fallen*; Russian military expenditure is now some 40 percent greater than that of the United States.

These things are known. Still uncertain is whether this nation, blessed with such splendid heritage, has the will to pursue with sufficient dedication a struggle to survive which, at best, we are on the verge of losing.

ORGANIZATION AND ORDER

✴

Two Declarations of Independence
(OCTOBER 1979)

By a striking (and not entirely fortuitous) coincidence, the year 1776 saw the appearance of two momentous statements of liberty, its prerequisites, its consequences, its vulnerability. The statements were the political Declaration of Independence by the American statesman Thomas Jefferson, and the economic *Wealth of Nations* by the Scottish scholar Adam Smith. Their virtually simultaneous appearance underscores the vital, but commonly underappreciated, fact that "societal order" subsumes intertwined political and economic aspects.

This is a world of scarcity. The condition of wanting more than we can have inevitably conduces competition and strife. A viable society must evolve and adopt modes of resolving conflicts. But there are ways and ways of maintaining order. The vision of Smith, highly influential in both Great Britain and the United States, was one of beneficial process and mechanism without tyrannical coercion. It was a picture of an economy characterized by private rights to the use of property and quite minimal, but essential, government; by individuals permitted, within broad but necessary limits, to use their resources as they think best, receiving the benefits and also bearing the costs of their own decisions; by "selfishly" motivated action channeled in a manner conducive to the general well-being. It was, in short, a coherent and persuasive picture of efficiency in a setting of freedom.

The Wealth of Nations appeared during the last decades of the interventionist age of mercantilism, and it did not

immediately win the field of debate and of policy implementation. But the experiment with freedom, both political
and economic, for all of the many dilutions, distortions, and
abuses to which it was subjected, had a fascinating and
robust history in nineteenth-century Britain and the United
States. It was a singular and generally gratifying experience.

But even success does not inevitably succeed forever. The
dominant character of world history has featured political
oppression and economic inefficiency. With the United States
now in its third century, it is increasingly apparent that she
is the last, best hope of Earth. But even this Land of the Free
has suffered, at an increasing rate since 1930, growing
political concentration and economic waste.

What do today's Americans want—and how much do they
want it? Will they meanly acquiesce, through either confusion or a fear of freedom, in stultifying regimentation? Or
will they finely strive for the principles of Jefferson and of
Smith—liberty with order, efficiency with equity, dynamic
growth with social stability?

The fate and welfare of all mankind hangs in the balance.
That fate will not be a happy one if the United States adopts,
either deliberately or by default, a static economy and a
centrally controlled society.

Order and Efficiency from Freedom
(June 1980)

If there is an *organization,* a well-defined, coherent *arrangement,* surely someone must be in charge. Who is in charge of
a free-market, private-property economy? Who decides what
to produce and in what proportions? Who guides the process
of production? Who decrees how the social pie is divided

among the members of the community and between present and future uses?

The answer is: No one—and everyone. There is no economic czar, no committee or bureau, in or out of government, who, in any interesting sense of the term, "runs" the American economy. Some people and some groups do have perceptible power. But we do not owe our relatively high level of well-being to them. On the contrary, to the extent that there are pockets of appreciable autocratic power, we are worse off.

Well, if no one runs the show, perhaps what we have is not a show at all, but anarchy. Nonsense. No one is "in charge" of the enormous gamut of food production—yet the people eat. Economic functions are performed; the economy works.

The American economy works very efficiently—within the increasingly severe constraints being imposed on it. To be very efficient, obviously it must be highly coordinated. The economy generates and represents *order*, not anarchy. It provides a *system*, a *process*, a *procedure*.

The order stemming from the system, process, and procedure enables us to adapt to a world of scarcity and to adjust to changes in that world. The evolved and evolving institutions of a free economy generate information about alternatives and preferences. They enable us to identify the options at any time and to register community choices among those options. They provide an order of efficiency, where efficiency entails use of scarce resources in accordance with freely expressed desires of the people. That efficiency cannot be matched by a centrally commanded social arrangement. Indeed, the essence of the centralized society is *substitution* of the preferences of Big Brother for those of a free people.

Market institutions do more than provide information on options and relative demands. They provide incentives to get done those things the community wants most. And the inducements are those of positive *gain*, not simply those of avoiding *pain*. The centralized government says: Do this or you will be put into a state of extreme regret. The market says: Do this and you will be made better off.

People in both production and consumption are drawn into coordinated activity of *mutual* benefit. Personal gain, not mutual benefit, inspires the market participation, but the shrewd Adam Smith understood the wider and happy implications: The trader, the investor, the producer in a free market "is . . . led by an invisible hand," as he put it, "to promote an end which was no part of his intention."

Freedom is not a luxury, affordable only in halcyon days. It is not only, in its own right, a critical characteristic of a civilized society. It is a prerequisite of, not a sacrifice to, order and efficiency. And inefficiency and disorder in a world of scarcity is a sin.

Economic Order: Big Brother versus Mutual Bribery

(JUNE 1980)

The means to satisfy wants are *scarce:* We want more than we can have. Scarcity gives rise to *competition* and *conflict*. And yet in a viable society we must live together in general confidence, with coordinated activity. How can there be peaceful and efficient coexistence of acquisitive and uncooperative people in a stingy world?

The motives of people are essentially the same everyplace —to increase material welfare and to express personality. But social arrangements, including economic systems, differ greatly in the extent to, and the manner in, which goals may be pursued. Scarcity exists in all societies; how *adaptation* to scarcity is made varies from community to community.

Use of violence is one way of resolving conflicts. Thomas Hobbes, the English seventeenth-century political theorist, explained the problem of order when people seek to satisfy their diverse desires with scarce resources: ". . . if any two men desire the same thing, which nevertheless they cannot both enjoy," he says, "they become enemies." And in the anarchical state of nature, "the life of man [is] solitary, poore, nasty, brutish, and short."

Hobbes resolves the problem of order by introducing a ruler to whom each man shall "give up [his] Right of Governing [him]self." People are to enter into a social contract with an absolute sovereign, Hobbes tells us, "to keep them in awe, and to direct their actions to the Common Benefit."

One may reject violence as a mode of interpersonal relations and still be dissatisfied with the Hobbesian Big Brother resolution of the problem. Instead of state-imposed order, how about mutual bribery? We tend to class as immoral all bribery. But is it immoral to induce people to do what you wish by making them *better off*? Let Adam Smith, the Scottish thinker of the eighteenth century, explain:

> Man has almost constant occasion for the help of his brethren, and it is in vain for him to expect it from their benevolence only. He will be more likely to prevail if he can interest their self-love in his favor, and show them that it is for their own advantage to do for him what he requires. . . . Give me that which I want, and you shall have this which you want. . . . It is not from the benevolence of the butcher, the brewer, or the baker, that we expect our dinner, but from their regard to their own interest. We address ourselves not to their humanity but to their self-love.

Is this a grubby view of the world and how to adapt to scarcity? Well, the world *is* grubby. We *are* confronted by scarcity. And so conflict *does* exist. Are we to adapt through giving up our individual freedom and responsibility to Hobbesian central control—or adapt through mutually beneficial coordination of self-interested actions in a free market? Acquisitive, self-serving drives exist. Are we to try forever, with Hobbes, simply to suppress them—or, with Smith, to channel them to fruitful ends? Are we to be content to constrain behavior and block energies from undesirable paths— or garner reciprocal gains of free men in pursuit of individually advantageous results?

Efficient Order: Fish, Birds, and Producers

(DECEMBER 1979)

Fish gotta swim, birds gotta fly—and both real people and politicians gotta blame problems on scapegoats.

When Eve blew it in the Garden of Eden, the devil made her do it. When athletic teams do badly, fire the coach. When students fail, the tests were "unfair." When we have inflation, blame it on big business, big labor, or OPEC.

Having botched diagnosis of our problems, we compound the error by simpleminded prescription. Increasingly, the prescription is to tell government to take care of us. And government is delighted to oblige.

Never mind the miserable record of government in producing wealth. Never mind that government has become primarily a vast engine simply for *redistributing*—and, in the process, *diminishing*—wealth. If you favor equity and efficiency, prosperity and progress, then turn to government —the same splendid officials in their bloated bureaucracies who have given us Amtrak, the post office, gasoline lines, housing shortages, inflation, and slavery to paper work. Apparently, nothing succeeds like failure: If massive government expenditure and debilitating government guidance have failed before, then do it some more. Spend more, regulate more. After all, that's the way virtually all the rest of the world has conducted itself virtually throughout 6000 years of recorded history—and as a result, the rest of the world is, as it generally has been, in great shape!

Now, there *are* problems in this vale of scarcity and tears. And there *are* people who wish us ill. This is a world of difficulty and strife. Perhaps it is inevitable, at least in our more depressed moments of confusion, that we seek the comfort of blaming our woes on a devil, we seek someone or some institution that will slay our dragons—perhaps a prince on a white horse, followed by legions of regulating and directing officials, if not the SS or KGB.

This is not really to suggest that politicians and their bureaucrats are different from the rest of us. They *are* greedy and coarse and selfish and aggressive—but so are we all. They are not to be trusted with discretionary, unaccountable power—but neither are you and I. No, they are not worse than the rest of us. But the corollary is often overlooked: They are not *better* than the rest of us.

So what to do? First, acknowledge that *no* social arrangement, *no* political and economic system, will resolve *all* of our difficulties to the full satisfaction of *all* of us. Given inevitable frustration, *minimize* the costs of existence. We minimize the costs of living together in a stingy world by maintaining those procedures and processes and mechanisms that yield *efficient order*. And efficient order must be based on the *individual*. Each must do his own thing, enticed and guided by the prospects of self-betterment, in a context that permits such personal choices among such alternatives as will promote the general well-being.

This kind of widely beneficial order channels the energies

and aspirations of individual people—contrasted to the kind
of tyrannical and stultifying order imposed from above. It is,
in short, the order of the *market*—not the order of the Gulag
Archipelago.

While fish are swimming and birds are flying, let producers
produce.

Scarcity, Ethics, and Capitalism

(J U N E 1 9 8 0)

A type of moralist or theologian fulfills a perceived obligation
to pontificate on economics. Few economists feel obliged to
agonize over the subtleties of morality and theology. Probably few economists have much of value to say about
goodness and naughtiness, heaven and hell. But then, most
ethicists and clergymen are equally innocent in economics—
they here seem, indeed, to be quite beyond salvation.

Recently, a conference fretted about the compatibility of
Christianity and capitalism. "Can a successful businessman
be a Christian?" Can a corporate manager repair to morality
when faced by "dehumanizing" options? Can a "reward
system based on self-interest incentives"—first in the schools
and then in the business world—produce corporate leaders
with a sufficiently "broad concept of the common good"?

Unsurprisingly, the conference concluded that men are
not angels—at least in the context of capitalism. Indeed,
men are *not* angels. But their nonangelic behavior is not a
result of capitalism. Angels, after all, do not reside in a world
of scarcity and resulting competition and conflict. It is
scarcity and the inborn—shall we say, God-given?—desire
to have *more* which engender rational acquisitiveness.

This *is* a world of scarcity. We cannot have or do all we desire. Supplies of iron ore and petroleum limit our production of goods; supplies of time and energy limit our prayer and meditation. Both the business mogul and the beatific monk, along with the rest of us, are forced to adjust to a world of finite possibilities.

There is nothing unique about business people or druids or capitalists in the confrontation of alternatives, the necessity of making choices, the consequent paying of prices and the bearing of costs, and the desire to maximize net returns. The employer, the employee, the unemployed; the theologian, the parishioner, the atheist; the Russian, the Cuban, the American—all must deal, in one context or another, with options, choicemaking, costs, and rational pursuit of objectives.

But the contexts, the ground rules and parameters of behavior, differ greatly. And capitalism *is* unique in its enormous breadth of allowed individual initiative, of market possibilities, of personal decisionmaking and accountability, of joining economic efficiency in accordance with community preferences with social mobility and political liberty.

All this is not to say that the capitalist world is lovely. In its basic nature, a world of scarcity cannot be very lovely. The real question, given our unavoidable constrained condition of scarcity, is how best to adjust, how most effectively to meld efficiency with freedom, with each contributing to the other.

We capitalist sinners will appreciate prayers on our behalf by those of self-satisfied piety. We, in turn, will pray for those who confuse the problems of scarcity with the free-market, free-society resolution of those problems. And all can pray for the mass of humanity entrapped in social arrangements that severely constrict the individual and his associations, damning with poverty and tryanny. Those poor souls are already experiencing hell.

Coping with an Unfair World
(February 1980)

This Land of the Free is supposed to be governed by laws of general, unambiguous, and minimal constraint, applied impersonally and evenhandedly, rather than by pervasive, dominating, discretionary direction by Big Brother.

Government by stable, limited ground rules rather than by ubiquitous intervention is not intended, in our splendid heritage, to be merely a fair-weather luxury. It has been the bedrock of our efficiency and our liberty. It is *not* an effective rebuttal to note failure to implement fully and perfectly the ideal. Ideals *should* exceed our grasp—or what's a heaven for? And to suppose that most peoples in most times have come closer to grasping finer ideals is to exhibit an embarrassing innocence.

Our proper concern is *not* the unattainability of full and perfect satisfaction of the ideal, but whether we *understand* the ideal and its prerequisites and whether we *accept* the ideal. It is difficult to believe that we well understand and accept the free society when we see all the tinkering by government—tinkering that we not only tolerate but widely demand.

The tinkering is not always trivial. Government tinkers with controlling prices and thereby creates shortages of gasoline and surpluses of wheat; it tinkers with wages and thereby increases unemployment of the young and untrained; it tinkers with so-called stabilization policy and thereby keeps the economy on a roller coaster of inflation and recession—sometimes going up and down simultaneously! With tinkering here and tinkering there, ever more widely and vigorously, it is inevitable that we live less well than we could—and less free.

Much of the broad support for discretionary government tinkering is couched in whimpering terms of "unfairness." We insist that central authority protect us from an unfair world, from each other, even from ourselves.

It is unfair to admit students into college or to hire and promote on grounds solely, or even primarily, of training, accomplishment, and promise.

It is unfair for scientists to have a larger demand for their services than that enjoyed by sociologists and other poets— or, more generally, for low productivity to earn small rewards.

It is unfair to a community for a store to move or a factory to close.

It is unfair to face international competition.

It is unfair to restrict any apartment buildings to adults or to convert apartments into condominiums.

It is unfair to allow all qualified drivers to operate taxis or to permit lawyers and doctors to advertise.

It is unfair for others to gain from an increase in prices for their products.

We had better decide, while we still have some chance to shape our own fate, what ideals are worthy of our support. On what basis—personal performance or bureaucratic preference—are we to receive rewards? On what terms, within what constraints, and with what ground rules, in the context of what institutions and procedures, are we to work and invest and grow?

In this vale of tears, much of the unfairness is perpetrated by bungling Big Brother acting supposedly to correct unfairness.

EFFICIENCY, FREEDOM, AND MARKETS

Freedom, Alternatives, and Markets

(October 1980)

Is there a genuine "yearning to be free"? We like to suppose so. But then, why do there seem so few places now and over history where freedom has predominated and characterized the community? Why does it seem so persistently beleaguered and so fragile where it does prevail?

The questions are best answered when we have a coherent and operational conception of the meaning of freedom, the prerequisites and processes of freedom, the costs and the accouterments of freedom and the alternatives to freedom. We had better distinguish those objectives and conditions which are complements of freedom and those which are substitutes. And, in all this, we must distinguish harsh reality from romantic fantasizing, with respect to both freedom and its alternatives.

There *are* alternatives to freedom and thus costs of freedom. Security and order may be deemed legitimate goals and genuine virtues. But in broad scope, security and order are *not* enemies of freedom; indeed, order is a prerequisite, and security is a consequence, of freedom. But there are some types of security and order—the types of the well-policed prison and of the grave—that are the antithesis of freedom. And even in this Land of the Free, there are those who evince a fear of freedom because they seek a security and an order of collectively assured, imposed, decreed, static nature.

For some of us, insulation through stagnation, protection through proscription, is a thoroughly uninteresting conception of freedom. Abdication of personal autonomy and responsibility for the warmth of the statist womb is a bastardization of the notion of freedom. And, ironically, after the costs of abdication have been borne, there is no assurance that the comforting warmth will be forthcoming. Having put oneself at the mercy of Leviathan, having passed the point of no return in our whimpering surrender, we will belatedly discover that there is little of either mercy or warmth.

Indeed, we are not likely, in this vale of tears, to find much mercy or warmth regardless of the costs we bear. Surely the essence of freedom in a world of scarcity pertains to *individual choicemaking*. When choices are made for, and imposed on, me, I am a puppet, a manikin without autonomy, a kept man. Even if kept well, I am not my own man: I am not free. But to have much autonomy, to be responsible for my own decisions, I must face the risks of experimentation, investment, change.

So there are risks in *any* case. I run the risk that Big Brother will not take good care of me by my own criteria and standards in a constricted society, or I run the risk of personal failure in an open society. You may prefer to take your chances with constriction and centralized direction. But at least have the sense not to tell me that that society is one of freedom.

What I seek, and am willing to rely on, is not the uncertain favor of the autocrat or the certainty offered by the Gulag Archipelago, but *alternatives*. Give me *options* by which I can make my own adaptions to a world of inherent risk. But meaningful alternatives require *markets,* where preferences and costs are registered and offers are transmitted. Free men require free markets.

Society, Liberty, and the Market
(SEPTEMBER 1980)

This is not an era notable for gentility, sophistication, and professionalism. Exacerbating the grubby coarseness of present society, and contributing to its fragmentation and indirection, is the steady dilution and disintegration of self-generating order and coherent system in public relations. Stable parameters of law progressively give way to discretionary decrees of men; accountable administrators give way to insulated bureaucrats; responsive legislators give way to an imperial judiciary.

These are not matters of trivial organizational and procedural detail. They have to do with the bases of our life—how we look at the world, how we anticipate, plan, and conduct our affairs. The essence of this country—this last, best hope of Earth—is liberty; the substance of liberty is individual aspiration, individual responsibility, individual accountability; the condition of individualism is opportunity and options, with personal decisions made on the basis, and in the context, of deductions in an impersonal market. Liberty, in short, requires and largely consists of a free and open marketplace—a marketplace of intellectual and cultural, as well as economic, interchange.

What is required for the viability and effectiveness of the market and thus for the order and efficiency that it conduces? Certainly not directives and constraints and quotas decreed by social engineers, whether these officious martinets are giddy sociologists and historians or regulatory bureaucrats or judges who make law. Such discretionary, ham-handed interventions are the antithesis of the self-equilibrating market, and those who use the power of the state to do the intervening are enemies, not friends, of freedom.

Nor is it required that each of us become an altruistic philosopher, eschewing self-interest and imbued with an overriding concern for the "public good." We need not individually dedicate ourselves to comprehending the "big picture" of society and to seeking "shared interests on the basis of which [our] differences can be composed."

To be sure, a flourishing society does require certain minimal levels of personal qualities and characteristics—foresight, discipline, rationality, integrity—in living with ourselves and with each other. But the market itself—with the information, options, and inducements it provides—strongly encourages and develops such qualities and characteristics, along with economic efficiency. The market itself registers preferences, resolves conflicts, and thus serves the public good.

There is nothing magical or metaphysical in all this. The open market is the most powerful and pervasive device ever to evolve in generating both freedom and efficiency. And in inducing freedom and efficiency, it provides essential cement that holds society together. If that cement is eroded by those morally superior reformers, then the society—such as it then will be—will subsist otherwise, through Big Brother and his SS or KGB.

Markets and Machinations

(OCTOBER 1980)

It would seem premature to proclaim the death, or even the terminal illness, of the democratic, capitalistic society. Still, there is reason to wonder how fully it will flourish and even if it will survive over a prolonged period.

What is the crux of the problem, the essential basis of the

wonderment? Economic illiteracy? Lack of philosophic sophistication? Well, yes, that is part of the general picture. But it has always been part of the picture. In no society have most people been elegant, rigorous scholars.

Perhaps more serious than ignorance is ignorance of ignorance—not knowing that we know little. Such innocence is more likely to lead to overconfidence and overexuberance in ill-advised experiments than to modesty. Certainly, the social and economic engineer too anxious to do good is not deterred by incompetence.

Even this is not the major source of danger for the free society. And that is fortunate, for it is no more realistic to expect widespread sophistication in economics than in molecular biology or jurisprudence. Further, preservation of the free society would not be assured even if the community were heavily infested with formal economists, for acquired sophistication does not guarantee wisdom. A good many economists are simply elegantly foolish.

While we cannot expect widespread rigorous competence in economic analysis, happily we do not require it for an efficient economy. What we do require is a free market, in which people—both producers and consumers—are permitted to utilize market information and respond to market signals in pursuing their independent goals through market-coordinated activities. In the free market, each of us takes care of his own affairs, and no Big Brother or economic czar need be in charge.

But suppose the essence of the game is not wealth production through the market but wealth redistribution through political machination. When we play the market game, typically individual gain yields social benefit as we are induced to work together. But when our strategy and best efforts shift from markets to machinations, the economy sputters, and society is splintered. When personal fortune is advanced not by being productive to the community but by currying the favor of government, individual gain comes at the expense of society. If we become sufficiently reliant on Big Brother, rational playing of *that* game and effective exploitation of the options *then* provided will entail ruin of the individualistic society.

Lamentably, we are well down the path to overreliance on the governmental security blanket. In 1981, half the population will receive half of a bloated federal budget as transfer payments—school lunches, food stamps, pensions, social security, medicare, unemployment compensation, family assistance, student loans, veterans aid. Program by program, such expenditures may strike us as reasonable. In the aggregate, they suggest rejection of personal independence through production, and addiction to personal subservience through subsidization.

Perhaps, after all, the illness *is* terminal.

Biting the Hand That Feeds Us
(NOVEMBER 1980)

A radio-network philosopher recently unburdened himself on the topic of American industrial efficiency, with particular reference to our international competitive position. He was concerned, with reason, about productive efficiency—although his jungle instinct was not adequate to yield comprehension of what is entailed in international comparative advantage. He lamented massive importations of automobiles, cameras, and such, seeming to suggest that ultimately we would be buying *everything* from foreigners.

What to do about the decline of the American economy? Well—let's do better! We must become industrially more efficient. That is a perfectly splendid prescription. But we must do so subject to the constraint that labor—especially, we may infer, our least productive labor—not be replaced, and probably not even displaced, by machines. How is all this enhanced productivity, unaccompanied by any inconvenience, to be achieved? Anyone pure in heart and anxious to do good knows the answer: We can save ourselves through —and only through—extensive national economic planning.

This sort of facile, populist sloganeering elicits warm applause from some audiences. But it does not provide guidance to the stipulated goal. What it does provide is revelation of fundamental confusion regarding the sources of wealth and the mechanisms of wealth creation.

When Eve and the serpent conspired to blow it, the Deity decreed that we would henceforth live only by the sweat of the brow, and we were thereby consigned to a world of scarcity. Come the revolution, we can have some fun chopping off heads and expropriating wealth. But the wealth we divide will not go far, and it will not last long. We will discover what we should have realized at the outset: To live well, we shall have to *produce* much.

In order to produce much, how shall we organize our affairs? What institutions, procedures, and mores are most conducive to effective productive work? How do we best induce and direct selfish, aggressive, acquisitive people to maximize and coordinate their economic efforts?

You make it worth their while. You reward them for being useful, for turning out lots of stuff desired by the community. You make them better off as a result of their productivity. You encourage accountability, work, saving, and investment; you induce the satisfying of consumer preferences rather than of decreed governmental preferences; you link pay with performance; you rely on the skills, ambitions, and adaptability of people assiduously coping with their personal circumstances rather than on the limited knowledge and abilities of autocratic, cavalier, unapproachable bureaucrats; you enable people, in pursuing their own interests, to determine paths of efficiency, with minimal burdens and misdirections yielded by taxation, regulation, and constraint.

In short, we progress as free men in free markets rather than retrogress still further through the antics of "economic planning." For it is in and through the market—maligned though it often is—that we obtain information, indicate preferences, and earn rewards.

Benevolence and Bribery

(AUGUST 1980)

Adam Smith, although an absentminded professor, understood certain key characteristics of the world better than do many modern sophisticates.

Professor Smith shrewdly taught that we obtain our dinner not from "the benevolence of the butcher, the brewer, or the baker" but by appealing to their self-interest, making it worth their while to supply what we want. Two hundred years later, the lesson still has not been learned by many. Perhaps such reciprocal bribery seems too grubby to sensitive souls. Or perhaps it seems cheaper to pout and insist that we be *given* what we want, as our moral right, rather than pay for it.

Judging from a newspaper story, an illustration of such precious naïveté is provided by certain movie directors, actors, and distributors.

Initially, color film was provided to the movie industry by Technicolor. Technicolor was replaced by Eastman Kodak in the early 1950s. The substitution was made by the industry on pragmatic grounds: The Kodak film, along with having technical advantages, was cheaper.

Most of the industry's money is made on initial releases. But a few outstanding movies and those aimed at children's audiences are good for re-releasing. So, although Kodak has always printed a "color stability" disclaimer on its film containers, some moviemakers are mad at Kodak because old films are fading.

Improvements can be made over film now generally used. But such improved film would cost more, and the movie industry is not willing to pay for what it wants. Instead, there is a campaign to "force" Kodak—as the newspaper story puts it—to provide the more costly film, evidently with no increase in price. Kodak is faced not by a *market* demand but a demand by *petition*.

Adam Smith's advice to the movie industry in its "crisis" would be: Don't rely on hysterics and histrionics; instead, try money.

One might expect a certain woolly innocence from the image-makers of Hollywood. But surely college students, with all their erudition, can be counted on for good sense. Well, maybe not.

A couple of years ago, the only chain grocery store next to the UCLA campus was demolished, with the land then used for construction of several movie theaters. No pig ever squealed more piteously than did the young scholars. Letters to the editor flooded the school newspaper. Some whimpered: How ever can we survive with no next-door grocery store? Some complained: We need the grocery store, and the community is obliged to provide whatever we need. Some jeered and threatened: This was another example of the rapaciousness of Daddy Warbucks, chasing the almighty dollar at the expense of people, and Daddy will be appropriately punished, come the revolution.

Of course, neither Kodak nor the grocery chain is morally obliged to provide merchandise at prices or in quantities inconsistent with maximization of profit. And it would be bad economics to do so—bad not only specifically for the seller but for the economy generally, for selling and pricing policies that ignore costs and best alternatives waste the resources of the community.

No Growth, No Wealth, No Freedom

(April 1980)

We are blessed with a clique of social philosophers and radical agitators who assure us that "small is beautiful" and warn that we live in "an era of limits." They garble the problem and its optimal resolution; they would misguide us with bastardized economics and totalitarian politics. A strategy of no-growth could be gracefully tolerated by those who already have it made, but the many below the top social and economic strata—for whom the no-growth spokesmen profess to bleed so readily—would be forever consigned to a static, hopeless subservience.

We do, indeed, live in an era of limits. We always have. This has *always* been a world of scarcity. Stingy nature and finite knowledge have *always* restricted what we can have and do. We do not require political and show-biz moralizers to inform us that we cannot have all of everything we want.

Confronted by a world of obvious scarcity, what is to be the nature of our response? It is inevitable that choices be made. To have some of this, we must forgo some of that. To get more of this, how high a price are you willing to pay, how much cost are you willing to bear? Choices, trade-offs, costs *cannot* be avoided. But they *can* be minimized.

How shall we go about the unavoidable task of choosing among alternatives? Well, first, *whose* preferences are to prevail? Who shall make the choices? Big Brother? A dictatorial elite now at the top of the economic pyramid—those who are now telling the rest of us not to expect or strive for economic advancement?

The hallmark of the free society is freedom. Within broad, clear, and stable rules of the game, each of us is to be permitted to handle his own affairs, using his own income and wealth, in accordance with his own aspirations and judgment, directly bearing the consequences, good and bad. For these private decisions to be rational, they must be based on knowledge of alternatives. So we must know of options and the costs of the various possibilities.

In short, we must have a *market* that gives undistorted information as well as a mechanism for carrying out transactions. A free market generates and disseminates essential information on preferences and costs—information that is essential if we want people to be free, and efficient in their freedom.

A free market informs and thereby coordinates the millions of people in the economy. Each of us adjusts as each of us thinks best, given our preferences and potentialities, and no commissars are required to direct us.

It may require a specialist in abnormal psychology to explain the no-growth autocrats. Do they feel embarrassed by their own riches and, in contrition, want the rest of us to don sackcloth and ashes? Do they hunger to control and mold society? Do they really believe that the key to survival is redistribution, rather than creation, of wealth? Whatever the explanation, they strain to subvert both freedom and efficiency.

The efficiency of freedom will not eradicate scarcity. Indeed, we want efficiency precisely because we cannot avoid scarcity. So we use the market to make the best of a lousy world.

Risk Is Not a Naughty Word
(AUGUST 1980)

It was an extravagance of rhetoric when a president told us that "all we have to fear is fear itself." We have reason to fear, among other things, lousy public policy. Indeed, fear, like pain, can help alert us to difficulties and dangers. But excessive fear, again like pain, can be stultifying and rob us of imagination and initiative. Petrifying fear, by evaporating strength and sense, can lead us to forgo exploitation of splendid opportunities, convert misfortunes into disasters, and make us into humiliated serfs.

This is the theme of an eloquent address by Walter B. Wriston, chairman of Citicorp, one of the world's great financial organizations.

Mr. Wriston deplores the unrealistic objective of "a totally predictable, risk-free society," the "growing thirst for an impossible physical and economic security. . . ." Indeed, the misconceived and misdirected "desire to avoid risk above all" endangers our economic efficiency, political liberty, and philosophic orientation.

Traditionally and productively, "the American spirit" has been one of "optimism and enterprise," yielding "a belief in individual responsibility and the superiority of the free marketplace, both intellectual and economic. . . ."

The dilution of that spirit has been abetted by mass communication, which has replaced sober and systematic reflection on basic issues with instant dissemination to the world of every criticism and panacea. "Things will inevitably go wrong. . . . But because all the failures, the mistakes, and the accidents intrude upon our consciousness in an almost unbroken stream, the clamor grows for a fail-safe society." And "it always turns out that the only way to avoid risk is to leap into the arms of an all-knowing government," with its indefinitely expanding bureaucracy.

Economic and political systems of free people will surely be "untidy." For there are alternatives, choices must be made, requiring estimates and assessments and predictions. Some investments and experiments and innovations will fail. But "the failures are the price we pay for the successes."

We are beneficiaries of grand successes. Change, in its nature, is unsettling and can be disquieting—as well as exhilarating and enriching. But it is not apparent that the pace of change is greater now than in some earlier periods: The two-thirds of a century prior to World War I has been called the "heroic age" of invention. And yet we seem now to have more fear, more complaints, more sense of guilt about change and the costs of adaptation.

We have put aside reasonable prudence and demonstrated much silliness in many of our constraints on business ingenuity and initiative, in taxation penalties and subsidies, in antiseptic regard for a harsh environment, in delimitations on medical innovation.

We flirt with the calamity of permitting "natural caution" to make us "terrified of uncertainty" and to lead us to "institutionalized timidity." "Uncertainty is an invitation to innovate, to create"; "uncertainty is the opportunity to make the world a better place."

GOVERNMENT AND POWER

Economic Power and Political Power

(JULY 1979)

Most of us are rightly suspicious of unconcentrated power—
at least when the power is wielded by others!

While concentrated, centralized power has the potential
for good, even more conspicuous is the potential for injury—
enforcing of the will of a few on the many, suppressing dis-
sent, reducing diversity, eliminating options.

But power comes in many forms, is obtained in various
ways, and is exercised in different contexts for different purposes. Compare concentrated *economic* power with concentrated *political* power. While it is easy to overestimate the
magnitude and the consequences of what is commonly perceived to be *economic* power, it is difficult to overestimate
the seriousness of undeniable *political* power.

Economic power is not readily defined or measured, but it
is customarily associated with "big business"—the "robber
barons," Daddy Warbucks and all that. But what do I have
to fear from, say, the president of General Motors? Does he
have either incentive or opportunity to harm me? People in
the marketplace have much reason to please me, to make
themselves valuable to me, so that I will reward them for
what they supply. A relatively large and wealthy firm like
General Motors became large and wealthy and retains its
power by being relatively efficient in responding to consumer demands. If you don't like GM products, you don't
have to buy them. And if you don't like working for GM,
you can leave.

Concentrated *political* power is quite another matter. People in governmental bureaucracies are not more evil than people in corporate bureaucracies, but they work under a different set of ground rules. Circumstances give them different options and different inducements. General Motors has little opportunity and no incentive to harm me; it has great reason to try to gain my favor. But taxing and regulatory agencies of government—local and state as well as federal—have much opportunity to harm me and little incentive to please me. What clerk at the Internal Revenue Service or the Federal Trade Commission will be promoted for being on *my* side? Far from having incentives to gain my favor, they are likely to get some of their jollies by tromping on me, knowing that they are largely unaccountable.

Of far greater danger is the fact that we have no option in accepting services of the bureaucrats—just try to stop paying for those services. Buying government services is basically different from buying products in the economic market. In the market, you can choose to buy or not to buy. And when you buy, you purchase just those things in those quantities you think best. But you have no choice in paying taxes, and, in making those payments, you are not choosing in detail or with precision just what the taxes are to buy for you. Indeed, all of us know of much use of tax collections which we do not like, and we know of many other instances when the resources sequestered by government are used inefficiently even when directed generally to services we want. The government, after all, is largely a coercive monopolist over which we have very imperfect control and which, indeed, exercises much control over us.

I have vastly more to fear from obscure functionaries in the bureaucratic mafia than from the president of General Motors.

Market Failure and Government Failure

(October 1979)

Many—even in this land of milk and honey—continue to scorn the decentralized, private-property, market-price-directed economy. So-called collective choice, partly through and mainly by government, is the alternative usually offered to "market failure." Supplanting the individualistic free market with centralized collective choice is, at best, a naïve proposal, disastrously designed by criteria of either efficiency or freedom.

We have been told much of market inefficiencies. Such failures can stem from circumstances and from activities—circumstances such as the costliness of obtaining economic information, and activities such as collusion.

Some failures commonly imputed to the market actually stem from government, with Big Brother adding to the burdens and reducing the options of market enterprises. Still, market failures do exist, and they should be acknowledged. But it is equally our obligation to note *government* failures. Indeed, market failures pale in comparison with the wastes, misdirections, and self-serving aggrandisements of government and its bureaucracy.

Blithely to assume that the answer to market failure is recourse to socialistic collective choice is especially frustrating when it is noted that much of government intervention in the market is not even intended to correct or compensate for market failure: Instead of *improving* the market on grounds of efficiency, the objective is to *dilute* and ultimately to *supersede* the market on amorphous grounds of equity. "Equity," as commonly interpreted, calls for wealth *redistribution* rather than wealth *creation*. After the revolution (or evolution), the dictatorial control of the onetime individualistic community will be conducted by those who so clearly detected *market* deficiencies but are virtually blind to *government* inadequacies.

This selective blindness is a conspicuous characteristic of reformers. We are required by elemental honesty to compare ideals with ideals, and actualities with actualities. It is not only dishonest and absurd but subversive to compare real-world economies with utopian governments. Utopia will always look better than real-world actuality.

The pertinent consideration is how we are most likely to survive best according to criteria of efficiency and freedom— to minimize the costs and the tears of getting along with each other in a stingy world. What kinds of institutions, procedures, rewards, and penalties are most likely to generate and perpetuate a relatively prosperous community of relatively free people?

We have been asking government to do more and more things which it can do poorly, if at all. We have underestimated the costs and negative side effects of government intervention and direction. Inherent in collective choice is a slighting of efficiency in responding to the revealed preferences of the individual members of the community; and the market—for all its imperfections—is our best hope for organizing greedy, aggressive people into a viable society which is economically efficient while preserving freedom.

Causes and Consequences of the Growth of Government

(FEBRUARY 1980)

Growing government—or already completely dominant government—appears to be universal. This is not a new phenomenon, even in the United States. During the twentieth century, tax payments have risen at a much faster rate than gross national product, and government employment has risen much faster than the total labor force. Indeed, government has been taking an increasing share of national income from the beginning of our history. And if present rates of change continue for another twenty years, nearly half of the economy's output will be channeled through government, which will employ a fourth of the labor force.

Why this persistent and sobering evolution toward Big Government?

One reason government tends to grow faster than the private sector is that costs of government can be spread among many people and benefits concentrated among relatively few. Costs are diffused and benefits are concentrated more easily through introducing new government programs and expanding old ones than through reducing or eliminating current programs.

Political coalitions *can* form either in support of expanding government activity and its selective benefits or, alternatively, in support of reducing government activity and its general costs. But with concentrated, conspicious benefits and diffused, camouflaged costs, the coalitions of *expansion* are the more effective in achieving their ends. More votes are gained by promising to increase benefits selectively than by reducing taxes generally.

Further, income is less equally distributed than voting

privileges. So the political mechanism is used to redistribute income generated by the economic process—although the adverse impact of such egalitarian machination on work, saving, and investment, by both the wealthy and the poor, reduces growth of the economy. And more and more people join the government establishment, adding to those with a personal stake in expansion of the regulating and redistributing bureaucracy.

So the socialist tide moves on. For a large proportion of the electorate "sells" its vote to candidates who "buy" the vote with promises both to bestow special advantages and to tax progressively the relatively well-to-do to provide general benefits to those less wealthy.

A major consequence of growing, more pervasive government is that access to, and use of, political power gains in importance relative to efficiency in economic activity. Even essentially economic decisionmaking is politicized. Corporations increasingly divert their efforts to manipulation of political power instead of concentrating on efficient production. Increasing attention is given to obtaining political favors—subsidies and protection from competition—and correspondingly less effort is directed to producing goods.

The very distinction between "government" and "business" becomes blurred. When economic activity becomes heavily intertwined with, and ever more subservient to, the political game, not only does the democratic process become ever more perverted and corrupted, but we produce less well—and, thus, we live less well.

The Simpleminded Answers of Government
(MARCH 1980)

For every answer, there is a good question. But for most questions, there are many bad answers.

This world of scarcity and grief provides a multitude of questions. Frequently, the public-policy responses to those problems are misconceived, basically misdirected, often doing more harm than good.

When faced by a conspicuous difficulty, act now and think later, if at all. Shoot from the hip—that is what is known as providing leadership, and the audience loves it. "Do something" now, for short-term effect; and deal with issues not as particular instances of general categories, applying basic principles encompassing indirect and side effects, but rather as unique and simple cases.

We want to help low-income people? Then pass a minimum-wage law. Gasoline and apartments are too expensive? Then destroy inflation with price controls. We are concerned about dependable and adequate energy supplies? Then severely regulate domestic producers (and be sure they do not make too much money), but subsidize foreign producers who collude against us. We suffer from low productivity? Then use tax laws and welfare programs to encourage consumption, discourage saving and investment, and penalize industriousness. Interest rates are too high during inflation? Then get them down by creating more money. We are prideful defenders of culture and heritage? Then scorn the principles and procedures that largely created this historical oasis of freedom and efficiency, and adopt the stance and strategies of our sworn enemies, variations on the theme which, through 6000 years of recorded history, has yielded poverty and tyranny for all but our masters.

Much, if not all, of this seems so plausible, so straight-forward, so incontrovertible. You simply do what is evidently required. You make come true, right now, the result you want.

And yet, analysis of even the most modest level of sophis-tication tells us that the apparently simple and direct policy often will not yield the desired results, and massive evidence rejects the siren song of the promises so glibly given at the outset. *Of course*, minimum-wage laws will hurt, not help, the untrained and inexperienced. *Of course*, price controls will not eliminate inflation, but will create shortages. *Of course*, adding to the money supply will make inflation worse and thereby increase, not decrease, interest rates.

We are being persistently suckered, being *exploited by* posturing politicians even as we try to *use* government to improve our lot. People are not stupid—but few are very good economists; they are not fools in their own jobs and areas of expertise—but they can be seduced by seemingly confident and supposedly knowledgeable people of authority.

We do well to deal very carefully with those of great authority—especially those of *political* authority, whose product, after all, is not commodities, which would make us better off, but machinations to control our lives, which makes us worse off.

Muddleheaded Minority Economics

(JUNE 1980)

It is not easy to do good well. Compassion is a virtue: Civ-ilized people sympathetically respond to those receiving a disproportionate share of the slings and arrows of outrageous fortune. But it is possible to be too anxious to do good. When compassion is not supplemented with rational analysis, resources are squandered—we are guilty of waste in a world of scarcity. This is particularly vivid in the context of racial and cultural "minorities."

No one denies that there are "minority" problems—even if disagreement is great on their nature, cause, and correction. Some of the widely perceived problems appear to be heavily sociological and psychological—problems of reliability and self-reliance, ambition and patience, planning horizons and investment. Much of the aid to minorities evidently has exacerbated some of those problems. It has tended to develop dependency rather than initiative; to break, rather than strengthen, the nexus between productivity and reward; to engender outrage over inequality from market activity rather than over constraints imposed by government which limit market options. The thrust of government effort has been on concessions and special arrangements to excuse poor performance rather than to improve performance; on short-term amelioration rather than on basic solution; on equality of state-imposed result rather than on provision of opportunity.

Many a minority spokesman has been seduced by this basically parasitic approach and has, in turn, helped to seduce those for whom he professes to speak. A dozen years ago, during the period of collective campus insanity, at least one university inaugurated a course in "black statistics." Perhaps courses were given also in "yellow chemistry" and "brown economics." Different people and groups will choose different topics to study and manifest different emphases, to be sure. But analysis is analysis, to be applied and assessed on its merits. There is no uniquely "minority" economics— or regional or national or sexual or religious or occupational economics. There is only good economics and bad economics—or, if you prefer, economics and, alternatively, sociological poetry.

But it is easier to exhibit outrage and darkly to threaten

political retribution than to analyze and to help make viable a national economy. From time to time, the Congressional Black Caucus seems to feel obliged to remind us of how easy it is to pronounce muddleheaded economics.

Recently, the Caucus visited the president. They expressed unwillingness to share inevitable costs of controlling inflation. Instead, they called for "an immediate attack on inflation in the proper way," as they put it, "by bringing down interest rates and by recontrolling and limiting the increases in prices. . . ."

Ah, yes, and we shall also keep the beach dry by commanding the tide to stay out.

Nominal interest rates have been high *because* of inflation, of course, and those rates will not fall back to historical levels until inflation has been brought back to historical levels. But price controls do not—*cannot*—eliminate inflation. They only make a bad situation worse.

While it is not easy to do good well, elemental economics really is not all that mysterious.

Equality of Opportunity or Equality of Outcome?

(NOVEMBER 1979)

This nation has had magnificent moral and philosophical underpinnings. The ideals have encompassed equality before the law, the corollary equality of social and economic opportunity, and the accompanying promise of rising material well-being. In both prerequisite and result, the orientation has been individualistic—opportunity for, and accountability of, the individual, with free men in free markets, engaging in essentially unfettered activities, bearing the consequences (both good and bad) of their own actions.

The ideals have never been fully realized in this vale of scarcity and human frailty. But there has never been a major society in which similar ideals were more closely attained.

However, in recent decades, the ideals themselves have been modified, bastardized, and effectively rejected.

The Great Depression understandably inspired pleas for government to "do something"—and it did it badly and wastefully. The 1950s greatly expanded government involvement in science and technology—with pure research and student test scores in mathematics progressively deteriorating. In the 1960s, the banner was "social justice"—and government mangled one social problem after another, until the 200 welfare programs of the New Frontier mushroomed into over 1000 by the mid-1970s. This decade has seen a distortion of the demand for social justice—it is now equality not of *opportunity* but of *condition*.

No longer sufficient is equal treatment under the law and equal opportunity. As observed by Daniel Bell, "Too many Americans who got that protection still came out losers. What is now being demanded is equality of result—an equal *outcome* for all." Robert Nisbet warns that the claimed right of "equality of condition" is a "poisonous value." "Impossible of achievement," he says, "it nevertheless excites cravings which escalate annually, cravings and expectations which will become more intense in very proportion to the total impossibility of their fulfillment."

Conspicuous in this new "revolution of rising entitlements" are a shift from production to consumption, a shift from wealth creation to wealth redistribution, a shift from individual opportunity to compete to communal assurance of outcome, a shift from free men in free markets to centralized dictation.

One manifestation of growing collectivism is the ongoing rise in government spending, which now absorbs over 40 percent of national output. Less obvious, but even more insidious, is government constraining, directing, subsidizing, regulating, requiring, prohibiting actions in a vast variety of social and economic activities.

More and more, consumer preferences and real costs do not determine use of resources, accomplishment does not determine rewards, personal accountability is not required, and personal initiative—except in enunciating "rights"—is not compensated.

What is the result of a massive destruction of incentives? Success! We shall achieve equality of condition—everyone will be reduced to the lowest common denominator. If everyone cannot be a winner, each one will be a loser.

ECONOMIC EDUCATION

"Economic Education" and the Nature of the Game
(March 1980)

Economics is important. Everyone lives in an economic world, and therefore everyone necessarily is a practicing economist. So "economic education" is important. Right?

Many urge more formal training in economics. Editorial writers defend the advantages, not merely to the individual but to the community generally, of learning more about economics. Some business firms have in-house programs of economic education. And several states have mandated a course in economics as a high-school graduation requirement.

How serious is the "general lack of understanding . . . of how the economy works"? One might infer that historically "economic illiteracy" has *not* been critical. After all, the long-term record of the United States economy in producing and distributing goods is excellent—over the past two centuries, we have had, in general, a flourishing economy. And we have produced much while maintaining a highly mobile, adaptable, open society.

But over those two centuries, there was little formal, tutored economic sophistication. How could we have acted so effectively in investing, producing, and selling while being so illiterate in technical economic analysis?

One of the beauties of the market-enterprise economy is that its operations require little of elegant economics and of central direction. No one—economist or bureaucratic czar

—was in charge of the show; none was needed; and, indeed, the economy operated vastly better than it could have under some imposed plan from headquarters. People are not stupid. They learn, and they calculate. But their calculations center well-nigh exclusively on their own personal, immediate affairs, where both their interests and their knowledge focus. The "big" picture of the economy is best resolved by self-interested, independent people taking care of their respective "little" pictures.

By and large, that is the way it has been—at least during the first century and a half of our national history—with free men operating effectively in free markets. The market itself magnificently coordinated and channeled all those millions of people with their individual interests and efforts. Our economic illiteracy was quite irrelevant to the level of our productivity. This is not to say that academic *study* of how a free economy operates is improper. Still, in large measure, such scholarship was its own end; it was not required for extensive social control.

But will the setting of our activity, will the game itself, be the same in the future? Even now can we be reasonably characterized as free men in free markets? Are we not becoming increasingly directed men in centrally controlled markets? It is expecting a great deal from "economic education" to save us from this socialistic folly.

We continue to be interested in our well-being, of course, but the evolving nature of the game calls more and more for political machination instead of economic production. Perhaps "economic education" of the future, after the free and efficient society and its economy have been subverted, will hardly be economics, but, rather, survival training in the bureaucratic jungle of Big Brother.

The Over-Selling of "Economic Education"
(APRIL 1980)

Some questions and problem areas are more conspicuous than others. While there may be more wonderment and anxiety about sexual matters—exhilarating as they are—than anything else, economics—depressing as it is—may be a candidate for second position.

When economic problems—especially inflation and unemployment—rise, so do economics editorials and enrollments in college economics courses. But there is also a general increase in "economic education." More and more school districts and states are pushing study of economics, the taking of an economics course even being a high-school graduation requirement.

The interest in so-called economics is on both a personal and a community level.

At the personal level, it is deemed desirable to learn early how to write and endorse checks and calculate the price per ounce of a can of beans. Such skills are valuable—but they have little to do with genuine economic analysis.

At the community level, it is hoped that greater knowledge of the principles of economics would conduce more sophisticated public policy, with economically literate voters electing economically literate representatives. One is reluctant to knock literacy. But, at most, better economic education is a *necessary* condition for improved policy—by itself, it certainly is not *sufficient*. For there are many motivations and considerations which impinge upon how one votes for candidates and policies—all sorts of personal perspectives and criteria and objectives may swamp the dispassionate conclusions of the economic logic machine surveying the various markets from atop Mount Olympus. And, in candor, your friendly neighborhood economist, for all his cleverness and rigorous technique, is neither omniscient nor infallible—especially when he has joined the government.

Economics (with a capital "E") may generalize that, by certain pertinent criteria, markets should be cleared, income should be distributed on the basis of productive contributions, exchange among consenting adults should not be restricted, and rights to use of property should be clear, stable, and mainly in private hands. But Economics itself does not pronounce such generalizations as definitive conclusions, subject to no qualifications or exceptions. Different economic criteria will yield different policy prescriptions. And there is no end to qualifications and exceptions presented on non-economic grounds by hysterical agitators and poetic reformers.

Better and wider appreciation of elemental economic analysis could be broadly useful. It could reduce the more blatant nonsense with which we are inundated, especially in election years. It could be a barrier to those who wish to seduce us, like dumb oxen, to put on the constraining yoke of Big Brother.

But it is unrealistic to suppose that every member of the community can be made into a sophisticated economist—or that that, even if accomplished, would guarantee the viability of the free society and its efficient economy. *That* requires not academic elegance in economics but an arrangement of institutions which will permit free men, with their untutored instincts and acquired aspirations, to handle their personal nitty-gritty affairs in free markets.

Economics versus "Economic Education"

(APRIL 1980)

One would hardly expect an economist to oppose teaching of economics. But he *can* be expected to demur when what is taught is *not* economic analysis and techniques of its application but, instead, bastardized garbage—fiction, poetry, dogma—dumped by inept instructors and authors on innocent students.

"Economic education" in the primary and secondary schools may be "education" of a sort—something *is* being presented to students. But we have reason to wonder if what is taught bears much similarity to economics.

A major problem in implementing "economic education" is the quality of instruction. You cannot teach what you do not know—and few "social studies" teachers know much economics. The person giving the high-school economics course is likely to be the track coach or the manual-arts instructor because he took a course in sociology twenty years ago.

Perhaps an even weaker link in the pedagogical chain is the textbook. With a good text, at least the teacher and the students could read the material together, to the benefit of all. A recent survey of how economic issues have been treated in high-school textbooks in history, sociology, and government provides grounds for concern, if not despair.

Major economic problems and policy issues are taken up in these social-studies textbooks. And, virtually without exception, the treatment is thoroughly mangled. Further, it is mangled with a consistent bias—whether or not intended —favoring government regulation of industry and union domination of labor markets and opposing free exchange and privately determined use of resources in open markets, all in a context of analytic confusion, historical error, and mischievous generalization.

According to these textbooks, free labor markets yield low wages and poor working conditions, with all gains from exchange and wealth accumulation going to the autonomous employers; technological advance and investment lower wages and increase unemployment; gains of workers can be imputed to unions and such legislation as minimum-wage laws; trade is the disposal of "surpluses," which leads internationally to imperialism; the result, as well as the intent, of regulation by such agencies as the Interstate Commerce Commission and of licensing of professions has been protection of the general welfare against rapacious businesses and incompetent or greedy practitioners; industry is plagued by too little competition and agriculture by too much, government regulation being required in both; the Great Depression was caused by a "structural imbalance" of the economy.

So goes the litany of ignorance, mistake, inconsistency, and collectivist dogma. Doubtless, the textbook authors are honorable. But, obviously, they are lousy economists, lacking a well-founded body of theory and effective methodology and relying on misguided jungle instinct, writing with seeming confidence and presumed authority on matters beyond their comprehension.

Confronted by such smug incompetence in the teaching of the young, the economist may be torn between laughing and crying. I, for one, am not laughing.

Mainly Microeconomics: Analysis of Relative Prices and Resource Allocation

✖✖✖✖

PROPERTY RIGHTS

Ideology and Economic Activity
(February 1980)

It is easy to suppose that production is purely a matter of engineering, along with available resources. After all, land is land, a machine is a machine, labor skill is labor skill, raw material is raw material. So we take these productive inputs and combine them as best we technologically know how in order to grind out the desired widgets and gadgets.

Of course, that *is* a large and critical part of the production story. But economists have long known that engineering and resources are not the *whole* story. One reason is that there are alternative ways to combine inputs in order to produce a given output—we can trade off, at the margin, more of one sort of input for less of another. Which of the combinations of inputs is best? Technology alone cannot tell us. The answer requires economic, or market, data—we must know the *prices* of productive services in order to produce a given output with the least cost.

Even adding economic calculation to the resource availability and engineering knowledge does not fully explain economic performance. Another variable in the picture is *ideology*.

Some economists have begun to investigate in detail, as have others in broader perspective, the impact of alternative political ideologies on economic efficiency. Largely unreasoned preconceptions, beliefs, and attitudes concerning social relationships, individual responsibilities, economic activities, and government obligations are reflected in the definition and enforcement of so-called property rights.

Rights of people to the use of resources, rights to the use of income generated by those resources, rights to sell their resources, and the present clarity and degree of future certainty of those rights, very largely determine not only the nature of the economy but the nature of society and of individual activity in general. Both the efficiency of markets and the character of the community, both what and how much we produce and the range of options available to individuals, are functions of the property ground rules.

Resources—including technology—are resources, and at any given time we are stuck with what we have found and figured out. But we can affect for what and how well those resources are used by specification of property rights.

People are neither stupid nor unconcerned about themselves; they constantly strive to increase their well-being through adaptation to their natural and social environments; they react with individual rationality to incentives and disincentives. Those incentives and disincentives are largely subsumed under "property rights." Communities differ greatly in their economic efficiency and in the attitudes and behavior of their people because of different options and constraints implied by their different patterns and procedures of property rights.

Property rights—the rules of the game—set the stage of activity for us all, determining, within limits imposed by nature and knowledge, how well we eat—and how free we live.

Property Rights, Human Rights, and Campus Radicals

(NOVEMBER 1979)

I don't mean to be beastly about it, but there does appear to be some degree of confusion among radical reformers concerning property rights. And campus radicals, be assured, can be as confused as any other kind.

The confusion begins with the very term "property rights." Property itself—a piece of land or an automobile—has no rights. Only people can have rights. So-called property rights are the rights of *people* to *use* of property. Those rights to use of property necessarily are limited: Within permitted limits, I can use my hammer as I please, but I am not permitted to use my hammer to break your window without your consent.

But the rights in question, even though limited, are mine, not the hammer's. There can be no conflict between the hammer and me over respective rights, for the property itself has none. Campus radicals are not the only ones who sometimes profess to see a contrast between "human" rights and "property" rights. And, of course, faced by that dichotomy—silly though it is—any red-blooded American would come out foursquare in favor of "human" rights!

Rights to the use of property will not be abolished by the revolution—unless the revolution leaves us in a state of complete anarchy. The rights can be redefined and redistributed by the revolutionary tribunal, and there can be institutional and procedural changes in *how* those rights are specified and allocated and how disputes over rights are resolved. But any society will have some system of property rights and their administration.

Indeed, the essence of a society is very largely determined

by its system of property rights—who has what rights to the use of what property, what are the classes of approved or prohibited use of assets, and who answers such questions through what processes. Property rights are the basic ground rules which determine what we are permitted to do and how we are permitted to do it. They provide opportunities and constraints. They are basic in defining how "free" the society is.

Now, campus subversives have some strong notions on who should control the use of assets. For example, they want to use any convenient wall of any building as a signboard. So college buildings are liberally decorated with gaudy pronouncements of a better, postrevolutionary world to come and with ringing calls to the barricades.

One might find amusing such youthful, even if ignorantly channeled, exuberance—except for a troublesome matter of dogma, or at least of tactics. For the revolutionaries do not dislike wealth itself; they spit only on wealth owned by others. They want wealth to be owned by the state—and the state to be directed by them. But here they are, besmirching state-owned buildings!

I could understand radicals making pigsties out of buildings at *private* schools, like Stanford and USC. But they surely are confused in turning *state* schools, like UCLA, into coarse and cruddy billboards.

Property Rights and the Fate of Whales

(OCTOBER 1979)

Whalers—particularly the Japanese—may be killing at such a rate as virtually to eliminate the species on whose survival their own future livelihoods rest. Why such seemingly irrational behavior?

No one owns the seas' resources. If ownership-control could be established, then the slaughter of whales would be moderated to ensure their future survival—as beef cattle exist as a viable species. No rancher would kill his entire herd, for today's gain would be far outweighed by the losses of tomorrow when he has no cattle to sell.

Japan and Russia account for about 95 percent of the total whale kill.

If a Japanese whaler has no assurance that the whale he saves today will be his to harvest tomorrow, then it is rational to "get while the getting's good." That assurance is not there when the rival Russian whaler can take the spared whale. The Russian gets the whale and may do so before it has matured and can reproduce, so the Japanese loses all around—unless he takes the whale *now*. The Russian whaler faces the same dilemma.

Thus, lack of control over *other* peoples' uses of the whale leads to overkill. By establishing such controls—known as "property rights"—we could be more optimistic about long-term conservation of whales. Contrary to impassioned histrionics, the problem is *not* one of unique "greed" on the part of whalers. They *are* greedy, of course—but no more greedy than ranchers, who do not kill all their cattle at once.

Yet outright ownership of the whales is an impossible solution: We cannot fence the oceans. Quasi ownership and partial control can be accomplished, in principle, by international agreement. The International Whaling Commission —including the United States, Russia, Japan, and twenty-one other nations—provides agreements on kill quotas and territories.

In recent years, the Whaling Commission has had some success in conservation; but there are inherent problems. The Commission can be effective in saving whales only if it sets biologically correct quotas *and* if those quotas are adhered to. But knowledge of whale demography is inadequate. Further, the Japanese have adeptly used economic carrots and sticks with enough Commission members to thwart or dilute most efforts to impose whaling constraints. Finally, the incentive for any one party to a quota agreement will be to cheat and take more than the quota. For the cheater will get the rewards, while the other countries will share the cost of having a reduced "pool" of whales. And the smaller the quotas, the greater the inducement to cheat.

Along with dangers of internal disintegration of the Whaling Commission, some whaling nations are not members. If nonmembers do not abide by the conservation efforts, they weaken the effectiveness of the Commission and increase incentives for member nations either to leave the Commission or to cheat on the quotas.

The threat to whales does not stem from a monstrous greed unique to whalers. Rather, it is a result of property rights which have been difficult to define and enforce. When the rules of the game are uncertain, resources are badly used.

Economics As the Protection of Whales

(OCTOBER 1979)

Whales have been killed to such an extent that survival of some varieties is in doubt. The problem is not peculiar greed of whalers but, rather, lack of clear definition and assignment of property rights in whales and effective enforcement of such rights.

When exclusive property rights are not stipulated and effective, we cannot expect long-term efficiency in use of resources. Resources that are available to everyone will not be rationally conserved by anyone.

International agreements on kill quotas for whales have had some success, but they seem insufficient. There are other economic factors, however, independent of problems of ownership and control, that may save whales from extinction.

The ocean is large, and while whales have known migration habits, they generally do not swim right up to the whaling vessels. They must be found. As the whale population diminishes, the more costly it will be for whalers to find the remaining whales. The costs involved per whale killed will increase as the numbers of whales available and caught diminish. When those costs exceed the value of the whale's carcass and its derivatives, it will no longer be economically feasible to hunt whales.

Whale products are used in food, fertilizers, oils, and cosmetics. But there are *substitutes* for everything. Whales are used in the manufacture of, say, cosmetics because alternative ways of manufacturing cosmetics are more expensive. But as it becomes more costly to produce cosmetics using whale derivatives, the alternatives finally become economically viable.

The same is true of all whale products: As the cost of catching the ever more scarce whales increases, the prices of those products must go up to cover the larger expenses. But as the price rises, substitute products—those made by means other than the now more costly whale derivatives—will become more attractive.

In the case of cosmetics, the price of whale derivatives evidently would not have to increase much. The United States bans the sale of cosmetics using whale derivatives, and we have found a substitute for the whale at an "acceptable" cost. Since other countries continue to use whale derivatives, we can infer that those derivatives are still cheaper than the ingredients in American cosmetics. But if whale derivatives become more expensive than their substitutes, all manufacturers will abandon use of whales.

Indeed, since the early 1960s, the world whaling industry has greatly diminished. Japan is the leading whaling country, and its declining fleet depends heavily on government subsidies. At a recent meeting of the International Whaling Commission, Japan was largely successful in harpooning proposed additional restrictions on whaling operations. Still, the United States whaling commissioner found a general feeling that, within a few years, whales will be priced out of the market.

There may not be many whales left when that day comes —but there will be some. The question is: Will there be enough for a viable population, or will we have gone past that point where a whale population can maintain itself?

No one can now answer that question. But there is reason to hope.

THE CONSUMER AND
HIS PROTECTION

Real and Bogus Protection of the Consumer
(February 1980)

All of us are consumers, and many of us are producers. Obviously, consumers and producers are *not* wholly separate groups, naturally opposed to each other. Instead, most of the adult population produce as well as consume, and most of what we consume we have had to produce.

But the bulk of what a given individual consumes is not directly produced by that person. Typically, the individual sells what he produces and buys his consumption goods from other suppliers. So it is appropriate that consumers be "protected," in some respects, to some degree, in some fashion.

But there are various ways in which the consumer can be protected. The most pervasive and ultimate protection is through normal market processes. For consumers are not fools; they are not incapable of learning about products and their producers.

Within the limits of their budgets, people choose the kinds and qualities of goods which, in their own individual judgments, will best serve their wants. Producers who respond poorly to the revealed preferences of consumers will lose wealth, even to the point of ceasing operations. At the same time, producers who please consumers will prosper.

The consumer protections inherent in free-market processes are little understood or appreciated by many. Indeed, confusion concerning the market and scorn for market operations are deliberately cultivated by self-designated saviors who are paternalistically overanxious to protect us helpless, dim-witted sorts.

So more and more reliance is put on governmental standards and requirements and decisions. Unhappily, the governmental intervention often does not supplement the market; rather, it suppresses and partially supplants the market, replacing impersonal efficiency in satisfying *community* preferences with erratic, wasteful discrimination and imposition of *bureaucratic* preferences.

Judicious government activity does have some potential for good. In particular, there are legal proscriptions of fraud, and government testing of products can enlighten consumers and thereby enhance the rationality of consumer choices.

But a vast amount of the activity is petty, irresponsible, unaccountable Big Brotherism. It is seemingly inspired by dictatorial tendencies, love of coercive power, desires to mold society and order the lives of other people. Tactically, it is sometimes a device to curry favor of special interests, not protecting consumers but rather subsidizing particular sellers. Whatever the motivations, much of "consumerism" leads to misuse of resources by the standards of consumers themselves, increased costs for producers and higher prices for buyers, bloated absorption by the bureaucracy, and further concentration of political power.

We do not live on manna from heaven—we produce what we consume. If so-called consumer protectionism misguidedly reduces consumption options and production efficiency, we consumers—along with us producers—lose from "consumer protection."

There's No Such Thing As a Bad Deal

(April 1980)

Since the serpent and Eve led us astray in the Garden of
Eden, this has been a world of scarcity. We cannot satisfy
all wants of *all* people *all*—or, indeed, *any*—of the time.

One consequence of scarcity is *competition*. We have conflict, injury, and tears. It is easy—because largely correct—
to view the world as one of adversaries and adversity. But
that is not a complete characterization. And a partial, selective assessment of our situation can inspire supposedly cor-
rective and ameliorative actions that make our sorry plight
even worse.

Our relatively open, adaptive, innovative society has been
based on the relatively open, adaptive, innovative market.
But how can a good society be based on a market arrangement of greed and competition? Wouldn't we be better off if
we more fully protected buyers from sellers and required that
all deals be made at fair prices?

There are problems in trying to protect the innocent and
in imposing fairness.

One problem is that many of those you wish to protect
are also those from whom you are trying to protect them!
Protect buyers from sellers? Each of us is a buyer, but many
of us also are sellers. As a buyer of X, you may lobby Big
Brother to decree a maximum price; as a seller of Y, price
ceilings look less attractive.

Do price controls make you better off even in your partial
capacity as a buyer? A ceiling price on gasoline or apartments
or loans is no blessing when, as a result of the imposed ceiling, you cannot find a seller or a lender, or if you can buy or
borrow only specified amounts after waiting in line and by
first obtaining coupons or permits from the government

bureaucracy. We cannot fool the market about preferences and costs—but we can *frustrate* market operations, to our disadvantage.

There is even more involved than taking account of the waste in frustrating the market. There is also the importance of properly viewing the nature of the interrelations of people in the market. It is, indeed, a world of scarcity and thus, inevitably, a world of competition. But if we are to have a viable society, it must also be a world of *coordination*.

In a genuine market, there is voluntary, uncoerced exchange. Governments and robbers do not *induce;* they *compel.* But in the market, no one buys or sells unless, in his own estimation, he will gain from the trade. If either individual were not convinced that the swap would make him better off, there would be no swap—and no mutual gains.

The traders need not like each other. Indeed, they may bargain over terms, each trying to get as much gain as possible. But each *does* gain from the trade, each *is* better off.

With free men in free markets, we have competition, but we also have a coordinated economy. Each trader strives for his own gain, but the market itself channels those self-centered strivings into coordinated efficiency.

There's no such thing as an uncoerced bad deal.

Mouse Wisdom: Profits and the Satisfaction of Community Preferences

(SEPTEMBER 1979)

Somewhere in my office live two mice. The wiser is Adam, of the Smith family; the other, who is bright but immature, is Karl, one of the Marx brothers. My little friends always listen to these broadcasts and then philosophize about life, scarcity, and other important things.

Recently, Adam and Karl discussed food production. Karl believed that the prime object of food suppliers should be to satisfy hunger, not to obtain personal gain. "How much better the world would be—more genteel and less wasteful—if mice were to give up selfish pursuits and, instead, work in the best interests of their fellow mice," remarked Karl. "Production should be for *use*, not for *profit*."

"I'm not sure," said Adam, "that reducing hunger and making profits are inconsistent, incompatible objectives. In fact, to reduce hunger most efficiently—that is, in ways preferred by consumers—may *require* pursuit of profit."

"I can't imagine why," snapped Karl, who professes to be offended by gamy materialism.

Adam pressed the point with insight. "How can we know what *kind* of food to produce and in what *quantities?*" he asked. "And how do we know for *whom* to produce that food?"

"Those questions of what to produce and for whom can be answered by the producers," asserted Karl, who loved mousekind in rather an autocratic manner.

Adam was not to be easily put off. "If I am a food producer," he said, "how could I know the preferences of consumers? Of course, I could *presume* to know the best interests of society by supplying the kinds and amounts of food I think mice should have. And I could allocate it to those mice I feel most deserving. But that would be very presumptuous."

"Nonsense," replied an irritated Karl. "Your motives would be noble, for you would be trying to help those ignorant mice who really don't know what is good for them."

"Well," said Adam, "neither of *us* has been appointed to tell mice what they want, or should want. It is *community* preferences which should direct production. And community preferences *can* prevail if I act to make profits in producing food. My profit reward is a measure of how effectively I have responded to, and satisfied, those preferences."

"I don't like where you are leading me," grumbled Karl.

"Look," said Adam, "my pursuit of profit is certainly more apt to satisfy mouse ends than if, for some odd reason, I were to disregard nitty-gritty profits and establish as my vague object simply the reduction of hunger. Customers give me market signals. They tell me their desires by the prices they are willing to pay; they don't want my preferences imposed on them. If I am efficient in responding to their preferences, I earn profits. And earning those profits is my incentive to give customers what they want. Producing for profit is producing for uses that consumers prefer."

Karl tucked his tail but insisted on the last word. "You," he told Adam, "would be a lousy commissar."

The Criminality of Satisfying Consumers

(JANUARY 1980)

A gasoline station owner has been found guilty of price gouging. Convicted of charging more than $1.50 per gallon, he was heavily fined and sent to jail for a considerable period.

The station owner was not attempting to become a national hero by selective civil disobedience. Indeed, he claimed that it was not his intent to violate the complex regulations governing the calculation of his maximum legal price.

Whatever the purity of his heart and his competence as an accountant, the seller was found guilty of overcharging. Should the rest of us rejoice that a scoundrel was discovered in his skulduggery? Should we be content with an economy that conducts its business by stupid regulations and their vigorous enforcement? Will we thereby make better use of resources? Better for whom and by what criteria?

Price ceilings on gasoline were dictated by Big Brother. The purpose was to establish lower prices than would exist in a free market. But with an imposed price below the market-clearing level, there will be a *shortage:* Low prices encourage consumption. It suggests a lack of either wit or integrity to force prices down by edict and then to evince surprise that the community wants to buy more than is available—and all the while to preach conservation!

But people cannot obtain more than is available. Somehow, the supply of gas is allocated among the competing consumers. Since this is not permitted through open-market bidding, people must make some of their payment in nonmoney form.

The nonmoney payment might take the form of ration coupons distributed by the same wise and kindly government that created the shortage by price controls in the first place. We have not yet taken that peculiar path. Instead, we supplement our low money payments by payments in time, aggravation, and uncertainty.

If we cannot clear the market through paying the money price at which quantity demanded is matched by quantity supplied, then we make part of the payment by sitting in line. Sitting in line does not make the total price lower, and it certainly does not create more gas. Instead, it wastes gas, and it wastes additional resources, and makes us much less efficient in conducting our affairs.

So there we wait in line for gas. We are *willing* to pay more than the legal maximum price. We should *like* to bid a higher price and thereby avoid waiting. The existence of the shortage means that we are frustrated in our wish to bid a higher money price.

If this is not the case, then how did our criminal seller find customers who would pay $1.50 per gallon? Why didn't they wait for an hour or two at the station across the street in order to get gas at only $1.20? The transactions at $1.50 were not coerced. The customers paid that price by their own decisions. They *preferred* to pay $1.50 and get the gas now. They had the option of waiting in order to pay only $1.20; the dastardly seller made them better off, in the customers' own estimations, by selling at $1.50.

But in the Alice in Wonderland world of Big Brother and his price controls, consumers are protected from options that can make them better off, and sellers are punished when they respond to the demands of consumers.

Markets, Government, and the Voice of the People
(JUNE 1980)

Procter & Gamble is a giant among giants. It supplies a great variety of well-known household goods and food items. Now it is entering the soft-drink business by acquiring most of Crush International. The government did not object some time ago to the acquisition of 7-Up by Philip Morris, and it is not expected to block Procter & Gamble from swallowing Crush.

Isn't that disgusting, even terrifying? If we "need" more investment in soft-drink production, then why doesn't P&G put its money into discovery and development of a *new* drink rather than taking over existing facilities? But maybe social well-being will not be best served by more bubbles in any case. Perhaps the firm should stick to its present products and turn out better or cheaper soap and coffee. Or, if it is to branch out, how about investing in energy? That surely is something we "need."

Evidently there has been no outcry from consumerist types

or politicians over the spending of tens of millions of dollars on frivolities like soft drinks and marginal amenities like soap and coffee. We may infer a general public feeling that P&G should be permitted to invest its resources as it thinks best, in accordance with its own assessment of market possibilities.

Oddly, it is a different story when the firm is not P&G but Exxon or Mobil or Texaco. Not content with controlling prices in the petroleum industry, stipulating and capriciously administering severe environmental requirements, and imposing special taxes, the community supposedly is aghast when oil firms diversify their investments into real estate, shipbuilding, and health care.

In actuality, despite all the handicaps and disincentives with which they are confronted, oil firms *are* investing massive and increasing amounts in energy. Exploration and crude-oil production account for two-thirds of total capital projects this year, exploration being the single biggest budget item.

What determines investment decisions? Corporate managers respond to signals, they make decisions on the basis of information and anticipations, in seeking to serve the interests of the owners—sometimes tens of thousands of owners—of the business. Those signals and that information come basically from the market, generated by offers and activities of producers, sellers, and buyers. With this information, returns and costs of alternatives are estimated. Producers and sellers who estimate well and act efficiently will prosper, to the benefit of their customers as well as themselves.

This free-market mechanism—recording information, generating decisions, and inducing coordinated behavior—is enormously effective in allocating resources *in accordance with the revealed preferences of the community*. But when the market mechanism is diluted and distorted by a shifting and discriminatory hodgepodge of governmental restrictions, penalties, subsidies, and directives, the received signals are confusing and discouraging. As political and bureaucratic whimsy are substituted for freely expressed community wishes, both the level and the efficiency of productive activity are lowered. Big Brother, by subverting the market, makes us both poorer and less free.

Super Scalping

(JANUARY 1981)

As the teams prepared to exchange hits and bruises in the Super Bowl, other exchanges were taking place on the sidelines. These exchanges were the purchase and sale of Super Bowl tickets at prices often far above the face values of the tickets. Widely denounced as a means of immoral exploitation of buyers, so-called ticket scalping is not unlike garage sales or the sale of beer.

In a garage sale, someone may offer an old television set he does not value highly. Only by bidding to pay more than the seller's valuation can a buyer obtain the set, but no buyer will offer more than his own valuation. Thus, the TV is transferred from a lower- to a higher-valued use—a transfer which creates *gains of exchange* which are *shared* by the buyer and the seller.

The gains of exchange are the difference between the buyer's and the seller's valuations of the TV. If the buyer values the set at $80 and the seller at $20, then the total gains are $60. How the buyer and the seller share those gains depends on the price. If the price is $70, then the buyer gets $10 of the gains, for he pays only $70 for a TV he values at $80. The seller gets the remaining $50 of the gains, because he receives $70 for a TV he values at just $20.

More complicated exchanges are essentially the same, even if they involve many middlemen. When beer is distributed, the producer, various middlemen, and the consumer all share in the gains. The productiveness of exchange is made apparent when middlemen can get a slice of the gains and still leave both the original seller and the ultimate buyer better off than they would be in the absence of exchange.

So it is with Super Bowl tickets. Thousands of tickets are given or sold at face value to numerous people. Initially, all the tickets go to the teams of the league and to the office of the league commissioner. The tickets of each team are distributed among players, coaches, and team administrators. Tickets are allocated also to sportswriters, politicians, season ticketholders, and others.

This original distribution of tickets does *not* happen to place them with people who most value them. So it is hardly surprising that many are traded—exchanges which move tickets from people who value them less to people who value them more. As with the distribution of beer, some of these exchanges involve middlemen who facilitate the transfer of tickets. Ticket brokers, acting as middlemen, have developed contacts with many of those who originally receive tickets. The brokers bid many of the tickets away from the original recipients and eventually sell them to people willing to pay prices much above face values.

The gains from transferring tickets to those who value them most highly are *shared* by the original holders, the ticket brokers, and the fans who are thereby able to attend the game. These exchanges are the same sort of phenomenon as the distributing of other goods: They realize a more efficient, more valuable allocation of scarce goods among consumers.

To prevent people from buying and selling as they think best is a peculiar way to try to make them better off. To complain about super scalping is super silliness.

Consumer Protection May Be Hazardous to Your Health

(AUGUST 1979)

Putting government in charge of protecting the consumer, it has been suggested, is much like putting Dracula in charge of the blood bank.

We all desire product quality and getting what we bargain for, but fulfillment of these desires entails *costs*. Not only can the costs be high, but bearing them will not inevitably achieve the objectives.

Costs are often in excess of the value of returns when government intervenes in the market to "protect" consumers. For consumer protection involves more than outlawing fraud and testing the physical qualities of products; it involves also *consumer preferences*. "Consumerism" very largely is a matter of bureaucrats imposing their own tastes and standards on a public that has myriad individual and differing preferences.

Government can sometimes enlighten consumer choices by gathering and disseminating product information. But to withhold products or to specify high product standards or to impose non-market-clearing prices, eliminates and distorts consumer choices.

Government has a long and lamentable record of paternalistic "protection" of consumers, resulting in waste, erosion of individual freedom, consumer frustration—even consumer deaths. All this in the name of "doing good," of course.

There is an enormous catalog of misconceived, often vague and inconsistent, very expensive, and capriciously administered consumer interventionism—air bags and other automobile specifications; price controls; restrictions on the payment and the rate of interest; professional training standards and licensing; regulation of advertising; building codes and land-use directives; regulation of transportation; tariffs; banishment of supposedly dangerous products; pollution standards.

Now, you may applaud some such cases of government specification and regulation while resenting others. I, too, might accept certain sorts of controls and imposed standards, even though most of the constraints strike me as highly inappropriate. But it is not to be expected that you and I and 200 million other consumers will agree on which regulations are sensible and which are silly. And I no more want your silly restrictions imposed imperiously on me than you want my silly requirements arbitrarily slapped on you.

Properly included in the great costs of consumer regulation is the general growth of government, the encouraged movement toward centralized and politicized control, the enhanced authority of the state to punish some and to subsidize others, the spreading encroachment of a largely unaccountable bureaucracy into activities which—at least in this Land of the Free—should be individually determined.

Beware the person who, with his peculiar brilliance and sensitivity, professes to know the "public interest" and who volunteers to drag us dull-witted types away from the dangers of "special interests."

Save us from our protectors! Who will regulate the regulators?

Regulators As Consumers: Controls and Competition

(December 1979)

Economists are a notoriously dour bunch. The reason, according to them, is that they so well understand this dismal world. They eagerly clutch any manifestation—or even promise—of economic rationality, of calculation of costs, of concern for efficiency, of provision of consumer alternatives.

A frustrating task of the economist has been the endless (and seemingly futile) explanation of the benefits generated by essentially unfettered competition—the lowered costs, the constant search for innovations, the rapid response to consumers' changing preferences. The analytical argument for competition is persuasive. But typically it has been swamped by industries pleading to be protected from competition, bureaucrats hungering to control larger empires, and politicians worrying about how best to appear active in defending our interests. We like to preach competition; we like even more to manipulate state-imposed monopolization.

We know, of course, that our friends in Washington are much concerned about our welfare and how it can be harmed by "reckless competition." Surely, one would think, the residents of that city would be the hardest to convince of the benefits of unbridled competition.

Well, perhaps not—at least, not when they are consumers. Consider the humble taxicab.

In most major cities of the country, you must have a special license to operate a cab. That might be a reasonable device —although subject to abuse—to help the city keep track of who is driving a cab in order to supervise safety regulations. But commonly the number of licenses issued is kept well below the number of perfectly acceptable applications for them—as evidenced by the high prices that must be paid for the licenses when bought and sold in the open market. A taxi license in New York City now sells for about $65,000.

What is the alleged reason for this government limitation on the supply of permitted cabs? You guessed it: Wasteful competition must be prevented. After all, we don't want the freeways and streets cluttered with hordes of yellow and checkered cars. Much better for us to wait longer and pay more for our taxi ride.

So once again the politicians and bureaucrats make the *consumer* worse off and the regulated *industry* (here the present owners of the taxi licenses) better off. Further, when consumers are frustrated by constricted supply, some would-be suppliers, too, are frustrated. A person with limited work experience, little wealth, and a poor credit rating will not be able to finance entry into the cab business.

Now, do our benefactors and protectors in Washington, most of whom are taxi riders, impose these same regulations in their own community? Not a bit of it. In Washington, the more taxis, the better! There, fees to drive a cab amount to less than $100, and there is no imposed limit on the number of cabs. Predictably, there are many cabs, and fares are low. And so our senators and congressmen and bureaucrats and their army of staff workers have to put up with the miseries of reckless and wasteful competition—including short waits for cabs and low prices.

Sometimes, it seems, what is good for the goose is not to be permitted to the gander.

Advertising by Professionals

(MAY 1980)

Advertising by lawyers, doctors, pharmacists, accountants, and other "professionals" has been severely discouraged. In professional circles, it still is not commonly applauded. Whatever may be claimed with respect to the "ethics" involved, prohibition of advertising walks uncomfortably in a free market.

A conventional view holds that advertising in general, through changing consumer tastes and establishing brand loyalties, tends to generate "monopoly power," raise prices, increase costs, create barriers to entry by new firms, and waste resources as the promotion efforts of the various firms within an industry offset one another. The conventional view is largely incorrect.

Information is valuable, scarce, and costly to acquire. Market processes are heavily directed to generation and dissemination of information. Advertising can reduce costs of conveying information which increases responsiveness of the market to alternative and differentiated goods and suppliers and to changing circumstances. It thereby *reduces* monopoly power, it *facilitates* entry and survival of new firms, and it *lowers* prices while increasing the quantity of the goods made available.

Advertising can also deceive. But deliberate deception is likely to be unattractive for firms seeking prolonged existence and repeat customers. Product sales will cover substantial advertising costs only if the seller provides, and continues to provide, a good product.

Professional codes of ethics have prohibited most advertising, purportedly in order to protect the public from being bilked by dishonest and inept practitioners, from inflated prices and deteriorated services, and from unseemly and debilitating competition. Such codes are unnecessary and can do harm.

Advertising by quacks will sometimes fool the most gullible. But commonly consumers will find protective institutional arrangements, while advertising will help to distinguish the relatively good practitioners. Increased consumer knowledge of the market for professional services and increased competition among suppliers will tend to reduce prices and increase the average quality of the services consumed by the community.

Efficiency of firms, quality of merchandise, attractiveness

of price, and amount of advertising tend to be associated. Bans on professional advertising do not protect consumers; rather, they serve the interests of the suppliers, who then find it feasible to act as members of a cartel. The collusion, administered through professional associations, is made viable through the state-enforced codes of ethics, which largely prohibit competitive behavior. To act competitively is deemed to be "unethical"—to professional *colleagues*, not to customers.

As with advertising generally, there are genuine considerations of propriety and aesthetics in advertising by professionals. And advertising, like all other forms of communication, can mislead and offend. But better occasionally to fool the few than to leave us all perpetually in vulnerable ignorance.

DEMAND, COST, AND MARKET ADJUSTMENT

Costs, Benefits, and Rationality

(APRIL 1980)

A radio commentator has noted the rising price of chest X rays and concluded that fewer X rays will be bought. But, the commentator wondered, *should* one apply the comparison of costs and benefits to something as important as health?

Many are reluctant to acknowledge that such weighing of costs and benefits is appropriate with *all* scarce resources. It is not a calculation recently invented just for an environment of heavy inflation.

Health care, oil, and potatoes are scarce: They carry prices, they must be paid for. Thus, the question: If I spend some of my limited income on an X ray, will I be better off than if I had spent those dollars on a tank (or two) of gas? Not to consider this grubby question of balancing alternative expenditures means waste in using one's income.

Sensible people—and most people *are* intuitively sensible in handling their budgets—have always balanced costs against benefits, even for things which poets say should not be corrupted by placing dollar values on them—health; safety in flying airplanes, driving cars, and producing energy; helping the unfortunate; education. But health, safety, welfare, and training are not free, whether the inflation rate is 2 percent or 20 percent: To have more of one means having less of another. We cannot escape the question: How big a price are you willing to pay, how big a cost are you willing to bear, to get what you want?

Perhaps mythology—but certainly not economics—holds that some things are "beyond" or "above" grubby price tags and rational calculations of costs and returns. Rationality, a few seem to suggest, is a luxury, something to forgo in the crunch of making important decisions. But "cost" *means* sacrificed alternatives; market prices reflect costs; foolishly eschewing effective use of economic information does not magically make anything free in this world of scarcity. And when things are not free, we have hard decisions to make. Those decisions of choice inevitably *will* be made one way or another. It behooves us to make them as efficiently as possible. And that requires use of market prices.

Without *measures* of *values* of alternatives, we cannot make intelligent choices among them. Without knowing what must be given up in order to obtain an item, we do not know if we are sensible to acquire it. So we have to have market data, or economic values, to supplement technological, engineering information in order to make good decisions.

Without a market to provide a mechanism for choicemaking and a method of recording people's preferences, those hard decisions will be made *for* us instead of *by* us. Freedom and efficiency go hand in hand. Are we to forgo our heritage of freedom of efficient choice and supinely acquiesce in what a handful of commissars and bureaucrats decree is best for us? If we are so cavalierly irresponsible, we shall deserve the tyrannical fate which will devolve upon us.

Rewards, Choices, and the Market
(SEPTEMBER 1980)

Let me tell you two real-life, fascinating stories.

One pertains to a recent network-radio commentary. The speaker has made a journalistic career of posing as one with moral superiority and urging that government clean up the shambles left in the Garden of Eden. His subject dealt with the pattern of income distribution. He did not—this time—complain about excess profits and exorbitant salaries of the Daddy Warbucks types. Instead, the villains were entertainers: athletes and pop musicians.

The commentator recalled the public wonderment half a century ago when Babe Ruth was paid more than the president of the United States. But now, in our degeneracy, it is easily accepted, when noted at all, when grown men playing boys' games and doped-up Neanderthals blowing horns, beating drums, and caterwauling receive hundreds of thousands of dollars per year.

The commentator asked how this sorry state of affairs came about, with quite useless people getting more money than is paid to those doing important things. His answer was that you and I—we little people, we working stiffs—have let it happen. He implied that we have been seduced into paying entertainers more than they are "worth."

Now, I, too, have doubts about the sophistication of a community that heaps extraordinary rewards on its gladiators and clowns. Some of the community's preferences seem a bit coarse. But we *are* dealing with *peoples' preferences.* And we may wonder also about the sophistication of a commentator's philosophy and analysis when he obliquely suggests that consumers should not be permitted—within very broad and carefully determined limits—to buy the services they want.

In my second story, an economist was interviewed by a reporter from a business magazine. The economist irritated the reporter in describing the efficiency of essentially unrestricted freedom of consumers in a market offering many alternatives. The reporter complained that it is surely *not* efficient to have fifty brands of laundry soap. Why not pick the best kind and produce only it?

The wise and kindly economist pointed out that there were many brands of soap because the community wanted them. Presumably, no one consumer bought all of the brands. But *each* of the brands was sufficiently demanded to induce a hardheaded, self-serving manufacturer to produce it. And the deity had not designated the reporter or the economist or an economic czar to pick the state-approved brand and to tell the consumers of the other forty-nine that they no longer could make their own choices. Efficiency, after all, is not solely a matter of technology in *how* to produce a given article; efficiency pertains also to *what* to produce. Who is to decide what to produce—Big Brother or the community at large?

The commentator and the reporter may be morally superior and exquisitely cultivated. But they have learned little about a free society and the free market on which a free society must be based.

Mouse Wisdom: Competition and Productivity

(OCTOBER 1980)

Adam and Karl, the two mice who live in my office, have again had an appropriately serious discussion of economic issues. This latest exchange was about the relationship of different forms of competition and productivity.

"If it weren't for our economic system of private property and market prices," mused Karl, "there would be no competition. Grubby activities to earn money in order to buy goods and services would be eliminated if everything were owned and distributed by the government. Heartwarming cooperation would replace divisive rivalry among mice, and output per mousehour would soar."

"You mean that more goods—more books, medical care, and cheese—would be produced?" asked Adam.

"Precisely!" exclaimed Karl.

"So mice don't have all of everything they want?" Adam inquired.

"Of course they don't," snapped Karl. "And they never will. It's because of scarcity that mice go to the trouble to produce anything. If we had all we wanted, we wouldn't have to produce. The reason for any kind of economic system is to organize and coordinate mouse activities, so that goods are produced in order to satisfy some of our infinite wants."

Adam pulled his whiskers and responded thoughtfully: "If mice can *never* have all of everything they want, then they must *compete* for scarce goods. Cheese is a good example—we always want more than we have. The amount available must be divided among many mouse mouths. Because there is not enough cheese, some wants cannot be satisfied. As a result," Adam continued, "mice are *rivals* for the scarce supply of cheese. And rivalry is *competition*. It is the *scarcity* of cheese and of other goods—not the economic system—that creates competition."

"It still seems to me," Karl grumbled, "that if things were collectively owned and distributed, then all this money competition in the open market would be eliminated."

"In one sense you are right," said Adam. "Mice would no

longer compete by productively earning money in order to buy things. But market *monetary* competition would be replaced simply by competition of another kind. Mice would compete by trying to win the favor of government officials, who would have authority to grant individual mice more or less cheese. You see, Karl, your scheme doesn't *eliminate* competition, it only *changes its form*. Mice would spend less time producing goods to please customers in order to earn money and more time pleading with officious government officials. Economically productive mouse behavior wouldn't pay as much as acquiring political influence."

"So," concluded Karl, "a private-property system directed through market prices makes us want to produce—and thereby make us all better off—in order to earn money we individually must have in order to compete for goods."

"Right," affirmed Adam. "Self-centered as we are—indeed, *because* we are greedy—we cooperate with one another in order to produce and earn more. Efforts of *each* mouse to get a bigger chunk of cheese result in more cheese production for us *all*. And productivity has always been basic to our well-being—at least, ever since the fiasco in the Garden of Eden."

Shelling Short on Peanuts

(DECEMBER 1980)

Surrounding the hearth this Christmas will be familiar treats to eat. But they may not taste quite the same. Peanut butter cookies without peanut butter? Peanut brittle with more brittle than peanuts? A dish of mixed nuts, but with something missing? That's right—no peanuts.

Fewer peanuts will be shelled and roasted this holiday

season, for there are fewer peanuts around—there is a crop reduction this year of more than 40 percent, an unhappy event brought about by abnormally dry weather.

Fewer peanuts is just something we are going to have to live with—and eat. We cannot alter what nasty nature has done to the peanut crop. But we can choose our *response,* our *adaptation,* to this heightened scarcity of peanuts. According to an editorial in a major newspaper, peanut shortages are "inevitable." That's because this year's crop will fall short of the peanuts we "need."

Don't believe it. We do *not* have to respond to a smaller available quantity of peanuts by experiencing shortages, for no shortage—peanut or any other kind—is ever inevitable. We do not have to experience long lines, bare grocery shelves, or panic buying. The prices of peanuts, peanut butter, and all peanut products will prevent shortages—if we let those prices perform their proper tasks.

One of those tasks is to *inform* us. Even if we never knew about the dry weather and poor peanut harvest, relatively higher peanut prices would tell us that peanuts are now scarcer. We do not like those higher prices, but that is because we do not like the fact that there are fewer peanuts available. Higher peanut prices only tell us of this unpleasant and immutable fact: They reflect reality. If a messenger brings us bad news, it is the bad news that saddens us, not the messenger.

By informing people of the increased scarcity of peanuts, higher peanut prices cause people to consume fewer of them. Contrary to the newspaper editorial, there is no specific quantity of peanuts that people *need.* The quantity we demand and use depends on many things, one of which is the price we pay. At higher prices, we *choose* to use fewer peanuts than we do at lower prices. Higher prices cause us to substitute other things for peanuts, such as more turkey sandwiches for peanut butter and jelly.

When available quantities of peanuts, or of other goods,

change—some goods becoming more scarce and others less scarce—their prices rise or fall, thereby causing our uses of them to decrease or increase. Higher prices cause us voluntarily to exclude those uses of goods which we do not feel are worth those prices. Lower prices lead us to use more.

Shortages are *not* inevitable. They will *not* occur unless we legally impose government controls which prevent prices, like the spurned messenger, from delivering their messages. With artificially low prices giving us false information about the scarcity of peanuts, we would want to use more than are available. *Then* we would see lines, bare grocery shelves, or panic buying. With a self-imposed shortage of peanut butter to spread with our holiday jellies, all of us would be in a jam.

What Price Zero Tuition?

(MARCH 1980)

Poets assure us that the best things in life are free. If so, then higher education is only a second-best commodity, for it is not free. Who pays for college educations? Who *should* pay for them?

Students are charged fees and sometimes tuition. But even in private schools, student payments rarely cover all costs. And in state schools, students pay only a small fraction of the costs.

There is a parasitic tradition against charging tuition at state colleges. This is one tradition even campus rebels defend, for their own pocketbooks are at stake! But it is a tradition that violates a sound principle: Those who *get* something which is costly should *pay* for it—recipients should make payment for what they receive.

Zero tuition is a public subsidy. The amount of resources

involved is considerable, and they have many alternative uses. In a world of scarcity, we cannot provide everything to everyone below cost. Providing a gift to some means a sacrifice for others. It is naïve simply to presume that *particular* members of this *particular* group should be subsidized and should receive this *particular* amount of this *particular* subsidy in this *particular* form.

Even if naïve, taxpayers have been generous to public colleges. And communities *have* received at least a gross, whether or not a net, payoff from their investments. But students are *twice* blessed. They gain, first, as students, receiving training costing many times what they pay in fees and ultimately returning to them an enlarged income many times greater than the educational cost. Over the years, they gain also as general members of the community. As members of society, they will pay taxes, of course—but all members of the community pay taxes, whether or not they go to state colleges.

Further, the bulk of the students come from relatively high social-economic levels. The poor provide a share of tax payments which is larger than their proportion of college students. The poor subsidize the wealthy to go to state colleges.

Even students with little money income are wealthy—if they belong in college. For college-caliber persons are rich in inherited mental traits. Such "human capital" *is* wealth, and we should distinguish between *wealth* and *current earnings*. The student's income may now be small, but his wealth —the present value of his future earnings—is large. Zero tuition certainly is not the only way to provide educational opportunity for the low-income but wealthy student, and it is not clearly the best way.

When students put aside the role of parasites, what need be involved is not a curtailment of college consumption *now* by students, but only a reduction of other consumption out of *tomorrow's* enhanced income. Students can draw *now* on some of *tomorrow's* income through borrowing and pay their own way. Borrowing replaces subsidization of students with investment by students in their own behalf. The direct beneficiaries of the education then cover the costs; those who get, pay.

Tuition, Costs, and Opportunities

(NOVEMBER 1980)

My noble dog, Winnie, is not the only creature who listens to these commentaries. A member of the audience recently took exception to some of my remarks concerning college tuition.

My correspondent purports to agree with the principle that "those who *get* something which is costly should *pay* for it." But she contends that society as a whole should pay for education, "since society reaps the benefit of developed minds."

There are difficulties with the argument for socialized payment for education.

Doubtless there are community gains from widespread, essentially universal education. But those gains are more conspicuous and more certain at the lower grades: There is general gain from people learning early to read and write and calculate and wash their hands. The gains from more-advanced training administered universally are less obvious. It may be that everyone should go to grade school; it does not follow that everyone should go to college, much less graduate school.

"Universal" advanced training yields returns which not only *diminish* but which can be *negative*. There is little question that colleges have been qualitatively diluted and have had their resources wasted by the expansion—or by the nature of the expansion—of both the student body and the faculty over the past generation. Dilution and waste are poor avenues for production of superior brain surgeons, astrophysicists, and economists. But inefficiency in use of resources is an inevitable consequence of camouflaged costs and buffering people from personal direct bearing of costs. When everyone subsidizes everyone to go to school, we tend to fool ourselves into believing that education is free—and this foolishness obscures and distorts market information on returns and costs.

For those who make relatively good use of their training, there will be rewards. In a world of free markets and individual accountability, those rewards will be adequate to engender the satisfaction of community preferences. It is not necessary to subsidize the initial training as well as to pay fully for the subsequent productive performance.

My critic suggests the desirability of equal educational opportunities. But it is a *non sequitur* to imply that equal educational opportunities require zero tuition or that zero tuition surely will result in equal opportunities. In fact, zero tuition has not yielded that result: On balance, the poor residents of Watts now subsidize the wealthy of Beverly Hills to attend the University of California.

We shall better use our resources—in education and in other areas—by retaining the connection of personal decisions with both costs and returns. If potential students anticipate ample rewards from education, they can decide to invest their own resources—both current and borrowed—in that education. Provision of funds for student borrowing can help would-be surgeons, physicists, and economists fully exploit their comparative advantages; willy-nilly provision of subsidies engenders a poorer education for parasites.

Government Planning and Agricultural Land Use

(S E P T E M B E R   1 9 8 0)

Why do public officials often malign the marketplace? Because the market uses resources according to the community's preferences, not the preferences of government officials. So it is not surprising, even though discouraging, to find impertinent politicians intruding upon, emasculating, and crippling the market in order to change the way our scarce resources are used.

In one conspicuous instance of pressure to impose governmental preferences on us, it is urged that Big Brother somehow save prime farmland from urban development. We are told how such development—houses, shopping centers, highways, factories—"gobbles up" or "steals" many thousands of acres of fertile land each year. It may seem initially plausible —as foolishness and sin typically do—that such conversion of land from farming to other purposes stems from lack of coherence and direction in resource use, and that government, of all things, must save us blundering souls from our irrationality and inefficiency.

The kindest interpretation to make of such proposals for further centralization and collectivism is that they reflect innocence of the nature of a free society and its price-directed economy.

Land-use planning to ensure enough land for agricultural output is an unnecessary attention for government. It is already provided through decisions of private individuals in the market, for "the invisible hand" of the pricing system allocates scarce land to those uses which are most valued by the community. Land for food competes with land for houses. Consumer valuations of the different uses of land are revealed by the prices they are willing to pay for food and for new homes. The more they are willing to pay for houses relative to crops, the more profitable it will be for home developers to bid land away from agriculture.

People want more and cheaper food, but they also want more and cheaper houses. Some of the most productive agricultural land is also the most productive land for new homes. When consumers value the use of some land in new homes more than they value it in crops, it is sensible to develop that land for homes. When farmers sell their land to home developers, they are releasing the land for uses the community values most highly.

This is how the invisible hand—the pricing system— "plans" the use of land. It is a planning that puts land into those uses which are most valued by the community, not by bureaucrats.

Not everyone will agree with the community's preferences. They may try to impose their land-use preferences on the rest of us. Government officials, eager to expand their bailiwicks, will have greater power if they, rather than the market, can determine how land is used. The power of government to direct the use of land can grow, however, only to the extent that the community surrenders some of its freedom to determine land use through the market.

We were born free. But freedom includes the freedom to acquiesce in giving away our freedom. And we shall not have the freedom to reclaim freedoms we have been seduced into surrendering.

Raising Baloney on Shrinking Farmlands

(January 1981)

It is popular to assert that our national farmlands are rapidly dwindling. Each year, new homes, shopping centers, and factories are built on prime agricultural land. Unless actions are taken by government, it is argued, food prices will skyrocket as our ability to supply food falls behind our demand.

Every year, some agricultural land *is* developed for other uses. But the argument that our farmland is shrinking and we are becoming less able to produce the food demanded is—baloney.

According to a study by the Federal Reserve Bank of Saint Louis, the amount of harvested cropland has varied appreciably between 1910 and 1979. The number of harvested acres did fall to a low point in 1969, but since then it has increased significantly. Indeed, there are now more acres of cropland than at any other time during the last four decades—and output per acre has never before been greater.

It is no surprise that the quantity of croplands has varied or that this quantity has recently been increasing. Much land not now suitable for crops could be made usable. Lands now in grazing or forests could be rapidly converted to crops *if* it were profitable. And that is the essential point: The amount of land used for crops depends on profitability. As profitability of land in crops changes, so, too, does the quantity of cropland.

During the 1950s and 1960s, prices received by farmers increased much more slowly than did consumer prices or prices of industrial commodities. As a result, profitability of using land in crops diminished, which caused the quantity of harvested cropland to fall. The first half of the 1970s was different. Bolstered by hefty increases in export demand, prices received by farmers increased faster than other prices. The profitability of land in crops increased, and that caused the number of harvested acres to grow by 51 million acres— 18 percent—between 1969 and 1979.

All this indicates that the market is an effective means of determining the quantity of harvested farmland. The market is a successful, decentralized land-use planner. Market prices present vital information to a multitude of private landowners concerned with their own individual fortunes. Those prices tell landowners about the relative importance to the community of different uses of land. If growing crops becomes relatively more important, then the profitability of cropland will increase, and the quantity of acres harvested will rise as producers, in their own interests, respond to consumer demands.

It is not true that centralized government planning is necessary, or even desirable, to assure an adequate amount of farmland. Government bureaucrats have no special knowledge, unique shrewdness, extraordinary analytic sophistication, or altruistic incentive in guiding today's use of resources for tomorrow's consumption.

The market is an effective planner, which has efficiently altered the quantity of farmland in accordance with preferences for food. It will continue to do so—if we have the sense to let it.

Mouse Wisdom and Draft Animals
(FEBRUARY 1980)

Adam and Karl—the two thoughtful mice who live somewhere in my office—recently discussed the military draft.

This was prompted by the announcement of the Mouse Chief that all mice nineteen and twenty months old would have to register with the Rodent Recruitment Service.

"I favor a mouse draft," Karl exclaimed. "It's not just that young mice—like young mice before them—have an obligation to defend their fellow mice, but the draft is also a cheaper way to raise an army."

Adam replied: "The draft is not necessarily cheaper."

"Nonsense," snapped Karl. "Less money would be spent on an army that is drafted, because we could pay them a lower wage."

"That's right," Adam agreed.

"You admit I am right!" exclaimed Karl.

"No, not really," cautioned Adam. "It is true that less *money* would be spent on an army of draftees than one of volunteers, but it is not true that this army of draftees is less *costly.*"

"Adam, that Tillamook you just ate is causing you to hallucinate," said Karl gently. "How can a drafted army, which is paid lower wages, not be cheaper?"

Adam slowly chewed another bite of cheese, licked his whiskers, and replied: "It's quite simple. The money spent on a drafted army does not measure the real cost of using mouse time there. The real cost of a mouse's time in the military is the value of the civilian job sacrificed. What do we have to *forgo* in order to have an additional mouse soldier? Say Fred Fieldmouse has a civilian job making this delicious cheese, where he earns ten thousand a year. The real cost of his spending a year in the army would be ten thousand dollars, the amount he would earn producing cheese. Even if he had no preference in cheesemaking or soldiering, the army would have to pay him at least ten thousand a year to induce him to stop making cheese and join the army. If the army has to draft him because he refuses to join voluntarily, it is because the army does not offer sufficient wages to compensate him for his lost civilian job."

Karl began to see the light. "You mean," he said, "if Fred were drafted and paid, say, six thousand dollars, the real cost of using a year of his time is still ten thousand?"

"Right," said Adam. "The alternative cost of the additional servicemouse is the ten-thousand-dollar cheesemaker we give up, irrespective of how much the recruit is paid. We can't avoid that cost."

"But note how the cost is borne when we have a draft," Adam continued. "If we draft Fred, taxpayers would compensate him for only six thousand dollars of the cost. The other four thousand, not compensated, is a tax imposed on him by the draft. The draft is a way to hide the real cost of an army, by shifting much of that cost onto the recruits. Instead of having taxpayers assume the full cost of paying enough to induce people to move into the armed forces, we force draftees to bear an enormous part of the cost as a labor tax."

"But I think that young mice have an obligation to defend their society," added Karl.

"I agree," said Adam, "and I am appalled by the egocentric boorishness of parasitic, loudmouthed young mice who flaunt their unwillingness to defend their country under any circumstances. But a labor tax on draftees is not the only way to meet our military necessities."

PRICE CONTROLS

✕

Price Controllers: The Camouflaged Enemy
(July 1980)

Much governmental intrusion and bungling takes the form of price controls—maximum or minimum prices specified by fallible people who confuse themselves with the deity.

The purpose of price controls is to suppress the free market. The market is one of the most efficient devices ever to evolve through human experience, providing information on costs and preferences; arrangements to bring together demanders and sellers, borrowers and lenders; and opportunities to pursue incentives of economic self-betterment. There is no better way to coordinate, for both individual and community well-being, the activities of millions of people in accordance with their preferences.

Price controllers substitute their preferences for those of the members of the community, for they substitute prices stipulated by them for prices the community would generate through the market. Price controllers, in superseding the market, are enemies of both efficiency and freedom.

Price controllers pursue their subversion in numerous contexts. Sometimes their decreed prices are *above* the market-clearing level. At unnaturally high prices, of course sellers want to sell more than buyers want to buy: We then are faced by "surpluses."

Surpluses are found in certain agricultural goods. Then the government either buys the excess quantity or pays growers not to grow the excess. Surpluses are found, also, in the labor market as a result of minimum-wage requirements. The least

productive workers, who presumably were to be the beneficiaries of imposed minimum wages, are priced out of the
market.

Maximum prices *below* the level at which quantities demanded and supplied would be equated give us "shortages."
We are blessed with many ceilings—and many shortages.
Big Brother has thus bungled with gasoline, interest rates,
apartment rents.

It sounds great at a political rally to promise low prices to
buyers—and buyers of a given commodity greatly outnumber sellers. With appeals to grasping viscera instead of
rational mind, the subversive demagogue can find a ready
response from the mob which is eager to strike back at those
rich bums who provide oil or loans or housing. It's us
deserving, downtrodden folk against those fat-cat exploiters!
Right?

Well, suppressing and superseding the market is *not* always
irrational. *Some* people can gain *something*, at least for a
short while. Plunderers can, indeed, get their hands on
unearned loot. But most people, the community at large, will
very soon feel the burdens and bear the costs of such vicious
foolishness. Ask the consumer who must pay more for food
than its economic costs, or the person who cannot get a job
because he would have to be paid more than he is worth, or
the person who cannot find an apartment although he is
willing to pay more than the legal maximum rent, or the
would-be borrower who cannot find a lender at interest
ceilings, or the motorist who waits for an hour to buy gas,
only to have the pump run dry as he finally gets to the head
of the line.

The price controllers, whom we put into power in a foolish
attempt to fool the market, have taken from us both wealth
and freedom.

Gas Shortage: Who Is the Villain?

(J U L Y   1 9 7 9)

Americans have been bamboozled—not for the first time—into holding strange beliefs about prices and shortages. These misconceptions create problems which should not exist and make bad situations worse.

According to newspaper polls, most people believe that gasoline shortages of the last year and a half have been a hoax and also that price controls on both crude oil and gas at the pump are desirable. It would take perverse genius to come up with a more absurd combination of beliefs. Such lousy economics harms us vastly more than does OPEC. It harms us not only by wasting our resources, but also by generating a frustrating situation to be exploited by the divisive demagogue.

We *have* had gas shortages. But we have had shortages *because*, not in *spite*, of price controls. The OPEC cartel has, indeed, reduced its exports of oil and succeeded in raising oil prices dramatically. Oil consumers thereby have been made worse off. But when oil-importing countries put controls on prices of domestically produced oil and on retail prices of gas, they turn a physical inconvenience into massive economic bafflement and waste. It is our own government-imposed price controls—not the production and pricing policies of OPEC, and not greedy oil companies or irresponsible consumers—which create gas shortages.

The meaning of "shortage" of a good is that more is demanded than is available—*at the going price*. The amount supplied is "short" of the amount demanded—*at the going price*. The excess quantity demanded results from the price being artificially low. If the price were higher, *less* would be demanded and generally *more* would be available (unless supply incentives are destroyed by taxes or other government policies). At a sufficiently high price, we will wish to buy no more than is supplied; then the market will be "cleared," there will be no "shortage."

Markets *always* are cleared in the absence of price controls; and the *only* way to avoid shortages (or surpluses) is to have markets free of price controls.

Even as Big Brother blames our problems on producers, suppliers, and consumers, *he* prevents the market from clearing through market-determined prices. And how can the frustration of our made-by-government short supply be resolved? We have again learned the inevitable sort of answer the hard way: Sit in line at the gas station for an hour or two —and get to the pump just after it has run dry.

When you squander your time and patience looking and waiting for gas, realize that your frustration is caused not by OPEC sheikhs or a sudden upsurge of domestic greed and irresponsibility but by our own ridiculous price controls.

High Prices and Long Lines, or High Prices and Short Lines

(SEPTEMBER 1979)

A radio commercial in Chicago provides an opportunity to focus on choices we face in the ongoing energy shortage.

The radio spot advertises a chain of gas stations; the voice is that of the company's owner. His message is that he has driven past one of his stations and noticed a sizable line of waiting cars. The businessman is boasting about the line, for, he asserts, it proves that consumers are pleased to wait to patronize his pumps, where the price per gallon is four cents below the competition.

But waiting in line is costly. "Time is money." If a motorist waits half an hour for a ten-gallon purchase and thereby "saves" 40 cents at the low-price station, he has been rewarded at the rate of 80 cents per hour for his patience.

The station owner should be grateful to his customers for their willingness to be compensated at far less than the legal minimum wage. But there is no reason to be grateful to federal government price controllers, who want to force us all to wait in line for such puny sums.

By suppressing the dollar price of gas, the Department of Energy has created the notorious gas lines. These price controls create shortages—even the feds admit the obvious —yet they are justified by Big Brother on the ground that the cost of gas must be kept artificially down because people cannot "afford" to pay more.

However, raising the *time* cost while lowering the *dollar* price defeats the purpose. The price of gas will still rise to a market-clearing level; but only part will now be paid in money, with the rest of the price paid in *waiting*.

Forcing people to burn up oil and time—along with composure—in first finding an open gas station and then creeping in long lines is a waste of resources. The Department of Energy itself estimates that gas lines around the nation would waste 100 million gallons of gas and $200 million of time each month. Allowing the dollar price to rise will hurt the pocketbook, to be sure, but it will not squander additional scarce resources. Rather, it will create incentives for producers to produce and for those consumers who avoid waiting in line to conserve.

Our gas station entrepreneur is free to offer lower prices and long lines to attract customers who will patronize his package in preference to the product of stations that charge higher prices for instant service. Such consumer choices are provided by a competitive marketplace. But it is folly to suppose that price controls—which would herd *all* of us into lines—can lower the *total* cost of gas for consumers. If they could, why not set the controlled price at zero?

No, a *full* price in time and money will be paid under price controls. And for the great majority of people, whose alternatives to sitting in a gas line are worth more than a dollar or two an hour, the controlled money-plus-time price of gas is higher than the uncontrolled price in money alone.

Gas Rationing: Trying to Fool the Market

(MARCH 1980)

What is gas rationing supposed to do for us? The usual, but incorrect, contention is that rationing would keep the price of gas below the free-market level. And there is the additional error of supposing that rationing would match gas supplies with demands in the various areas of the country and avoid gas lines.

If the specified ceiling price of gas is below the market-clearing level, there will be a shortage. The community wants to buy more gas than is available, so there will be queues at gas stations: Since Big Brother prohibits paying the full *money* price, part of the price will be paid by waiting in line.

In order to avoid creation of lines, ration coupons have been proposed. Each coupon would permit buying of a unit of gas, and the government would issue just as many rights to buy gas as there is expected to be gas available.

Does everyone get the same number of coupons? Some people don't drive. And those who do vary greatly in pertinent circumstances—nature of their jobs, location of home relative to places to which they want to drive, gas mileage of their cars.

So introduce variation in the scheme: Permit buying and selling of the ration coupons. Wouldn't that avoid creation of lines at gas stations?

Coupon trading could clear the *coupon* market, but not the *gas* market. Per-capita consumption of gas is not uniform across the country. Coupons would be shifted through the coupon market to areas of relatively great demand. But what would shift the *gas* to keep supplies in conformity with demands?

In a free gasoline market, prices of gas would be bid up and seller receipts would be larger in areas of relatively great demand. The higher prices and greater receipts would provide signals and incentives for the shifting of greater supplies to such markets. But that mechanism cannot work with the scheme of price controls and coupon rationing.

Gas prices in the various markets would be pegged and thus could not reflect different and changing market demands. And dealers in markets of heaviest demands would not be accumulating additional coupons necessary to obtain larger inventories, for they would pick up a coupon only when selling a unit of gas, and they could not collect more coupons after their pumps ran dry. Only by some *bureaucratic* action—delayed and arbitrary—could gas supplies be occasionally reallocated. Meanwhile, gas lines would be growing.

Finally, not only would there be a *time* price of getting gas, even the *money* price would rise. The money price of the gas itself would be pegged, but not the price of the ration coupons. Those who favor rationing in order to assure their access to gas at a low price would bid up the price of coupons. The *total* of the gas price plus the coupon price would move up to a market-clearing level, although gas suppliers would receive only the low pegged price.

In this bizarre game, gas buyers do not get away with a lower price or obtain greater and more certain supplies than a free market would provide; gas producers are denied supply-motivating receipts equal to the community's valuation of the gas; and we heap upon ourselves unnecessary costs and aggravations in a silly effort to fool the market.

An Epidemic of "The New York Disease"

(NOVEMBER 1979)

A political cause is spreading which may leave the rest of the country in the ridiculous and disastrous condition of New York City. Such is the promise of the rent-control crusade. For New York, which has maintained rent controls since World War II, provides a sobering laboratory: The city suffers an *annual net loss* of 28,000 rental units.

Rapidly rising rents are a problem for millions. Yet the average rental fee rose by only 70 percent between 1967 and 1978, while the general price rise was over 100 percent. We can hardly blame high rents on unique greed of landlords.

Persisting inflation remains the underlying culprit, with growing construction and maintenance costs and property taxes. The threat and sometimes the reality of rent controls help to make conversion of apartments into condominiums more attractive, which further reduces supply and raises rents, which strengthens the pressure for controls. So goes the spiral of economic deterioration and hysteria—with the number of rental units in the United States actually *falling* at an annual rate of 1.5 percent.

Instead of creating the problem, government could in various ways encourage a widescale reduction in rents. Sweeping away layers of regulatory red tape, reducing property taxes, and, perhaps most important, ending restrictive zoning laws which enable already established upper-class homeowners to exclude middle-class apartment construction —all would push apartment supply up and rents down.

But the law of supply and demand has few charms for the rent-control lobby. The lobby has summarized its tactic in the rhetoric of a movie star. "What we have to do," says this reader of scripts, "is eliminate the greed quotient."

The rent controllers would have us believe people will build, maintain, and offer the same amount of housing at a low price as they would at a higher price. They talk as if they do not grasp that, in making a decision to provide housing, builders and investors weigh their alternatives. If treasury bills or GM stock or condominium construction offer higher returns than rental units, this is evidence that the community *prefers* money to be invested in these alternatives. Artificially lowering rents by political means will inevitably shift investment from apartment buildings to other economic uses in higher demand.

Who gains and who loses from rent control?

The gainers are those who already have apartments (if they do not want to move or care much about property maintenance); those who administer the expensive control machinery; rebels and radicals looking for a populist cause; and noncontrolled communities who attract construction resources sensibly fleeing controlled areas.

The losers include local landowners and developers—but it is fun to abrogate *their* property rights, for, after all, such grubby people have beady little eyes, set too close together. The losers include also those the rent controls were designed to help—the low- and middle-income people who are looking, with increasing desperation, for rental housing.

The road to perdition is paved with good intentions, it is said. Probably so. But also with an occasional cobblestone of deliberate subversion contributed by our collectivist comrades.

Housing and How to Induce the Goose
to Produce
(FEBRUARY 1980)

We do not have enough resources to satisfy all wants of all people all the time. The inescapable fact of scarcity engenders competition. The best we can do is arrange our activities in such fashion as efficiently to coordinate the activities of grubby, aggressive people.

In this world of scarcity and conflict, it takes little genius to see problems. But it takes uncommon sophistication to deduce optimal resolutions of problems. Unhappily, economic issues are treated increasingly as matters of wealth *redistribution* instead of wealth *creation*, of granting discriminatory favors of *consumption* instead of encouraging *production*.

This is illustrated by the problem of supply of apartments. Housing is not manna from heaven. It must be produced with scarce resources. Vacancy rates are very low—we want more apartments. Costs must be borne in the production. How are we to induce builders to bear the costs of producing more apartments?

There are two approaches to inducing greater supply. We get producers to produce either by making them *worse* off— perhaps hang them by their thumbs in Siberia—if they *fail* to do what we want, or by making them *better* off as a reward for doing what we want. The major source of the economic strength, as well as the freedom, of our society has been reliance on market incentives rather than political punishments, on inducements of gain rather than fear of coercion.

Efficiency and freedom have been our heritage. But Big Brother—and Little Brother, too, at state and local levels—is not known for sophisticated appreciation of how a free society and its efficient economy operate. The socially fruitful channeling of individual ambitions is too subtle for them, too indirect, leaving too limited a role for the bureaucrat.

And so, with respect to supplying housing, what do our governmental leaders and protectors do? First, they note that there is, indeed, a scarcity of housing, along with scarcity of about everything else. They note, too, that tenants greatly outnumber landlords. Next, it is important not simply that government *do* something but that it be *apparent* that government is doing something to protect the masses of real people from the landed enemy.

What does government do? Induce more production over the long run? Induce efficient allocation of what exists in the short run? Of course not. For that would require reliance on the market, and government is a suppressor of the market.

Instead, government first creates a housing shortage by imposing rent control. Then it restricts conversion of apartments into condominiums. Now it still further diminishes the attractiveness of investment in housing by denying landlords the right to limit their clientele to adults.

Obviously, it is expecting too much that politicians comprehend and take seriously such esoteric notions as economic efficiency, liberty, property rights, and their interconnections. But surely they could be expected to see that if we want more housing, we should encourage investors to build it, and that rent controls and severe restrictions on what owners can do with their property really, truly are *not* the way to induce production.

A *Housing Horror Story*

(APRIL 1980)

Midnight is a good time for horror stories.

Imagine a city with a fixed number of apartments and a growing number of people wanting to live in apartments. It requires little sophistication to predict what will happen to rents once the quantity of apartments demanded exceeds the quantity available. Even Mortimer Snerd can see why rents are bid up. Whether or not landlords are uniquely "greedy," they can charge no more than what tenants will pay.

But why are there no more apartments? Rents are rising because there are not enough apartments to satisfy demand at the old rents. The increasing rents are evidence that people are willing to pay for more apartments; the higher rents are *market signals*, indicating that rewards are available to producers of additional apartments. Like you and me, real-estate developers want to prosper. So, in their own interests, why don't they quickly respond to the market signals and produce the demanded rental units?

Suppliers *will* find it advantageous to respond to market incentives—and disincentives. When they receive undistorted signals directly from demanders, then demanders, too, will be better off from the positive response of suppliers. But if the signals from demanders are filtered through government restrictions and processes, what is received by suppliers are *warnings* more than prospects of rewards.

So why are apartments not being built? Because the city has imposed ceilings on rents and limited issuance of building permits through zoning and environmental regulations. What message is now received through the static by potential real-estate investors? Not only are rewards of productive activity severely curtailed but bureaucratic vacillation and harassment, procedural delay, and public vilification are added to the normal costs and uncertainties of the market. Is this an attractive city in which to build?

Remember, the problem at the outset was too few apartments. But now, with elimination of incentives, there will be no more built even though the community wants them. So where does real-estate development money go? Well, if this horror story is about the Los Angeles area, the money is going out of state, where there is no threat of rent control and housing investment is welcomed.

Not only is apartment construction and maintenance inhibited but apartment *conversion* to condominiums is induced—*if* permitted by Little Brother—by first the prospect and then the reality of rent control. But as one lie leads to another, so one restriction on free market activity leads to another—and soon condominium conversion is controlled to try to ease the costs imposed by the original rent control. The *Los Angeles Times* has summarized it well:

Having said to the owner in the rent-control ordinance, You can't make your normal profit on rents, the city would now say, You can't make your normal profit on condo conversion, either. What then is the owner to do? First, he will look for a way to make a return on his investment through some other device not prohibited by the government, just as he turned to condo conversion after rent control. If there is no other way, he will . . . let his rental property run down. He will also not go further into the business of rental property, for there will be nothing in it for him. Like rent control, a prohibition on condo conversion would perversely make housing not better, but worse.

A Shortage of Clear Thinking on Clearing the Market

(JULY 1979)

Why do people often object to goods being sold at market-clearing prices? When the market for widgets is cleared, people want to buy just the number of widgets at the going price that widget suppliers want to sell. Buyers can buy all they want *at that price*, and sellers can sell all they want *at that price*. Neither buyers nor sellers are frustrated, and their respective preferences are reconciled. The market works—when we let it work.

A couple of years ago, the Los Angeles County Museum of Art decided to sell tickets to the King Tut exhibit at a price of just $2, with a limit of four tickets per family. Would-be purchasers stood in long lines in the rain, and all 660,000 tickets for the four-month exhibition were sold in only four days. It was obvious that more tickets were wanted at $2 each than were available: Putting the price too low created a "shortage" of tickets.

Theater brokers had some tickets. Of course, the brokers did not ask the same low price as did the museum; soon the price had been bid up to $20. Some in the California legislature were outraged by this "gouging" and wished to outlaw such greedy behavior. It wasn't "fair" to charge $20 for tickets that had been sold originally for $2, so people should not be allowed to spend their own money as they pleased!

Does the $20 price serve any function other than to enrich the original purchaser? Yes. The higher price allocates tickets to those who want them most, in accordance with preferences revealed by market bids and offers.

At a price of only $2, I might use my ticket to see the

exhibit. But if I had the option of selling the ticket for $20, I might prefer to take that money and visit a fine restaurant: I would value the meal more than seeing the exhibit. On the other hand, the person who bought the ticket from me preferred the exhibit over $20 worth of other things he could have bought.

Each of us consenting adults would gain from the exchange, for each would value more what he acquired than what he had to pay to get it. If reselling the ticket at a higher price were prohibited by Big Brother, each of us would be precluded from making his best use of his own money: I could not sell my ticket and then buy other goods I preferred, and the would-be buyer of the ticket could not see the exhibit.

The museum itself could have received the difference between the pegged price and the natural price if it had charged a market-clearing price in the first place. Setting the original price too low resulted in people wanting more tickets than were available. Letting the higher market-clearing price now prevail is the way to *reallocate* the tickets to those who most want them.

In a world of scarcity, it is peculiar to prohibit people from making use of their resources by their own criteria and wishes. Such prohibition is not only wasteful; in this Land of the Free, it is also unseemly.

Minimum Wage: Maximum Folly

(OCTOBER 1979)

The national unemployment rate for blacks fourteen to twenty-four years old is some three times the rate for whites. This unhappy fact is exploited by those who seek to expand government welfare programs and to promote unionization. Yet that unemployment obscenity has been created largely by just the kind of federal "help" provided to deal with economic hardships.

The telling clue about unemployment among black youths is that it used to be no higher than for whites. Professor Walter Williams, of Temple University, notes that thirty years ago the unemployment rate for young blacks was actually a bit *lower* than the rate for whites. Dr. Williams, himself a black, writes: "Has society become *more* racially discriminatory since 1948? Or were black youths *more* qualified than white youths in earlier times? To answer either question in the affirmative," he says, "requires an imagination bordering on the psychotic. Most statistical evidence supports the theoretical prediction that increases in the level and extent of coverage of the minimum-wage law have an adverse impact on minority youth."

So we come to the minimum-wage law—a law first sold over forty years ago on the claim that it would raise living standards of the poor. The law now covers over 80 percent of the labor force and makes it illegal to hire or to work for less than a specified hourly wage, today nearly $3.

Most minimum-wage-level workers are new workers, either young or returning to a job after twenty years in the housewife business. The most important thing these laborers can acquire is on-the-job training, which will enable them to progress beyond menial first employment.

But to get on-the-job training requires *having* a job. Minimum-wage laws forbid the employing of new, unskilled workers at their low market value. And those whose labor is not worth $3 are not likely to be hired at that artificial wage. Setting a floor on wages above the market-clearing level creates a *surplus* of low-productivity labor offered for sale.

Some who do have jobs will receive higher wages as a result of the law. But with labor services now more expensive, total employment is reduced. And those who lose jobs or fail to get jobs they would have had at lower wages are the very ones—the less educated, the less experienced—the law presumably was intended to help.

Is it better to have a job at, say, $2 an hour than to be unemployed at $3? If government could make unskilled workers more valuable just by passing a minimum-wage law, why stop at $3 an hour? Why not raise the minimum to $10— or to $1000? Untutored jungle instinct is enough to tell us that a minimum wage of $1000, instead of making all of us rich, would put all of us in the unemployment line. This hypothetical unemployment line would be precisely the same kind of phenomenon as the real unemployment line of today's young and unskilled, many of whom happen to be black.

Dr. Williams rightly concludes: "The minimum-wage law is certainly not a poverty weapon." For the jobless, it is closer to being a booby trap, helping to perpetuate poverty. The minimum wage is the maximum folly.

THE CORPORATION: CONTROL, POWER, PROFITS, AND SURVIVAL

The Criminal Law and Economic Regulation
(APRIL 1980)

How shall we define the proper relations between *governmental power* and *economic activity?* Aspects of that problem often pertain to the impact of governmental regulation on economic enterprise. Regulation, in turn, commonly relies on the criminal law.

The criminal law and the threat and use of criminal penalties have been long and extensively used to influence economic behavior—in antitrust laws, price and rent controls, marketing of securities.

The criminal law has not only been routinely used in major regulatory legislation, it has also been used in cavalier, unsystematic, and inappropriate fashion. It can be reasonably contended that efforts to employ the penal law as a device of economic regulation have had a demoralizing effect on the law itself and the institutions of criminal justice, with significant associated social costs.

The central purpose of the criminal law is preventive: Minimize behavior which may endanger persons or inappropriately interfere with use of possessions. The law is provided severe—and dramatic—penalties of enforcement. History provides ample evidence that governmental power is prone to abuse, that the criminal law is capable of being perverted into an instrument destructive of basic political values.

Effective law enforcement is essential for a viable society. But for a free society, it is essential, too, that governmental authority be constructively contained. And use of the criminal law for economic regulation tends to erode those principles primarily relied on to contain the powers of government in the criminal area.

Consider three such principles of containment of government:

a) The penal law should be as clear as possible.

b) Guilt is personal.

c) Most fundamental, criminal penalties should be imposed only on those who deserve to be punished—those who intended harm or at least were reckless.

Each of these principles has been weakened where the criminal law has been directed to objectives of economic regulation.

Perfect clarity is not to be found in any area of the law, but vagueness is peculiarly—and perhaps inevitably—conspicuous in economic regulatory legislation. While guilt should be personal, it may not be possible to identify a guilty corporate officer. There is then adopted the unsatisfying tactic of imposing penalties on the corporation itself, with punishment of innocent stockholders. Notions about what actions deserve punishment are products of society, defined and limited and supported by the moral sense of the community. But commonly economic regulatory statutes are simply morally neutral—conduct is decreed punishable even when not offensive to the community—or pertain to unresolved moral issues.

Lacking general support for its laws, a government may resort to greater force or other unappealing machinations.

The penal law may have a proper role in economic regulation. If so, it must be founded on just and relevant principles and applied with fairness and consistent good sense. These criteria have been often abused, and such departures from principle harm us all.

Misplaced Trust in Antitrust

(AUGUST 1979)

Government regulation of business activity stems from many sources. It is based on provision of law, conclusions of courts, and predilections of prosecutors, regulators, and legislators which are notoriously vague, contradictory, and vacillating.

Great uncertainty on the rules of the commercial game leads to great inefficiency in the market. Vulnerability to costly legal challenge by government inhibits entrepreneurial boldness. Innovations and investments which would have been undertaken in a more predictable environment are restricted or forgone. And since we must produce much in order to live well, workers and consumers are hurt by stunted economic growth as surely as are business managers and stockholders.

All this is apparent in the antitrust laws, their provisions, their interpretations, and their implementation. Antitrust agencies characteristically have been more interested in industry *structure* than in corporate *performance*, in degree of market *concentration* than in business *costs*. In trying to identify "noncompetitive," "trade-restraining" business activity, there is a persistent temptation to look at sheer size: If a firm is, in some sense, very big, there is a common presumption that it is very bad.

That is a presumption unworthy of Mortimer Snerd, much

less a senator or an Antitrust Division lawyer. For firms survive and grow large by being economically successful. Typically at very considerable risk, they make themselves efficient in production and attractive in the market. They prosper and expand through being rewarded by customers who prefer them and their products. And sometimes efficiency leads to such reductions in costs and prices as to evolve an appreciable degree of industrial concentration— concentration which can be long maintained only through continued superior market performance.

We all are in trouble when firms are hassled through the antitrust laws, not because they have actually restrained trade through dirty tricks or colluding or otherwise subverting competition, not because they have restricted output and raised prices, as any self-respecting monopolist is supposed to do, but because they have competed all too effectively and prospered as a consequence. And increasingly, successful American firms have had to survive foreign as well as domestic competition.

It is peculiar policy, indeed, to punish good market performance—performance which, in the quality and the price of the product, is good in the eyes of consumers. And benefiting consumers—not fragmenting an industry into many firms and not protecting firms from more efficient competitors—was the explicit purpose of the original antitrust legislation nearly a century ago.

Doubtless, overzealous application of nebulous antitrust laws can provide populist politicians and their bureaucrats with hearty delights. But when costs and prices are thereby kept high and initiative is reduced, not only may we wonder about the policy's fairness, we must also realize that the intended beneficiaries—consumers—are actually victims.

Concentration and Monopoly: Is Big Bad?

(APRIL 1980)

It is widely believed that when output of any industry is concentrated in a few firms, it is the result of skulduggery and gives rise to various bad things which result from "monopoly power."

Indeed, it is part of the populist folklore that *bigness* of a business firm—bigness in absolute size or bigness relative to other firms in the industry—can develop only from dirty tricks by rapacious "robber barons" and can result only in exploitation of the defenseless community. Everyone knows that big firms (which are always highly profitable) drive out and exclude smaller competitors through "cutthroat" pricing while, at the same time, ripping off consumers by charging inflationary monopoly prices which, somehow, in some sense, have been "fixed" and made inflexible.

Such grab-bag criticism and complaint comes from many politicians, media types, activists seeking a cause, and even judges and the Antitrust Division of the Department of Justice. To some extent, the antibigness prejudice stems from ancient scholarship, which suggested that the structure, or concentration, of a market is a reliable index of undesirable monopoly power. But research of the last decade provides a basically different view of bigness, business survival, and economic efficiency.

Of course, *inflation* is not a consequence of business concentration. A rapid, persistent rise in the price level is due to the sins not of Daddy Warbucks but of governmental monetary authorities. Prices in general continue to rise because the government continues to create too much money.

The price increases in highly concentrated industries have not been greater than those in relatively unconcentrated industries. And *within* concentrated industries, the largest firms typically sell at *lower* prices than do the smaller companies. This is not "predatory" pricing; it reflects lower unit costs of production—the larger firms, with economies of scale, are more efficient.

Further, there is no established linkage between price flexibility and market concentration. We can expect price changes to be affected by cost changes at different rates of output, and different cost patterns can be associated with different degrees of concentration. But, again, market concentration is not the same thing as, and does not necessarily give rise to, monopoly power.

The hypothesized link between concentration and monopoly power rests heavily on an alleged persistent pattern of *profit rates*. Supposedly, profits are greater, and remain greater, the more concentrated the industry—and, it is suggested, the greater profits stem from collusion. But in actuality, there is no persistent correlation between industry concentration and profit rates: Over time, there is a *shifting* relation between concentration and profits.

Profits stem not from collusion among firms but from superior performances by firms—superior performances in efficiently responding to indicated preferences of consumers. Leading firms maintain their leading positions through lower production costs and competitive pricing. Bigness is not badness, but stems from efficiency; concentration does not mean lack of competition, but evinces effective competition.

The Mystifying Myths of Monopoly

(JANUARY 1981)

In few areas do we more persistently repair to myths than with respect to "monopoly" and "monopoly power." Americans more than most suffer from a monopoly phobia. The phobia stems from interrelated myths.

A basic myth is that market competition carries the seeds of its own destruction, inexorably leading to monopolization or cartelization.

A second myth is that monopolies are always successful in raising prices, profits, and market shares.

A third myth follows: Market concentration of industries has increased during the twentieth century.

Indeed, a fourth myth insists that concentration now is definitive, with all major segments of the economy dominated by one or a very few firms.

All this horror generates a fifth myth: Restraining, controlling, interventionist action by government is required to prevent formation of, or depredation by, monopolies.

A more specific sixth myth is that both the purpose and the effect of government regulatory commissions have been to restrain monopolistic practices and enhance competition.

Behind such naïveté is perhaps the champion myth that government is inherently the great enemy of monopoly, encouraging competition for the benefit of consumers, actively opposing monopoly, and never encouraging, much less creating, monopoly.

Even the most addlebrained among us realize that literal monopoly—that is, a *single* seller of a good with no close substitutes—is extremely rare, if it exists at all. But the mythmakers profess to be terrified by *collusion,* with a few robber barons effectively conspiring against the public.

Imagined collusion provides grist for lurid novels and asinine movies. It bears little relation to reality—not because of lack of desire to collude but because of massive operational difficulties in colluding.

Collusion to set prices above the free-market level requires *curtailment of output.* Curtailment of output—and perhaps market division into noncompetitive sectors—requires clear agreement among the colluders. *If* agreement can be reached, there are powerful incentives to cheat, secretly to shade the price or to encroach on the market of a fellow colluder. Somehow, there must be effective ways to detect cheating and to punish detected cheaters, while still holding together the cartel. And the more successful the collusion and the longer it is successful, the greater the likelihood that the cartel will be challenged by firms that are not members of the in group.

In actuality, the basis of profits and market survival has *not* been collusion or even industry concentration. Such limited correlation as there is between profits and concentration is attributable to *efficiency*. Businesses that are large and profitable are efficient—efficient in providing goods which the community finds valuable.

It is important to set aside myths of monopoly. The importance stems not primarily from the appeal of fairness, or from the aesthetics of analytic accuracy, but from considerations of our own nitty-gritty economic well-being. In berating a mythical Daddy Warbucks, we foolishly slice our own throats.

Profits: An Engine and a Rudder

(J U L Y 1 9 8 0)

When managing their individual affairs—earning and consuming their own daily bread—people typically are pretty sensible and shrewd. But no one is born with knowledge, and we can be led astray on matters largely beyond our personal experiences.

We are commonly led far astray by newspapers, agitators, and political types on the subject of *profit*. Even economists and accountants have troubles in clearly defining and consistently measuring so-called profit. And the community at large considers "profit" to be a six-letter dirty word.

Everyone knows—doesn't everyone?—that profit is received by corporations, which are owned by a few rich people. These bloated, rapacious parasites get profit by ripping off the rest of us, who are poor but honest workers. And the enormous profits—which are corrupt extortion, not produced earnings—serve no good purpose, simply letting Daddy Warbucks reap where he has not sown.

The general perception of the rate of return on investment is of monstrous exaggeration. It is commonly believed that the annual rate of return for corporations is on the order of 30 or 40 or 50 percent—instead of the actual representative rates of 4 or 7 or 10 percent for successful firms.

Less than half of corporate after-tax earnings are paid as stockholder dividends. And the recipients of those dividends are hardly confined to cigar-chomping, bonbon-nibbling rich; individual owners of stock number in the tens of millions. But the major owners of businesses are institutional investors like union pension funds, charitable foundations, and insurance companies.

The other half of corporate earnings are reinvested by the firms. Indeed, in recent years, the major source of business investment has been retained profit. Unhappily, this has not been a big enough source. The rate of business investment in this country is far below that of other major industrial nations. So is our rate of personal saving. So is our structure of tax incentives to savers and investors. So is the seeming attitude of the community toward the rewards of efficient work and successful risk-taking. And so is our rate of productivity increase.

Most of what we consume today stems from various kinds and degrees of risk-taking yesterday—risk-taking in estimating future preferences, incomes, prices, technological and market alternatives. Profit prospects—prospects not only of *earning* but of being permitted by the community to *receive* profits—provide the rationale and the driving force of current investment. Profits are not only rewards for successful risk-taking; in addition, they are an indicator of performance and a predictor of future performance by the business managers to whom investors entrust resources. And profit possibilities provide the essential guide to those business managers in their allocation and combination of resources, for profit-making firms are firms which have done well in responding to preferences of consumers.

Profits, then, far from being silly tribute to an undeserving leisure class, are a critical element—both an engine and a rudder—in that efficient economy which is the foundation of a free society.

"Unearned and Undeserved Windfall Profits"

(July 1979)

In a free-market economy, those who produce much receive much. If they produce things or own things of high market value, they receive rewards from the community which puts that high value on their output and assets. Is that the way an open and efficient market *should* work?

Nineteen years ago, I bought a house for $34,000. Six years ago, it was appraised at $50,000. Now I could sell my old house for about $200,000, mainly because of government-created inflation. If I sell, should I be permitted to keep such "unearned and undeserved windfall profits" (to use a presidential phrase)?

A young woman whose bust measurement is larger than her IQ is discovered by a movie producer. Although she has no talent and has acquired no acting skills, she is capable of stirring lust in even a president's heart, and she becomes a sexy millionaire—"unearned and undeserved windfall profits."

Through an accident of nature, you are among the best in running and bouncing or hitting a ball. You have risked nothing in investing in such skills, for you have the capacity to be very good only at playing a boy's game. You now do so for several hundred thousand dollars a year—"unearned and undeserved windfall profits."

Perhaps you are not convinced that such windfalls should be taxed away. Even if deemed by high authority to be "unearned" and "undeserved," they *belong* to the recipients. It is *their* income, *their* property, you say, not to be expropriated in this Land of the Free for uses of politicians. That would be "unfair." Even "inefficient." You insist that, in a "free" society, people should be able to spend their money as they wish, making their choices among goods and among the producers of those goods, thereby bestowing rewards on the basis of their own preferences. And you think that market registering of such preferences is effective in getting suppliers actually to provide what you prefer and efficient in rationing what is available.

You are right, of course. Essentially unfettered choices by consumers, and profit-inspired responses by sellers to those indicated consumer choices, are the essence of market activity. Those suppliers who best respond to consumer choices —whether because of shrewdness, boldness, wise investment, or the luck of the draw—will prosper most. They prosper because their products and their assets are useful to the community. The revealed preferences of demanders have provided both general incentive and specific guidance to suppliers.

Yet we have so-called public servants who wish to single out and label certain market rewards as "unearned and undeserved windfall profits" and then, by some arbitrarily esoteric formula, take those rewards for their own purposes. This belligerent silliness not only offends propriety and subverts the free society but harms us by reducing the supply of those things the community has indicated it values highly.

Evil Oil Companies and Their Pure Critics

(NOVEMBER 1979)

The many who operate at the shallow level of slogan and shibboleth are having a circus with the reported increases in oil-company profits.

There are references to "incredible" and "obscene" profits and to "unfair" and "unreasonable" prices (even though prices at the gas pump are now subject to effective controls). The president dignifies his office with promises of "punitive action" against oil firms, congressmen threaten nationalization of the petroleum industry, and there is even a bill before the California legislature to establish its very own state gas and oil corporation.

Such outbursts and machinations are calls to the viscera, not appeals to the mind. They do not obviously stem from, and are not evidently supported by, either analysis or factual review, other than merely noting a short-term increase in measured profits.

It is enough that we are supposed to have an energy "crisis" and that the crisis must be blamed on someone. Government can hardly be expected to admit its own fundamental role in generating, exacerbating, and perpetuating our problems, even though utterly miserable government energy policy has been the source of most of our peculiar energy difficulties.

Who, then, is the enemy? Why, the most conspicuous villain is the *producer* of the desired commodity!

Is the petroleum industry a monopolistic, price-gouging recipient of extraordinary profits?

For several decades, the price of gasoline, while rising, has persistently lagged well behind prices in general, except in the unusual periods of 1974 and the last few months. From 1974 through 1978, the consumer price index rose more than did gasoline prices; the *real* price of gas actually fell. Not until May 1979 did the gasoline price index catch up with the general price index.

As for monopolization, the petroleum industry is one of the least concentrated. And the degree of concentration has been *falling* for nearly a decade. In 1977, the largest producer of crude oil—Exxon—accounted for less than 8 percent of the total; the four largest producers provided less than one-fourth; the top eight produced a little over one-third, and the forty biggest accounted for less than two-thirds.

But what about those profits? Even though gas has generally been a bargain and the oil industry is not monopolistically dominated by one or even several firms, doesn't the industry have an unusually high rate of return?

The rate of return on equity for the largest twenty-five oil companies has been almost identical to the rate for all manufacturing companies. Indeed, in six of the eleven years from 1968 through 1978, the rate of return in oil was slightly *less* than in total manufacturing.

The stock market has not been fooled. While different oil-company stocks have had varied histories, look at the stock-price record of Exxon, Gulf, Mobil, and Texaco over the last two years. Since summer 1977, the average increase in these four stocks has been a whopping, scandalous, indecent, obscene 4 percent!

Of course, all this information is highly secret and not available to the president, the Congress, and the California legislature.

Big Profits and Massive Confusion

(DECEMBER 1980)

The high and rising price of oil has increased the wealth of the oil industry—although crude-oil *refiners* have lost from higher prices of their raw material while large gains have gone to crude-oil *producers.*

There has been wealth redistribution in the overall economy as well, with oil-industry profits recently having become a much larger share of total manufacturing profits. A leading business magazine finds this alarming, asserting that the oil industry is absorbing more wealth than it can invest efficiently and is depriving other producers of resources they require to develop more valuable projects.

The magazine is simplistically confused in predicting "lower economic growth as more and more [nonoil] companies find it increasingly difficult to acquire funds for capital investment." As pointed out by Armen Alchian, one of the world's premier economists, the assertion of the magazine reverses the actual relationship between production and financing.

Companies find it difficult to attract investment funds because they can't show prospects of *profitable* projects. A lack of profitable investment *prospects,* not a lack of sufficient *funds,* is the problem. No one need abandon profitable ventures because of lack of funds; rather, projects are abandoned because of lack of profitable *prospects.*

The illusion of the problem of the oil-price increase stems from confusing past profits as a source of funds with future profitability of new investment. No industry or firm has to have earned profits in order to have funds for profitable investment.

Past profits are irrelevant to financing profitable prospects.

The computer industry initially had no profits, but it attracted enormous investments that proved profitable. Where did those funds come from? Not from its past profits—there weren't any. It got them from *savings*—from people who were willing *not* to consume some current income because they were attracted by the prospect of a profitable investment.

Several oil-industry spokesmen have contributed to the confusion. They have argued that, unless allowed to keep past profits from the crude-oil price rise, they could not make future investments in exploration and in other sources of energy. But those particular profits are not required for that particular purpose. Past profits have nothing to do with either creating or financing future profitable investments. So long as the prospects look attractive, funds will be available from people seeking a share of the profits.

Yet, as Professor Alchian discerns, there *is* a valid idea that has been confused with the preceding nonsense about financing growth. If wealth is *expropriated* by confiscatory taxation, then future investments that look profitable will be ignored, for investors will reasonably believe that future profits also will be confiscated. It is the *prospect of future confiscation*, not the absence of past profits of the producer, that inhibits investment.

Oil Profits and Efficient Investment

(DECEMBER 1980)

During the mid-1970s, profits of the oil industry were quite stable while profits of other manufacturers were rising rapidly. In the last two years, oil profits have grown greatly, both absolutely and as a proportion of total profits.

When considering oil-industry profits, the numbers are big and the stakes are large. All the more reason for exhibiting some sophistication in sorting out the issues and implications. Confusions abound and largely reflect lack of comprehension of, and resulting lack of confidence in, our highly efficient capital and production markets.

One of the alleged new problems resulting from the recent increase in oil profits is called "recycling the profits." That may suggest that profits earned in oil production are sucked out of the economy and disappear into a black hole, to the impoverishment of us all. Actually, the "recycling" pertains simply to what particular assets are to be acquired by those who have become richer: What to do with the increased wealth? But there is nothing special or unique about that "problem." It is solved every day in ordinary markets. Markets are constantly—and efficiently—adjusting to changing fortunes.

But even though free markets operate mechanically well, will the wealth be invested wisely? It is sometimes contended that, since oil executives are not experts in other industries, they will not be successful investors elsewhere with their new funds.

Indeed, oil executives are *not* commonly experts in other industries. Nor are ordinary stockholders who invest in various businesses. It is not required for efficiency that either oil executives or stockholders be Renaissance men with the knowledge and skills to administer all the endeavors which are candidates for their investment. For investors are not managers. Investors select and hire managers. There is nothing to suggest that investments by oil companies in other firms would create inefficiencies in use of resources. Or is it to be argued with a straight face that, mysteriously, ordinary stockholders are better selectors of managers than are other proven managers?

Some allege that oil companies have more wealth than their managements know how to invest well, while other companies must abandon worthy projects because of lack of funds. They propose that oil companies be forced to distribute profits more fully to their stockholders, who then can invest the funds. But investing of funds would not thereby be improved. Oil-company executives will strive to invest where it is most profitable, in light of technological possibilities and community preferences. Why would one expect dividend receivers to do better? There is no reason to presume that individual stockholders can perceive investment opportunities more reliably than can managers of oil companies.

Ham-handed proposals to abrogate rights to use of property can be attributed to various things—muddleheaded economics, socialistic mythology, thirst for autocratic power. Whatever their intellectual and psychological origins, they subvert the market and its freedom and its efficiency.

Corporate Power and Halloween Economics

(November 1980)

Halloween comes but once a year. But Halloween economics —more grotesque than the face of a witch—goes on all the time.

It is increasingly fashionable to speak of corporate control of our lives—to allege that, by seeking profits, corporations abuse the community's preferences and thereby cause pervasive maladies, from inflation to maldistribution of income to smog.

Of course, it can be comforting to blame some readily identifiable bogeyman. Perhaps because of their size, large corporations—and thousands of corporations are *not* very large—are often seen as a sinister force.

Focusing discontent on an imaginary malefactor can rid one of the task of comprehending economic events. It is not perfectly easy to understand why the prices of food, housing, and gasoline rise, why some in a free country are wealthier than others, and why air is befouled. It is convenient to blame supposedly inhuman and purportedly inhumane corporations and their pursuit of profit for our problems. We are encouraged in this silliness by those who either do not comprehend the free market and its efficient economy or prefer a society of Big Brother and his commissars.

Some corporations do own vast resources, and corporations in the aggregate do produce most of the products we consume. But the corporation has emerged as the dominant business institution in our extraordinarily productive economy because of its ability to *serve*, not to *contravene*, community preferences. By limiting possible losses of owners to their stock investments, the corporation has been able to attract the funds necessary for large-scale production which efficiently provides goods at lower costs. That large size also has enabled stockholders to buy services of managers and of other specialists, thereby freeing the owners from the complex tasks of management.

Even when large, corporations do not have the power to coerce consumers. Businesses try to persuade consumers to buy their various products, but it is the consumer who chooses to accept or reject among the variety of offerings. Consumers have been rejecting many automobiles of American producers because those cars have not been the kinds consumers now prefer. This punishment, administered by consumers, has sent domestic producers to government to seek relief from foreign competition. It has also induced dramatic attempts by domestic manufacturers to revamp their products in accordance with revealed consumer preferences. Both of these efforts—to seek political protection and to satisfy economic demands—underscore an absence of power of the industry to control consumers.

The survival of any corporation, large or small, depends ultimately—in a free market—on its ability to provide what the community prefers. When successful, a corporation is rewarded with profits; when unsuccessful, it is punished by losses. To argue that corporations violate the community's interests by pursuing profits is to conjure up economic goblins and recite the incantations of Halloween economics.

Nasty Profits and Wholesome Subsidies in a Topsy-Turvy World
(DECEMBER 1979)

The media have been heavily preoccupied with two items in recent weeks. One is concern with the *abundance*—or overabundance, whatever that might mean—of oil-industry profits; the other is concern with the *absence* of profits in the case of Chrysler Corporation.

The response of policymakers in Washington has been, in effect, to squeeze both sides toward the middle. They are trying to apply the finishing touches to a so-called windfall-profits tax to take all but a small fraction of increased oil-industry revenue resulting from the rise in worldwide energy prices. Presumably, the managements of the firms and the thousands of shareholders of the firms are not to be entrusted with their own money. As for Chrysler, the White House has proposed a taxpayer guarantee of $1.5 billion in loans—a bailout twice what the company dared to ask for.

Apparently, nothing fails like success, and nothing succeeds like failure. It is a monstrous subversion of freedom and efficiency alike to deny both the right to succeed and the right to fail. We can reasonably wonder how far our society expects to travel on an incentive scheme which singles out the profitable for "punitive" tax increases and pours revenues into enterprises that flunk the market test. This will promote investment not in productive capacity and consumer satisfaction but in political dealing. Thus we actually encourage the dreaded "special interest" through further politicizing economic decisionmaking.

The popular biases which support both the Chrysler subsidy and the oil-company tax reveal a penchant to see "profit" as something nasty and inimical to the interests of consumers and taxpayers. Profit, it is proclaimed by the unwashed and their political spokesmen, is nothing but a rip-off, an unearned levy on society.

Profit, in its accounting essence, is simply the difference between a product's price and what it costs the firm to produce the product. The firm's revenues represent the value that purchasers place on the product, and the costs reflect the value of the resources that went into making the product.

If a firm makes a profit, the community has demonstrated that it puts a higher value on the output of the firm than on the resources used by the firm. That firm has an incentive to expand its operations, and, by expanding, it is responding to consumer preferences. Conversely, a firm making a loss is using resources more valuable than its output. It should reduce output—perhaps all the way to zero—thereby releasing resources to be used in ways the community deems more valuable.

Neither the oil companies nor Chrysler got an order writ on tablets of stone to put their money where they did. Investors in each case attempted to cash in on their educated assessments as to where they could maximize their revenues vis-à-vis their costs. That the petroleum industry has experienced a profit is cause for consumers to cheer—not for joy over the good fortune of the (ugh) oil producers, but because those efficient people, out of greed, have served the community so well.

Corporate Democracy: Ownership
and Management
(MAY 1980)

People will somehow work together. It is not only physical closeness which leads to association. Even if we were much fewer in number, there still would be advantages in coordinating some activities. Various modes of joint endeavor have evolved. They have been tried, accepted, modified, and have persisted because they were found to be mutually and broadly useful. Among the most valuable has been the *corporate* form of commercial organization.

There are a few in our midst—commonly with vocal power more evident than analytic competence—who oddly look upon the corporate mode of association as part of The Enemy of mankind. Astonishingly, they deny any positive relation between the corporate organization and the relative freedom and prosperity of modern economies. Unhappily, their innocence—if innocence it is—does not embarrass them into a silent search for understanding.

In one of their more conspicuous manifestations of confusion, the anticorporate clique pictures the corporation as a thoroughly disembodied, as well as malevolent, creature—allegedly, inhuman and inhumane corporations lead lives of their own in conflict with us people. But, at the same time, it is complained that corporations include too many people!

Proponents of so-called corporate democracy might be expected to rejoice in the fact that some 30 million Americans are direct owners of corporations, with over four times that number being indirect owners through such other associations as insurance companies, credit unions, and pension funds. But our self-styled and self-appointed saviors speak darkly of "the separation of corporate ownership and control"—few of those who own corporations do the managing of the businesses.

It requires only a modicum of sophistication to comprehend that the separation of voluntary investment and ownership from the specialized functions of management is a major source of benefit to all involved, including the numerous owners.

Many of us are pretty good in doing what we do best. But rarely is complex, specialized business management what we do best. It is a beneficial division of labor for me to put my investable resources into the hands of full-time business managers. I do not have the time, expertise, or inclination to run even Exxon, much less a dozen additional corporations, while continuing to do my own thing.

When I buy stock—that is, shares of ownership—in Exxon, I understand perfectly well that I will have no perceptible voice in managing the outfit. I was neither coerced nor defrauded in buying the stock. Indeed, I buy it precisely because I *choose* to participate in anticipated rewards of business ownership *without* bearing the costs and inconveniences of management.

Further, by separating myself from the activities of management, I can diversify my personal portfolio. And that portfolio can be easily rearranged whenever I think best. I could hardly ask for more "democracy" and more protection from inevitable vagaries of commerce than an arrangement which permits me at any time to pick my investments from the thousands of stocks available.

There is much efficiency and no oppression in permitting me to choose my business activities and investments in the open market.

The Corporation and Survival of Freedom
(MARCH 1980)

Most of history has been characterized by political domination of individuals and curtailment of associations of individuals. The experience of the United States has been an
aberration of world history. But that magnificent experience
may be ending. Even here, political power is superseding
personal freedoms, which are based on private rights to the
use of property. Political power has been eroding private
rights under the guise of controlling corporate power.

The persistent and pervasive growth of government promises the demise of the private corporation. This despite the
enormous usefulness of the corporate organization as a means
of pooling investable funds, with its advantages of limited
liability, of continuity, and of specialization.

Partly under the rubric of imposed so-called social responsibility, corporations are constrained and directed in
such manner as to reduce the value of corporate ownership—
indeed, of contractual agreements and responsibilities generally; raising capital becomes more costly; and the firm
either is dissolved or becomes a ward of the state. In democratic principle, government protects rights; in bureaucratic
practice, government often reduces and redefines rights.

"Property rights" are delimited rights of people to use of
property. When those rights are diluted or made less certain, the value of the property falls. Increasingly, government has been attenuating property rights:

—Government *revokes* general classes of rights, making it
now illegal to use property in ways previously sanctioned
(for example, antipollution requirements, "affirmative ac-

tion" and occupational-safety programs, price controls, land-use restrictions, limitations on closing and moving of plants).

—Government *abrogates* specific contracts (for example, denying contracted rights of creditors of Penn Central Railroad and of New York City).

Revocation and abrogation of property rights takes place in response to "crises" which government itself has engendered but which are commonly ascribed to failures of "the market." People in the market have ingeniously adjusted to changes in the rules of the game—but such adaptations to increasingly tenuous and uncertain property rights reduce wealth-producing private investment.

Entrepreneurial government authorities not only reduce the value of privately held rights but in addition increase their own control over uses of property. Conversely, stability in private rights is, by its nature, a constraint on what government can do.

In this contest, the political sector is likely to dominate, if not obliterate, the private sector. Constitutional restraints on abrogation and revocation of rights are increasingly ineffectual. And little reliance can be placed on the electorate in halting the erosion of rights, for the attraction of special governmental favors outweighs the general interest in community well-being.

GOVERNMENT TINKERING

Horses Sweat, Men Perspire, and Women
Glow at 78 Degrees
(MAY 1980)

The administration's edict last summer [1979] that public
buildings not be cooled below 78 degrees or warmed above
65 degrees has been a fiasco. Therefore, the edict has recently been extended. It illustrates the can of worms opened
when government tries to impose a rule of behavior in a
situation inevitably yielding complications best handled by
the market.

Ludicrous in some respects, this is supposed to be serious
business. The 78/65-degree rule could affect 5 million buildings, and it was hoped to cut total oil use by about 1 percent.
A long set of regulations was issued, and penalties can come
to $10,000 a day.

It was acknowledged at the outset that enforcement would
be very difficult and costly and could not be either comprehensive or equitable. In actuality, there has been no attempt
to enforce. Not a single fine has been levied, and the Department of Energy doubts that a prosecution could be successful.

It is not easy to comprehend just what this unenforced—
and probably unenforceable—program is, for there are seemingly endless exemptions and optional modes of compliance.
Private residences, hospitals and medical offices, and elementary schools are among the exemptions; so are hotel
rooms—but not hallways, lobbies, and meeting areas. Other
exemptions include special arrangements for movie theaters,

buildings with high humidity or where equipment or materials could be harmed, and stores which can get an engineer to certify that total energy consumption would rise if the 78-degree rule were followed.

Actually, what is required is not that *thermostats* be set at 78 degrees but that *temperatures* not be below that level. That seems sensible; but it also increases the difficulties of checking compliance. Even that is not the end: Only the *warmest* room sharing an air-conditioning unit—for example, the kitchen of a restaurant—need be as warm as 78 degrees. So the details go, on and on. . . .

The costs and difficulties are more than administrative problems. As men perspire and women glow (with running mascara), commerce is curtailed, both human and mechanical productivity is reduced, and there is waste of products. There has even been concern about the ice melting in hockey games.

But the most fundamental objections pertain to the program's lack of coherency. It is another piece in a piecemeal approach to the question of how to adjust to a situation of scarcity. We live in a complex world, with myriad individual preferences and circumstances. Central government cannot efficiently lay down specific rules—even with a mind-boggling list of exemptions—which will foresee and approximately reflect those differences.

The *Wall Street Journal* has summarized the point and the moral:

> Since some businesses, like restaurants, obviously need to operate in lower temperatures than others, the sensible approach would seem to be the free market, rationing lower temperatures to those willing to pay the electric bills. Instead, government regulators find themselves creating outrageous loopholes in the attempt to fit their rules to reality. And the federal government has taken control of one more area of our lives.

Choking on Clean-Air-at-Any-Cost

(AUGUST 1979)

Everyone wants clean air. But clean air, like most other good things, is not free, to be had just for the individual asking or the government ordering. *Cost* must be borne to cleanse the air to any specified extent. The more pollution we eliminate and the faster we eliminate it, the greater the cost.

"Cost" is sacrificed, forgone alternatives—what must be *traded off* to get the desired thing in question. At the margin, how much is it rational to give up in order to eliminate a given bit of pollution? And with each additional improvement imposing increasing cost, how much *more* should be sensibly sacrificed to go still another step in clearing the air?

There *are* costs and adverse consequences in pollution control, even if the more strident environmentalists find it convenient to ignore them. Some of these repercussions—higher prices, unemployment, greater taxes, expenses of compliance, harassments and delays—can be relatively apparent. A mind-twisting legalistic and bureaucratic maze at different levels of government makes much of today's plant-and-equipment investment procedure resemble the Wonderland of Alice. The productive portion of the economy is choking on near-paralyzing requirements, uncertainties, and lost options, converging on an economic dead end.

But the costs—the forgone alternatives, the missed opportunities—include *intangible* components easily ignored even by those who wish to calculate reasonably. These real but invisible costs are the factories *not* built, the output *not* produced, the jobs *not* created, the productivity and wealth *not* increased.

A consequence of environmentally pursuing too much, too soon—striving for goals which, at least for now, are unreasonable—is a reduction of both production and freedom. There are important choices to be made in deciding how much cost we are willing to bear in order to obtain a given gross benefit in a given time. Free people in free markets—and people are not free if markets are not free—will determine those choices efficiently, in accordance with their own preferences and criteria. But those choices more and more are being made for us and jammed down our throats by a belligerent bureaucracy, egged on by those superior citizens who hunger to order the lives of the rest of us.

This is hardly an all-or-nothing world. Most people are not willing to maximize plant construction and operation at "*all* costs." At the same time, we can wonder if pristine air is worth the bearing of "*all* costs."

It is unrealistic to suppose that everyone will agree on the best balance of costs and benefits. But we will not come close to consensus—or to efficiency—through our present convoluted, inconsistent, uncertain, overlapping, ham-handed, and sometimes basically misdirected bureaucratic requirements and processes.

Pollution: Costs and Corporate Responsibility

(JULY 1979)

We have heard much about the "social responsibility" of corporations and the proper standards of business "morality." A secretary of commerce has advocated construction of an index to measure the social behavior of corporations—a grade card to indicate who has been naughty or nice. Of course, those who make charges of pervasive corporate irresponsibility admit to being pure in heart and willing to lead us all down the paths of righteousness.

Sin and virtue have little analytic content in assessing legal market actions. Instead, what is "good" and "bad" in economic activity has to do with *returns* and *costs*—that is, with rationality in our use of scarce resources.

Problems of *pollution*, unfortunately, are commonly put in terms of good or bad social behavior. Pollution is bad, so polluters are bad. And good people supposedly must do all that is required to keep bad people from imposing costs on the rest of the community.

At best, such simpleminded moralizing reflects innocence about the nature of costs, who imposes costs, and who bears them.

Suppose a chemical company disposes of wastes in a stream. The firm has imposed costs on fishermen.

If the firm is now prohibited from using the stream, should good people applaud? The firm is then forced either to stop producing or to find more costly ways to dispose of its wastes—fishermen have imposed costs on the firm and its customers.

There are costs involved in *either* case. Harmful effects obviously come from polluting the stream. But harmful effects come also from prohibiting pollution. It is not more "wrong" for consumers of the firm's product to put costs on fishermen than for fishermen to impose costs on the consumers.

The proper objective is *not* to avoid pollution. The only way to stop pollution by people is to stop people from living—the ultimate environmentalist solution.

Rather, we rationally strive to use our scarce resources so as to make our *net* gains as large, and thus our net costs as small, as possible. When resources are used, we obtain *returns*—and we bear *costs*. We want to make the costs as small as possible for a given return. In some cases, costs can be minimized by reducing pollution; in others, *increased* pollution is required. Clean water, like other resources, should be used as long as the return outweighs the cost.

To be sure, there are legitimate questions of who will reap the returns and who will bear the costs. But answers to such questions require analysis, not hysterical vilification of Daddy Warbucks.

All this may not sound very glamorous. Some like to talk as if all good things—including energy, cancer research, and clean water—are costless. But what *we* speak is economics, not poetry; it is rationality, not demagoguery.

Pollution Control: Taxes versus Regulation

(DECEMBER 1979)

The gains from control of industrial pollution are apparent. The various *costs* of control programs are not as readily seen or as commonly analyzed. And yet, rational environmental policy, like any other policy, must proceed from calculation of costs as well as benefits.

There is a twofold question in pollution-control policy.

First, *how far* do we want to go in reducing pollution? In playing to the gallery, the easily shouted demand is to eliminate *all* pollution. But that answer is sensible only if there are no costs involved. Pure air or water requires trade-offs—alternatives must be sacrificed, with costs of additional purity ever increasing. By definition, it is irrational to attain a still higher level of purity when the benefits of the greater purity are not as valuable as the costs entailed.

The second aspect of the policy problem is the *best way*

to achieve any given objective. Since we have to pay some price for what we attain, we surely want to pay the smallest possible price. There are alternative ways to induce pollution control. What is the *cheapest* way?

Government typically evinces the sophistication and refinement of a wounded water buffalo. Unsurprisingly, current pollution policy relies on direct government *regulation*. It is a strategy which provides an awesome combination of inefficiency, unfairness, and opportunities for bureaucratic abuse. Our remarkable regulatory system includes both federal and state requirements and administration, involving setting of standards, adoption of implementation plans, and specification of a variety of detailed regulations and controls for different areas, circumstances, and plants—all stemming from statutory provisions that are often vague as well as complex.

An alternative to the convoluted, ham-handed regulatory approach is a pollution *tax*, a unit tax on the emission of pollutants. Each firm, facing a common tax rate for polluting, will then make its own decisions with respect to pollution abatement. The firm will find it economic to reduce pollutants as long as its cost of doing so is less than the tax.

Under the present regulatory approach, firms naturally resist investment in costly abatement equipment, especially when the regulations are subject to sudden, if not capricious, change. There is incentive to dicker with regulatory authorities, pleading special circumstances and seeking exceptional arrangements by bureaucratic discretion, with a tendency to reward high-cost firms. With the taxation approach, the incentive is reversed, the inducement being to seek less expensive ways to reduce pollution. The essence of the game is to avoid the pollution tax: The more efficient firms will have smaller costs of pollution abatement while the less efficient will have to pay the tax.

The tax approach has deficiencies and difficulties. But

they seem to be problems inherent in *all* feasible pollution-control schemes, not unique to tax plans. And the tax approach is enormously superior to the regulatory system on grounds of efficiency and preservation of the impersonal rule of the law.

Balancing Time, Gas, and Lives

(S E P T E M B E R 1 9 8 0)

There are many things you would do or acquire if there were no price to be paid or cost to be borne. If the activity or the good were "free for the taking," you would take much more that you now demand. That is a lesson learned early in handling our individual affairs. But it is a lesson easily forgotten and garbled when politicians handle our affairs.

Consider the fifty-five-mile-per-hour speed limit. It was legislated to reduce waste of gasoline. But in order to determine if gas is wasted when we drive faster than the decreed limit, we must take into account *costs* as well as *benefits* of driving at an imposed lower speed.

Part of the *benefit* of driving more slowly is obvious: We consume less gas. The *cost*, perhaps not so obvious, is the time spent driving instead of doing other things. The gas is valuable. So are the alternative uses of the time. Which is *more* valuable?

Joe Blow—who may be a chemical engineer working on synthetic fuels—spends an additional hour driving each month because of the lower speed limit. But his gas consumption is smaller by two gallons. Are the fuel savings worth the sacrificed time? Joe has spent an additional hour on the highway to save two gallons of gas valued in the market at only $2.60—less than the legal minimum wage. Joe has been forced to waste resources in the aggregate in order to consume less of a particular good. If the time saved from driving faster is worth more than the additional gas required at higher speeds, it is efficient, not wasteful, to drive faster.

But there may be a second benefit from the speed limit. While the limit was originally lowered to save fuel, it is alleged that traffic fatalities have been reduced. And human lives, we are sometimes told, are of infinite value. If so, the speed limit should continue to be lowered as long as that would save additional lives. Indeed, we should reduce that limit to *zero*—ban driving (and all other forms of travel)— for only then would all travel deaths be eliminated. We do not go to this extreme, because the costs of eliminating travel would be greater than the benefits in saved lives.

We like to talk of human life being invaluable, but we do not act that way. In actuality, at the margin, we trade off safety for things of still greater value. Automobiles are not the safest mode of travel. And light cars are not as safe as heavy cars. But we use cars, despite their danger, for speed and convenience; and we use light cars, which are especially dangerous, to reduce gas consumption.

We reduce consumption also because the *price* of gas has risen. It is hardly surprising that average highway speeds have been falling as the gas price has been rising, although the fifty-five-mile-per-hour limit has been on the books since 1974. The self-benefit law of economic demand is more powerful than the imposed law of government.

All this does not definitively tell us if the speed limit is good. But it does remind us that we are faced with *options* and thus with *costs* in considering the wisest combination of spending time, spending gas, and spending lives.

Egalitarianism, and the Efficient, Fair Society

(FEBRUARY 1980)

". . . to each according to his needs." That Marxian motto of income distribution is devoid of analytic content, and it is not salvaged by interpreting it to mean that incomes should be equal.

Still, for reasons best analyzed by the specialist in abnormal psychology, egalitarianism has had persisting appeal. Those who espouse the egalitarian norm look to use of state power to eliminate the differential between norm and reality. Elimination of income differences would require use of coercive power, reducing both the range of voluntary activity and the productivity of society.

It seems commonly assumed by egalitarians that people are equally endowed and equally motivated in economic activity. A companion assumption is that "social justice" requires, and largely consists in, equal incomes. With these assumptions, it follows that differences in incomes result from some malevolent force that perverts the natural course of events.

Egalitarian rhetoric suggests that incomes—at least, incomes larger than average—are not *earned* through productive activity, but are unfairly *extracted* or *extorted* or *stolen*. There is somehow a manipulated carving up of a fixed, predetermined pie, with the size of the social output not at all a function of productive incentives and disincentives.

But if economic aptitudes and motivations actually were uniform, then an open, adaptive, enterprise society would yield economic equality. However, egalitarians reject the enterprise society. Advocacy of interventionist measures to gain equality thus reflect actual *dis*belief in uniform aptitudes and motivations. So we are to impose equal rewards despite unequal productivities. It may be suggested that there are a few problems of equity—as well as of efficiency—with equal incomes in the face of different performances.

A basic characteristic of an enterprise economy is that income is distributed as a market valuation of productive input. Physical *productivity* is determined by endowed talents, developed character, acquired skills, and supportive productive services. The *value* of that output stems from assessments in the marketplace, from revealed preferences of people engaged freely in exchange.

Differences among producing units in physical yield and differences in market valuations of outputs generate differences in payments to owners of resources. Whatever one's moralistic, philosophical, or aesthetic reaction to this inevitable generation of differential income, the differences are not wholly random; they are part of a rational, coherent mechanism. Indeed, the free-market mechanism very powerfully tends to induce economic efficiency, thereby enlarging the social pie to be divided.

And receiving shares of the social output on the basis of contributions to that output seems hardly inappropriate even on the nebulous criterion of "fairness."

The Welfare Industry and Handicapping the Poor

(October 1980)

The "welfare industry" is big: Many thousands of administrators transfer tens of billions of dollars through dozens of programs to many millions of recipients. Despite the compassion which supposedly has motivated the explosive growth of the industry, it is not self-evident that most of the welfare recipients are genuine beneficiaries.

Tom Bethell, writing in *Harper's*, finds that, in promoting the welfare industry, spokesmen frequently use quixotic double-talk. The basic strategy is to sell welfare *expansion* as welfare *reform*. The strategy is applied in various tactics.

An appeal to *reduce administrative costs* can mean dilution of eligibility requirements and reduction of enforcement of remaining requirements. Some fraudulent *violations* are acknowledged, but with the implication that the only proper concern is *abuse* of the welfare system, not the system itself. "Need" and "equity" are related, but competing, criteria: The first principle of welfare is need, but geographical equity calls for "averaging up" low-benefit states in pursuit of high-benefit states—while high-benefit states then must increase benefits to reflect the relatively greater need of their beneficiaries. State differentials lead to proposals for federal control of all welfare, in the name of *simplifying the welfare mess.*

The fundamental dilemma of welfare turns on *work incentives.* When an individual receives welfare benefits approximating the highest income he can realistically expect to earn, he is not irrational to eschew work. Since welfare benefits are tax-free, earned income has to be appreciably greater than benefits for the individual to break even through employment. Even when benefits are less than wages, loss of benefits when employment is accepted constitutes a huge tax on work. It is unrealistic to rely on an idealized "work ethic" for those who—as Mr. Bethell puts it—"are faced with minimum-wage and manual-labor jobs that are far less appealing than the occasional visit to the welfare office."

In field experiments, welfare income guaranteed for several years was accompanied by reduction of work and—perhaps more surprising—increase of divorce. Further, as welfare support has increased, the average period on welfare has lengthened. All this at least delays and distorts efforts of the poor to achieve economic advancement.

Other than reducing welfare payments, the only way to offset the work disincentive of welfare is to provide so-called earned-income disregards—allow people to remain eligible for some welfare for some time while earning income to a substantial level. Allowing people to continue to receive benefits after taking a job would reduce work disincentive—but it also "extends welfare and its attendant costs and problems into the middle class."

The relatively poor will always be with us. But few are doomed to poverty—unless the welfare system makes them "permanent economic invalids."

Micronesia: Trying Badly to Do Good
(JULY 1980)

Evidently, it is not easy to do good well. Even with intentions pure as the driven snow, it is difficult to be efficient in helping masses of people. Still, it requires perverse talent to do actual harm by trying to do good, to make people worse off by a program of aid. But you can count on government for unpleasant—and expensive—surprises.

According to a report in the *Washington Post*, the United States government has bungled its Pacific Ocean trusteeship of Micronesia, which includes the Mariana Islands. The record is unamusingly ludicrous.

Since the early 1960s, the government has well-nigh smothered its wards with patronizing assistance—to the detriment of the Micronesian economy and people.

For one thing, a third of the labor force—double the proportion in the United States—is on the government payroll, in largely unaccountable activities in undemanding jobs at relatively high pay. That stultifying tactic alone is enough to do wonders for the productivity of the economy.

Then there is the food dole from the United States Department of Agriculture, along with other gifts. Some 95 percent of the population is eligible for free or subsidized food. So there goes another major incentive for productive activity.

Government programs not only are inefficiently and even dishonestly administered, but are basically misconceived and misdirected, fostering dependency and indolence rather than self-reliance and self-sustaining economic development. The aid programs are in the form of direct, short-term benefits instead of procedures to help the Micronesians help themselves over the long pull.

And, in fact, the domestic economy has been devastated. Why produce food locally when the people will not buy it because they get free imported food? In just one decade, the production of fruit and vegetables fell 97 percent.

The *Washington Post* finds "the almost universal judgment that [over three decades] . . . of American trusteeship in Micronesia has created a society dependent on government jobs and benefits, an island welfare state whose people are so inundated with free handouts that they are abandoning even those elemental enterprises—fishing and farming—that they had developed before the Americans came."

The obvious explanation of this fiasco, *Fortune* magazine suggests, "is that our government *likes* to go around introducing the welfare state. In fact, our government consists in large measure of people whose careers are dependent on the infinite expansion of handouts to people who don't need them."

But the obvious will not do for the "investigative reporters" of a well-known TV documentary program. Their explanation is—imperialism: We have deliberately made the islanders dependent on us so that we can keep control of the islands so that we can test missiles there. Clever devils, those Pentagon types, with one part of government persuading another part to subvert an entire society.

We need not impute the lousy policy to subversion. Bungling is explanation enough. It is not the first instance of a very heavy price paid for the foolishness and ineptitude of social engineers trying badly to do good.

Compassion and Comprehension
(APRIL 1980)

This is a world of tears. It requires neither extraordinary perception nor peculiar sensitivity to detect difficulties which inflict grievous harm. But simply noting problems and their human consequences does not magically generate optimal resolutions. Indeed, far from good answers springing full-blown from the mere voicing of questions, the emotionally involved observer—or the demagogue playing to the gallery —often rushes in with simplistic solutions where angels and analysts are more sensibly cautious.

Illustrations abound of supposedly direct public policy "solutions" which—with their controls and directives—actually are harmfully misdirected. An illustration is proposals to inhibit, through various directives, penalties, and restrictions, the closing and moving of business plants.

It is easy to see the temptation to restrict by government the closing and moving of supposedly privately owned plants. The workers in the affected plants are at least inconvenienced in the short run, and the costs for some can be great. Evidently, it is not so easy to see that, for the economy and society generally, including workers overall and in the long run, such restrictions on business decisionmaking do more harm than good.

In a thoroughly stagnant world, there would be neither occasion nor opportunity for adjustment. We would freeze relationships both among people and between people and things. We would produce the same goods in the same ways in the same proportions, and there would be no geographic, economic, or social mobility. This would be "stability" of a sort, but not an equilibrium many would applaud.

For most people—especially those *below* the top social-economic strata—the best hope is a stability *not* of stultifying *outcome* imposed by Big Brother but of ground rules which permit efficient adjustment to evolving technological and economic circumstances. Let there be invention, innovation, and discovery, with new products and new technology —and discarding of old; let people effectively express changing preferences and pursue diverse objectives. But if change is to be accepted (and it cannot be wholly suppressed), there must be adaptation to change. In a world of scarcity, it behooves us to minimize the costs of adaptation.

By the criterion of efficiency, we do not wish to hamper reallocation of resources, by plant closings and relocations or otherwise. By the criterion of compassion, we *do* wish to ameliorate the peculiar adverse effects on individuals. And by criteria of both efficiency and compassion, we *must* facilitate resource mobility—that is, reduce the costs of adjustment in a world characterized by occasion for adjustment. Inhibiting plant closings and relocations limits, not expands, economic options which are the basis of growth; such subversion of private economic decisionmaking increases, not decreases, the costs of adaptation, especially for those least prepared to bear such costs.

If compassion were a sufficient condition for deducing solutions, problems would not long continue. But neither suffering, on the one hand, nor commiseration, on the other, is an adequate substitute for analysis and comprehension.

Economic Subversion: Another Attack
on the Corporation
(MARCH 1980)

The defense of freedom and efficiency can never be finally won.

One reason for the never-ending struggle is that the world continues to change; adaption to change imposes injury on some even when others are benefited; it is tempting to try to resolve each problem and soothe each injury directly and immediately; and in this incessant effort to patch and insulate with *ad hoc* machinations, many turn, almost instinctively, to government. Whenever a problem seems, or threatens, to arise, impose a governmental constraint or directive here and provide a subsidy there, case by case, with little regard for analytic long-run validity or operational feasibility.

A recent illustration of this proclivity to shoot from the hip, with little regard for either the real nature of the target or the appropriateness of the bullet, are proposals—at both the federal and the state levels—to inhibit the closing and the relocating of business plants.

One common feature of the various proposals is to require warning that a plant is to be closed or moved. The notice period is as long as two years—unless demonstration is made to a government commission that there is "adequate justification" for quicker action.

Even with such advance notice, there may be penalties—fines or eliminated tax benefits—on firms which fail adequately to justify the plant closing or moving.

Finally, there are provisions for substantial government and corporate assistance to released employees and to the community where the plant is located.

This new, audacious assault on the open, adaptive society and its free-market economy is breathtaking, utterly alien to those presumptions and processes which have distinguished our national history and generated our national success. It is part of the massive offensive on the very conception of private rights to use of property. Tactically, the growing and increasingly effective efforts to dilute, revoke, and abrogate rights of private use of property have centered on the corporation.

All this is not an issue of empty dogma, a matter simply of slogan and motto. Nor are restrictions on corporate mobility most basically a constitutional question, although surely there are legal questions pertaining to interstate commerce. Such constraints on business decisionmaking strike at the essence of the activity and adaptability of the economy.

There is an inevitable dynamism of a modern economy. The level of economic activity ebbs and recovers; demands shift from commodity to commodity; technology develops; sources of materials and energy evolve; the world setting—economic, political, military—can alter abruptly. That there will be ubiquitous and unceasing change is certain. The question is, how effectively will we adjust to change? Delaying, hampering, and penalizing efficient change strikes at the sinews of our strength.

Those who act to attenuate private initiative—and accountability—in a market economy, those who seek to make us increasingly wards of the heavy-handed and bungling state, those who foolishly seek total protection from risk and full compensation for all injury in a world of inevitable risk and injury—those are not friends of freedom.

Silly Strategy and Terrible Tactics

(April 1980)

In public policy, there can be a great gap between objective and realization. A blunder inspired by good intentions is still a blunder—and the major victims may be the intended beneficiaries.

Consider a proposal making the rounds at both the federal and the state levels. Daddy Warbucks sometimes closes a business plant, for he—unlike us pure types—is greedy and wants to make more money than he deserves. When the plant is closed, workers lose jobs, and communities lose taxes. That is a problem—at least for some in the short run. So let's solve the problem straightforwardly by making it difficult— through directives and penalties—for Daddy to close the plant.

Why would Daddy *want* to close the plant? Because of perverse pleasure in the miseries of downtrodden mankind? Maybe. After all, the head of a business can't be *very* nice. But it is possible also that the decision was a rational response to changed circumstances—changed demand or technology or input prices or supply availability or government regulations.

Further, rational reallocation of resources benefits not only the firm but the economy generally. The firm is an institutional device by means of which information on costs and community preferences is collected and assessed for decisionmaking in use of resources. If the firm does well in its decisionmaking, it will prosper. But it prospers *because* it has efficiently responded to market circumstances, including consumer demands.

Would-be regulators of the economy often find it convenient to ignore the nitty-gritty production process. We live according to our output. One can object to *what* we produce, in what *relative quantities* we produce it, the *ways and circumstances* of the productive activity, and the *distribution* of the output. But, in any case, the game begins with production. And it is unforgivably simpleminded to suppose that we will long continue to produce much when the organizers, directors, and risk-takers in the production process are hamstrung in their decisionmaking by increasing operational constraints and increasing uncertainty about the market ground rules.

What is a silly strategy at the national level is a terrible tactic at the state level. Inhibiting market adjustments through the national economy is wasteful; and waste, in a world of scarcity, is a sin. But for a state to hinder economic adaption not only is wasteful in general but concentrates the burden of the inefficiency on the state's own economy!

You want to help workers of your state by increasing demand for their services? Then—obviously—don't discourage the demanders by imposing special, unique constraints and costs on their operations. Where businesses are heavily hassled about closing or relocating old plants, business decisionmakers are much less likely to open new plants.

Government has a vital role in the market. But the role is to help provide a predictably stable setting within which energetic, ambitious, innovative people will be induced to be productive. The supply of manna from heaven being finite, we shall live well only if we produce much. Inhibition of plant closing and relocation would not aid production.

ENERGY: EXPERIENCE,
POLICY, AND SOURCES

❧

Change, Crisis, Adaptation, and Innovation
(MAY 1980)

History is just one thing after another. Some happenings are unfortunate. But the human race has survived much adversity. Indeed, instead of being steadily beaten down and weakened by hardships imposed by a stingy and capricious environment, people have laboriously and often ingeniously bettered their lot.

How has this survival and this improvement come about? A case study of long-term adjustment and progress is provided by the resolution of an early raw-material crisis.

In medieval Europe, wood was used extensively in both construction and heating. But the economic expansion of the early modern period—the fifteenth and sixteenth centuries—generated an increasing demand for energy, as well as building materials. By the mid-1500s, England was the first to feel "the wood crisis."

The crisis was not one simply of physical inconvenience as forests were depleted. The situation was reflected also in a prolonged rise in *prices* of firewood and lumber.

Coal had been used in small quantities for centuries. But mining coal was less attractive than cutting trees, and burning coal created unpleasant fumes. So wood was used primarily—until the price of wood rose to high levels. Unsurprisingly, coal became more acceptable as it became relatively cheaper. Wood continued in high demand for construction, but coal became the key source of heat, and coal exports paid for some of the wood imports.

All this was not merely making the best of a bad situation. The English standard of living *rose*. And it rose in major degree because, not in spite, of the massive adoption of coal in the 150 years between 1550 and 1700. By the end of this so-called crisis period, England, which earlier had been a relatively poor nation, was perhaps the most prosperous in Europe.

Extensive use of coal itself required technological development. The increasingly sophisticated use of coal led, in turn, to a scale and a variety of commerce and production which would not otherwise have been possible. A distinguished economic historian has observed: ". . . the technological advances of the Industrial Revolution were largely the culmination of the innovative period associated with the conversion to coal."

This story of challenge and effective response, of imaginative technology and flexibility, yielding a growing national output, is gratifying and instructive. People faced by constricting supply and increasing costs found incentive to seek alternatives; they found it advantageous, in their individual interests, to exercise initiative in adaptation, invention, innovation, and investment; guided as by an invisible hand of the market, they efficiently adjusted to their evolving options.

It would have been a different, and dreadful, story had the crisis been confronted by imposition of centralized plans administered by a stifling bureaucracy, punitively taxing current major producers, quixotically subsidizing minor producers, and hysterically closing off options of enormous future benefit. Therein may be found a moral of modern applicability.

Energy, Government, and Shortages

(FEBRUARY 1980)

This is a world of woe and wickedness. Under the best of circumstances, we will have difficulties. But there are problems and problems. We shall never escape the constraints of scarcity. But we need not make our situation still worse by adding *shortages*.

Scarcity stems from people wanting more at any given time than stingy nature can then provide. But *shortages* are self-imposed. They are self-imposed by a confused community that permits its greed to be misdirected by a posturing government anxious to manipulate the lives of its citizens.

Consider our energy problems. Almost everyone says we have an "energy crisis." Petroleum is our most conspicuous source of energy; and petroleum is produced from limited sources and sold in various forms in various markets. Everyone knows that. So if we have energy problems, it might seem to be because either we are on the verge of abruptly exhausting petroleum sources or the market is incapable of inducing petroleum producers and distributors to operate efficiently. Unhappily, many believe that, too.

Market decisions are made by all of us—consumers and producers—on the basis of changes in relative prices, as some things become more or less expensive compared to other goods. If the community's demand for commodity X goes up or if the cost of producing X increases, then the price of X tends to rise—if Big Brother permits marketplace variables to vary. The rise in the price of X is a *signal* and an *inducement* to people who want to use their resources efficiently. It is information which rational people take into account as they adjust in a world of scarcity. The higher price of X leads people, first, to *reduce consumption* of X—

they economize; second, they *substitute other goods,* alternatives which now are relatively cheaper, for some of their previous use of *X;* and, third, they *produce more X.*

This applies to petroleum. If the price of petroleum is pegged by government below the market-clearing level, people want more than is available at that artificially low price. The price control inevitably has created a *shortage.* But if the price is now permitted to rise to its natural level, consumption will be reduced and redirected while production is increased. Shortages cannot exist in a free market; they cannot be avoided in a controlled market.

In all this, there need be no reason to panic, there need be no "crisis," no occasion for presidential fireside exhortations or for expensive expansion of the government's regulatory legions. Sensible people, concerned with their own individual well-being, if permitted to do so, will quickly respond and efficiently adjust to changing circumstances. They will receive the market messages and act on the market information.

Regrettably, paternalistic government persists in underestimating both the effectiveness of the market and the ingenuity of people. Government thereby creates and perpetuates commodity shortages. Government adds to our woes.

Diagnosis Before Prescription: What the Energy Problem Is and Is Not

(AUGUST 1979)

Before a doctor can usefully *prescribe,* he must accurately *diagnose.* So it is with economic policymaking—we must first get straight what the problem is.

The fundamental long-run *energy* problem is the tendency for energy costs to rise. An expanding world economy and increasingly sophisticated production techniques probably will cause energy to become more expensive relative to other resources over the coming decades. The long-run problem is *not* an *absence* of energy—projections of a doomsday in which energy supplies have run out are unfounded. And shortages are *solely* a result of price controls, which prevent clearing of the market.

Self-interest and market incentives, if allowed to operate, will induce and direct adjustments in both consumption and production. These adjustments will reflect the reality of higher costs. Faced by increased energy prices, users will reduce total consumption and switch to relatively cheap types of energy, and suppliers will find it feasible and rewarding to expand output from both conventional and newer sources.

The government does *not* need to subsidize home insulation. It does *not* need to tell automakers to improve fuel economy. It does *not* need to allocate fuel, either geographically or between gasoline and heating-oil production. It does *not* need to ration gasoline. It does *not* need to tell industry to switch from oil and gas to coal. People, both consumers and producers, will make efficient adjustments without being forced—and without presidential moralistic exhortations or calls to the barricades. Such rational responses involve changes in the ways energy is used, but they do not imply a "crisis," much less an impending catastrophe.

Substantial adjustments to higher energy prices are going on now, independent, and at times in spite, of federal policies. The United States economy is using over 10 percent less energy per dollar of gross national product than it did in 1970. Market-induced conservation can be expected to continue—to a *rational* extent. Economic efficiency calls for extended consumption of energy as long as the benefits outweigh the costs. Too *little* energy is consumed with artificially *increased* energy costs; and too *much* is consumed with artificially *restrained* costs. Meddling, hyperactive government has been guilty numerous times of both errors, sometimes inducing too little energy use and sometimes too much.

To say that the economy *can* most efficiently adjust on its own to a future of higher-priced energy is hardly to say that it will be *allowed* to do so. Federal energy policy typically has been grievously misdirected, largely because of misconceptions of the energy problem. Inept problem diagnosis and debilitating policy prescription have not helped the health of the American economy.

Free Markets and Energy Policy

(NOVEMBER 1980)

When the implications and consequences of muddleheaded government economic policies remain hidden or are distorted in description, citizens can be seduced into supporting perverse policies which transfer to inept government their freedom to make their own efficient choices.

The cleverly insidious reporting of pretentious nonsense was recently illustrated by a comic strip. A free market in oil was ridiculed by the cartoonist as a way to "squander" our nation's scarce petroleum until it "runs out" and meanwhile to provide "obscene" profits for oil companies. To have a free market in petroleum or energy was absurdly presented as having *no* energy policy. The implication, of course, was that coping with the scarcity of energy requires government action—taxes and subsidies; price controls and allocations; discrimination among products, processes, and producers.

If the cleverness of the cartoonist were matched by competence, he would understand that the scarcity of energy is not unique, for *all* economic resources and goods are scarce. He would realize that we do not need a government energy policy of discretionary intervention and control any more than we need such a government policy for beer, beef, or bath oil. He would comprehend that the market, or pricing system, most efficiently organizes our production and directs our consumption, even for energy, and that it does it in such a manner as to satisfy the community's preferences—preferences which may, indeed, be different from those of government bureaucrats or cartoonists.

The pricing system guides our behavior as producers and consumers in a remarkably unobtrusive way, like an "invisible hand" that coordinates our many separate, individual activities.

When a good becomes more scarce, either because consumers demand more or because less can now be supplied, consumers will bid up its price. By increasing the profitability of supplying oil, the higher price tells producers that the community wants more resources directed to oil, or to oil substitutes, like coal and nuclear power. A higher price also tells consumers to use less. As producers, in pursuing their own interests, respond to the community's call for additional supplies, the good's price will fall relative to other prices. Profitability of producing the good also will fall, back to rates which are in line with other industries.

These events did happen in the oil industry after the initial price increase in 1973, when OPEC reduced its supply. After climbing rapidly, the relative price of oil dropped, as did rates of profitability in the oil industry. When OPEC again reduced oil supplies last year, the relative price of oil jumped once more, as did profit rates in the oil industry— rates which have since begun to decline again.

Increased prices and profitability are the community's way of directing resources to supply more energy in ways the community prefers. Government policies which distort those prices and restrain that profitability muffle the consumers' voice—a muffling proposed in the name of the people, of course. Government bureaucrats, instead of consumers, then make choices about energy.

Save us from comic-strip economics!

Energy Technology, Economic Efficiency, and Consumer Freedom

(OCTOBER 1980)

The Department of Energy, in bureaucratic tradition, strives to substitute government decree for producer and consumer voluntarism. It now has proposed energy-efficiency standards for appliance manufacturers. For example, manufacturers would not be permitted to sell refrigerators that use more electricity than thought desirable by our government guardians.

Energy efficiency is certainly important. Indeed, the efficient use of *all* economic resources is important, for all those resources are scarce. We *efficiently* employ a resource when only the most valuable uses of it are satisfied. The remaining, less valuable uses cannot be met.

Government types tend to forget that efficiency is not a matter of physical technology alone—and thus is not achieved simply by decreeing engineering standards. Efficiency is a matter also of satisfying consumer preferences—and thus requires a weighing of costs along with benefits, rather than looking at benefits alone.

There is a method by which our behavior can be directed, so that we voluntarily choose to exclude all of the lower-valued uses for which there is not enough energy. That method is the pricing system—a system of prices which tells us how scarce resources are. Should a resource, such as electricity, become more scarce, that fact is evidenced in a higher price. Electricity consumers are not happy about the higher price. But like a thermometer which records fever, the higher price of power reflects reality. Breaking the thermometer will not reduce the fever; nor will artificially holding down the price of electricity change the fact that it is now more scarce.

The higher price of electricity sets into motion a voluntary but efficient adjustment. If electricity were selling for 5 cents per kilowatt hour, consumers—rationally, in their own interests—would have eliminated all uses of electricity not worth at least 5 cents to them. Should its price now rise to 10 cents, then consumers would choose to buy less by excluding additional uses of electricity—those uses worth less than 10 cents.

Electricity would be efficiently used, for consumers would use it in only the most valuable ways. Further, they would demand appliances that use less power, and manufacturers— rationally, in *their* own interests—would produce those power-stingy appliances in order to earn profits.

With electricity now more expensive, those producers that supply appliances using less electricity will be very popular. They will be rewarded by consumers for their technological efficiency. Consumers respond to higher electricity prices, and producers respond to consumer demands. We *economize*—that is, we conserve resources while using final output only in ways most valuable—through freely exercising the interrelated production and consumption options of the market.

Through government decrees, free-market adjustment is replaced by coercion in the name of efficiency. But freedom and efficiency are complements, not substitutes. In destroying freedom in order to obtain efficiency, we destroy both.

Further Conservation or More Production: The Role of the Market

(AUGUST 1979)

There is a global energy problem. There has *always* been a global energy problem, for energy is a scarce good. But the problem has become more apparent recently because of rising energy costs.

Even if OPEC behaves itself, energy costs will continue to rise, partly because much of the relatively easy adjustment to more pressing energy scarcity has already been made. As we move beyond marginal, simple "fixes" of conservation, there will be required much more elaborate equipment and basic process redesigns: Conservation not only is not free, it inevitably becomes increasingly costly.

Consider the administration's urging that industry conserve natural gas and petroleum by switching to coal. It has been estimated that such a conservation switch would cost some $200 billion in plant and equipment. That is about $45 billion more than all of industry invested last year. For General Motors alone, converting plants to coal would cost more than $2 billion. In addition, use of coal involves much higher operating costs than does natural gas.

Increasing automobile gas mileage provides another illustration. This year the average new car provides 19 miles per gallon—up from 14 five years ago. Federal regulations require 27.5 miles per gallon just six years from now. It is estimated that it now costs about $1 billion to achieve a half-mile-per-gallon improvement in average fuel economy. The most cost-effective mileage improvements are made first, so cost goes up as still further improvements are made.

Eventually, it will cost less somehow—and there are various possibilities—to *produce* an additional gallon of fuel than to *save* a gallon by vehicle design changes, which are increasingly expensive. Then we shall be able to buy more transportation through additional energy *production* than through further *conservation*.

But with government-mandated fuel-economy specifications and continuing government controls on energy prices, we are not likely to shift emphasis from conservation to increased production at the appropriate time to the appropriate extent. For the signals required to make such decisions are information provided only by a free market.

Indeed, in the absence of permitted response through the calculus of the market, will the marginal shift from further conservation to increased production be made at all? Without market signals provided by market information, we are flying blind. That's an inexcusably clumsy way to operate an economy.

Monopolists and Substitutes for Oil

(JANUARY 1980)

At an OPEC conference, the spirit of the oil-price-fixing conferees was effectively summarized by the oil minister of Libya. "The industrialized countries can pay whatever we ask," he said. "They have shown they can stand a price increase."

So far, while he exaggerates, he is not far wrong. Behind this camel-trading view of the market is "inelastic" demand. If the price of a good goes up, quantity demanded declines. There are many instances, though, when the fall in demand is so small that the increased price more than makes up for the loss in sales, so the seller's receipts rise.

The demand for oil exhibits inelasticity. The quantity demanded is not highly responsive to price changes, especially in the short run. It is true that the industrialized world has made some energy adjustments. Industrial and personal conservation measures, along with production of automobiles with greater mileage, have lessened the demand for oil. And the quantity of oil demanded has been reduced roughly 1 percent for every 10-percent increase in the price of oil. But the observation of the Libyan minister is largely justified.

More drastic conservation measures could be implemented, but not without consequent depressing effects on economic activity. But there is another way to reduce the amount of oil consumed besides legislating ourselves into an excessively lowered standard of living. That is by finding viable *substitutes* for oil. For it is the number and quality of alternatives for a given product that determine the sensitivity of sales to a price change. With suitable substitutes for oil, a price increase would lead to a substantial reduction in the quantity of oil demanded: People would shift to alternatives which then were relatively cheap.

For now, there are only two significant alternatives to oil: coal and nuclear power. With present technology and long construction lead times, sun, wind, geothermal pressure, waves, bird droppings, and the like are marginal, supplemental sources and by themselves cannot provide the enormous and growing quantity of energy required for a complex, industrialized economy.

Historically, coal was largely abandoned in favor of oil. Oil is cleaner, more healthful, and safer than coal. Nuclear power has proved itself still cleaner, more healthful, and safer. Logically, oil should be gradually abandoned in favor of nuclear power.

OPEC members have observed, however, that America and other countries are unwilling to revert to unclean and dangerous coal and are paranoid concerning nuclear power. In other words, we are ignoring our major options. This gives OPEC a quasi-monopoly position in the energy market.

There is little reason to whimper when monopolists behave like monopolists. But there is no sense at all in continuing to help monopolists—as our government policy has helped OPEC—to build and maintain power over us. We break monopoly power only by availability of alternatives. So long as we strangely deny ourselves adequate alternatives, the oil-exporting countries will have us over a barrel—or else have us wearing one.

"Almost Unbelievable" Foolishness About Nuclear Safety

(JULY 1979)

In essence, the issue of using nuclear power is technological and economic. But the debate has become heavily emotional and ideological. And when emotion and ideology take the place of analysis, we can expect a great deal of silliness—and shrillness.

Last spring there was an accident at the nuclear plant on Three Mile Island in Pennsylvania. Despite bungling by personnel at the plant, built-in multiple safeguards prevented community damage, and no one's life was lost.

A conspicuous Hollywood figure, who loves dramatic roles in the public arena as well as on the silver screen, professes to resent noting of the fact that no one was killed at Three Mile Island—or, we add, at any other nuclear plant. She is quoted as telling a university audience: "They say that Three Mile Island proved that nuclear is safe because no one died. That is so cruel in my mind," she says, "as to be almost unbelievable."

The actress was reciting a thoroughly remarkable script. First, *no* responsible individual has said, or would say, that "nuclear power is safe." *All* sources of energy and *all* uses of energy—by the nature of energy—are unsafe to some extent. Why doesn't the actress distressfully acknowledge the thousands of annual deaths from generating electric power by fossil fuels? Why is she not agitated by the tens of thousands of annual deaths from use of internal-combustion engines?

While *all* energy—including nuclear—presents hazards, we shall continue to use energy, doubtless in increasing amounts, from various sources. In deciding what sources in what relative amounts, comparisons are in order. And it does not require the genius of Einstein to comprehend that *zero* deaths are fewer than the yearly 50,000 from automobile accidents or even one death.

Why is it "cruel," in what the actress chooses to call her "mind," to note the remarkable safety record of nuclear power? Would she have preferred a Three Mile catastrophe which might have killed, say, 50,000? Is it really irrelevant that no one died at Three Mile Island? Is it actually naughty to acknowledge the fact that no one died? Well, I guess we all suffer from our funny little frustrations.

A good deal of silliness and shrillness can be—and must be—tolerated in a free society, of course. But we all are vastly endangered when many people begin to believe error and distortion of such monumental magnitude as to be "almost unbelievable."

UNIONS

❧

Labor Unions: Rights and Free Riders

(July 1980)

Everyone but the anarchist agrees that there is a legitimate
role of government. Certainly, a social arrangement of private rights to use of property requires government, for those
rights must be specified, assigned, interpreted, and enforced.

For there to be government, there must be some degree
of some kinds of coercion. In our political heritage, the
coercive powers of government are to be severely delimited.
Still, powers of government must exist if governed society is
to exist. Characteristically those powers are exercised on the
basis of majority vote, and dissenting voters cannot choose
not to be represented by those who win elections.

Some argue that majority vote also legitimately estab-
lishes coercive powers of labor unions. If a majority of employees of a firm vote to be represented by a particular union,
then dissenting employees cannot choose not to be represented by that union.

But *unions are not governments.* They are private associations of people in their private capacities. The essence of
government is that its services—however delimited—are
uniformly provided to, and universally supported by, the
citizenry. The essence of private associations is voluntarism:
People are free to join or not to join. Freedom of association
precludes coercion.

But to the extent there may be gains to workers from
activities of a union, we have the "free rider" issue: All affected workers benefit, so is it not appropriate that all

workers pay union dues? There are problems in the free-rider argument.

First, the situation is not unique to unions; in our inter-relations, everyone receives numerous benefits for which he does not pay. There are spillover benefits to the community from various associations—churches, clubs, teams—which no one is required to join or support. I benefit from your good manners, your well-kept lawn, your well-kept wife. But I am not forced to contribute to meeting your expenses. Why should I be forced to help finance a union, which may not be as attractive to me as your smile, your lawn, or your wife?

Second, those who fret about *free* rides might concern themselves also with *forced* rides. If it is reprehensible to receive unsolicited gains without paying, why is it accept-able to force payments when the supposed gains are not only unsolicited but may be unappreciated? I may consider the gains from the union to be less than the union dues; indeed, I may assign *negative* value to the union's activities. Then, where is justice in forcing my affiliation with the union?

Finally, I may be dubious not only of the value of the union for me but also of the value of unionization for the economy. Unions are institutionalized agreements among sellers of labor services not to compete with each other. They are avowedly instruments of collusion. Cartelization of business firms not only is illegal but almost invariably is ineffective. But union cartelization, promoted by govern-ment, may be reasonably deemed subversive of the market—to the detriment of the community generally.

In short, the free-rider argument for coercing member-ship in unions is both philosophically unacceptable and theoretically confused.

Public Employee Unions: A Special Problem
(JULY 1980)

Unionization in general has had much difficulty and some legislative, judicial, and representational setbacks in recent years. But unions of *government* personnel have become more conspicuous and militant. Policemen, firefighters, prison guards, hospital workers, teachers, postal workers, garbage collectors, and public transit workers increasingly threaten to strike—and not uncommonly make good on their threats, with predictable disruption and violence. A news magazine has commented that such strikes "are becoming one of the normal summertime discomforts of urban life."

Government has granted significant privileges of collective bargaining and of striking to unions in the private sector. The justifications of such powers for private-sector unions are not appropriately applied to public-sector unions. Some sharp distinctions are to be drawn between "public" and "private" unions.

First, employees in the private sector are paid from earned business receipts, while government employees receive funds provided through coerced, nonoptional tax payments. If public unions are granted mandatory collective bargaining and permission to strike or to use compulsory arbitration, then wage rates are determined by negotiations with unions; if tax revenues are currently inadequate to pay for the negotiated wages, taxes are raised—and effective taxpayer control over aggregate taxes disappears.

Second, compulsory public-union affiliation and exclusive representation are inconsistent with a government "of, by, and for" all the people. Whatever may be said for compulsion and exclusivity in the private sector—and it is not persuasive—no group properly has a monopoly in access to government or in representation of other citizens in their dealings with government.

Third, in the private sector, customers do not pay for output not produced during a strike, but tax payments continue even when government services are not rendered.

Fourth, most government services, in contrast to private-sector goods, cannot be readily supplied by substitute producers, either because of their nature or, more commonly, because of imposed state monopolization. To permit suspension by strike of police services, in particular, is to question the very necessity of government.

Fifth, since government is largely a monopolist in providing its services and obtains its receipts mainly through obligatory taxes, government managers, interested largely in the short term, are more inclined than private-sector managers to meet union demands to any extent necessary to avoid, or quickly settle, strikes.

Finally, denying collective bargaining and strikes to public employees recognizes their special position. Necessarily, people in government exercise unique, coercive authority in collecting and spending taxes—and, to protect the rest of the community, that calls for special restrictions on their behavior.

Public unions, with the ultimate permission to strike, are repugnant to, and seemingly incompatible with, the individualistic, decentralized society.

Academic Unions: A Futile Defilement
of the Temple
(September 1979)

Recent years have not been entirely happy for labor unions. Membership has remained nearly unchanged absolutely and has fallen as a proportion of the total labor force. Big labor has taken hurtful and embarrassing defeats in conspicuous legislative contests. It has been losing most of its representation elections, along with public esteem.

But the unions also have had some successes. In a particularly sensitive battle, unionization has gained in an area —college faculties—which might reasonably have been deemed quite alien territory for ungenteel, unprofessional collectivism.

In contrast to the rapid growth in enrollments and federal funding of higher education in the 1960s and early 1970s, the coming decade portends severe financial difficulties. Many schools are expected to close.

The economic status and job security of faculty will be seriously affected. While declining enrollments reduce demand for college teachers, the *supply* is projected to increase. Under such threatening circumstances, collective bargaining could appeal to faculty members.

However, there is little reason to suppose that unionized action by college teachers would strike such terror into the hearts of state officials, boards of trustees, or society at large as to be effective in wringing more employment or better employment terms. Indeed, in collective bargaining, just what can the faculty *give* or *threaten* in order to *get?* The climate has been such since the campus insanity in the 1960s, intensified by the tax revolts of the 1970s, that faculties will do well to mind their manners lest they be slapped even harder by a disgruntled community.

Studies provide no convincing evidence that unions have succeeded in raising compensation of unionized faculty relative to nonunionized. If organized pressure has not produced substantial gains in propitious periods of relative academic prosperity, there is little basis to suppose that unions will be successful in times of retrenchment. Certainly, unions cannot reverse population trends or preserve jobs at institutions that close due to diminished enrollments.

Although benefits from collective bargaining are illusory, associated costs are real. Teachers must pay dues, fees, and assessments to support the organization. Negotiation, grievance proceedings, and fact-finding are costly, diverting resources from education programs and salaries. Collective bargaining alters the structure of campus governance, leaving a smaller role for the individual faculty member, his department, and his academic associations. Standardization of pay—a major union goal—reduces rewards for outstanding performance and leads to a decline in educational quality. Union agreements may require all faculty to support the union financially, and the traditional protection of tenure is sacrificed.

The beneficiary of collective bargaining in higher education is the union. Academic freedom and educational quality will be casualties of collectivism.

Mainly Macroeconomics: Income and Monetary Analysis

᙮᙮᙮

GNP, UNEMPLOYMENT, THE BUDGET, AND FISCAL POLICY

GNP: Production and Well-Being
(JANUARY 1980)

Gross national product—fondly known as GNP—is a money measure of aggregate output, the dollar value of all goods and services produced in the economy over some accounting period. It is an imperfect measure, and a few have suggested throwing out the notion.

There *are* problems and limitations in using GNP figures, especially in noting changes in GNP over time.

For one thing, the dollar value of a basket of goods is determined by both the *physical quantity* of goods and the *price tags* on those goods. From 1978 to 1979, GNP in this country went up over 11 percent. That sounds great. But prices went up 9 percent, with real output increasing just over 2 percent. There is a big difference between 11 percent and 2 percent. In dealing with GNP, watch out for inflation.

Another problem pertains to *qualitative* changes. Automobiles and refrigerators are hardly the same commodities today as they were ten or thirty years ago. But these differences are not indicated simply by the numbers of units produced and their prices at different dates. Nor do GNP figures indicate other qualitative by-products of the production process, such as the costs of polluted air and the returns of consumptive variety.

There is also the complication of *population* change. If real output goes up 15 percent over a period while the number of people increases by 20 percent, output per person actually falls. Some countries have such a large rate of population increase that most of their output is absorbed in merely maintaining per-capita income: They run hard just to stay in the same place.

And what of income *distribution?* Several oil-producing countries have recently experienced huge increases in GNP per person, but 95 percent of the residents have not gained.

So there are these and other technical issues in interpreting GNP data. There remains an even more basic matter of exactly *what* is being measured.

GNP is only a money measure of the economy's *output*. It is not a comprehensive measure of the community's *well-being*. The human condition is a function of many variables of psychology, sociology, philosophy, theology, as well as economics. How do the races, the generations, the genders get along? How well established and how well respected are the standards of the community? How confident and how dedicated are the people—and confident and dedicated with respect to what?

Now, GNP is pertinent to many of the more subtle aspects of life. People are more likely to be content and live harmoniously when the economy is flourishing. But GNP figures themselves—the money value of production—do not include measures of propriety, gentility, courage, discipline, enthusiasm, love . . . which most fundamentally determine the quality of people and of their lives.

But, then, the GNP concept was not intended to encompass such things. What GNP does measure is very important, however. Properly used, GNP data can tell us useful things about some vital aspects of the world and its well-being.

Unemployment: Varied Reality and
Simplistic Measurement

(M A Y 1 9 8 0)

The "unemployment rate"—measuring the proportion of
the official labor force who are not working but supposedly
are available for work and looking for work—is one of the
more glamorous indicators of the state of the economy. It
attracts attention from editorial writers. Politicians point to
it with gratification or dismay. Purported economic policy
goals are stated in terms of the rate, and actual policy actions
are taken on the basis of it.

With so much heartburn and activity hanging in the balance, we should ask how good the unemployment measurement is, and how well that measurement has been conceived,
and how appropriately it is generally interpreted.

The collection of national data has recently been improved. Still, it is a *sampling* procedure and indicates only a
certain probability of accuracy within a certain range. Measurement problems are even more acute when dealing with
states and local areas. And the dubiousness of such regional
data is critical, for very large amounts of money are allocated
under government programs on the assumption of a degree
of statistical accuracy which does not exist.

It is tempting to presume that the unemployment rate
should be *zero*. After all, unemployment is a bad thing, isn't
it? Actually, some unemployment is efficient: An adapting
economy in a changing world requires shifting—and thus
some temporarily unemployed—resources. The measured
rate not only is inevitably greater than zero, it misleads by
lumping together different categories. For example, unemployed as young as sixteen years and interested in only *part-*

time work are included with those seeking *full-time* jobs. Including the part-time unemployed adds about half a percentage point to the unemployment rate.

A real, but governmentally induced, increase in unemployment stems from minimum-wage and unemployment-compensation laws. Whether or not these programs are desirable in their own rights—and there is little good to be said for imposition of minimum wages—they add another percentage point or more to the jobless rate.

Another governmentally induced, but *fictitious*, increase in the reported rate stems, since 1972, from including people who are only nominally registered as looking for work in order to qualify for various welfare benefits. This new inclusion of people in the measured work force has bloated the overall unemployment rate an additional percentage point.

Together, these three factors account for nearly half of recent official unemployment!

In addition to the aesthetics of measuring accurately something meaningful, there are concrete policy implications. The so-called unemployed now include people in a hodge-podge of circumstances, many of whom are not, in any conventional sense, unemployed—and, indeed, in some instances are naturally discouraged by welfare programs from seeking jobs.

Expansionary government actions to reduce nominal unemployment to anything near zero will not help many of those we wish to help. Instead, through engendering inflation and inefficiency, they would weaken the economy—and the poor are, by definition, those with the least protection from, and adaptability to, a weakening economy.

Rational Investment in "Unemployment"
(MAY 1980)

Is unemployment a bad thing? Yes, of course—under some circumstances. Losing a job can not only mean loss of substantial wealth, it can entail gut-wrenching trauma.

But not all unemployment is a disaster. Typically, a large proportion of those counted as "unemployed" are either in a routine, anticipated period of temporary layoff or voluntarily switching jobs.

So-called unemployment is, to a considerable extent, rational *investment* in job search. The length of time the person is categorized as "unemployed" is determined by his decision on how much of his time and other resources he thinks it optimal to invest in acquiring market information—given his skills, the state of the labor market, and the extent of welfare assistance which subsidizes his job search.

Suppose your employer tells you that business has fallen and he cannot afford to keep you at your present salary, but you can stay at a 20-percent cut. You refuse to take a pay reduction. After all, you are no less productive today than you were yesterday. Indeed, your jungle instinct tells you that there is *someone* in this huge economy who is ready to hire you at more than your old wage.

Your jungle instinct may be right. But *who* and *where* is that potential employer, and just *what* are those favorable terms of employment? You don't know. That valuable market information is not obtained costlessly or instantaneously. You are going to have to search for the information.

Sampling the market to learn of employment possibilities will entail out-of-pocket expenses—costs of transportation, telephone calls, mail, employment agencies, a haircut. There will also be income forgone as you devote time to the search.

For there *are* jobs you could have right now: *I* stand ready to hire you as my lackey at a wage of one cent per year.

People who really do want jobs remain unemployed for some time, not because there are no jobs but because the jobs or terms of employment are deemed unacceptable. There probably *are* better alternatives—including leisure— than being my stooge at virtually a zero wage.

How long do you search for the best alternative? The costs continue to accumulate, perhaps at an increasing rate as you go further afield. Your knowledge of the market also will increase, but at a decreasing rate. Eventually, you decide to take what you deem to be the best job available to you now.

But note: During the entire period of investing in information collection, you were classified by the government as "unemployed." Would you—and the employer who finally hired you and the consumers who ultimately bought your product—have been better off to keep the unemployment rate always at zero? The only way to avoid all unemployment is to lock people into their jobs and deny them the opportunity to sample the market in order to identify alternatives.

There *are* such societies of zero unemployment. Perhaps by 1984 we *all* can live in the Gulag Archipelago.

The Consumer Price Index and
Scientific Measurement
(SEPTEMBER 1980)

The consumer price index has been called our most strategic economic measurement. Millions of people and billions of dollars are involved, with income of half the population directly affected by it. But the consumer price index is a "quick and dirty" measure, highly flawed in its representation of actual changes in the level of prices, its main virtue being simply that it is made available each month.

There are unfortunate implications of the imperfections of the consumer price index, and science alone will not be enough to obtain acceptance of corrections of the miscalculations.

First, in a period of inflation, there is much additional government and private spending tied to the index. Since the index exaggerates the change in the price level, spending is increased too much. And the greater spending contributes to still further inflation. With so many people aided by the induced additional spending, we cannot realistically expect to correct the price index until inflation abates. So the repercussions of the faulty index delay improvement of the index.

Second, overstating the rise in prices—the index jumping from under 13 percent to over 18 percent in two months last winter—creates a degree of panic, including nervous twitches in the Federal Reserve, leading to policy overcorrection. The rate of change in the money stock has actually been *negative* in recent months. Conversely, when the index exaggeratedly falls—dropping from over 18 percent to nearly 11 percent in just one month—public complacency can be engendered. Correction and persistent containment of inflation calls for stable monetary policy, eschewing the herky-jerky episodes of creating money first too fast and then too slowly, which have characterized the history of the Fed.

Third, misleading measurement can so distort our perceptions of reality that seemingly rational market reactions actually are misguided. Excessive swings in the badly calculated consumer price index generate excessive changes in the "inflation premium" in nominal interest rates, along with overcorrections in monetary policy. But it should be added that we can have poor policy prescriptions even with good measurement. Good measurement is necessary for good policy—but, by itself, it is not sufficient.

Finally, it is reasonable to suggest that measurement of prices should be a matter of dispassionate, formal professionalism—the use of technical tools is to be confined to technicians for solely technical purposes. But many people—some well organized—have a heavy stake in what is recorded (and misrecorded) by the consumer price index. So we have the spectacle of political machination intertwined with technical measurement, with the machination polluting the measurement.

Limited Government and the Defense Budget

(FEBRUARY 1980)

Most historians know a lot. Many of them understand little. And some either do not know much or find it convenient to be very selective in what they tell.

A member of this latter group—characterized by either incompetence or lack of integrity—was recently given more than half a page of a major newspaper for an essay. With compassion, he finds "conservatives" suffering from "galloping schizophrenia." Their alleged disease is manifested in seeking two incompatible goals: namely, limited government and military strength.

Our historical analyst discovers that "our own generation . . . has the distinction of proving that it costs more to be at peace than at war." And in just the last several years, he says, we find in this country "concentration of an all-embracing military power." Indeed, our society is cursed by "probably the largest and most powerful power complex in history," which, he purports to believe, dictates our economy, our psychology, and our culture.

Well, we all are entitled to little psychoses in interpreting society. But the absurdities might be at least diluted by getting some fundamentals straight.

The general growth of government is *not* a new phenomenon, and it is *not* associated uniquely with the military component.

United States defense spending *has* risen greatly in *current* prices over the last twenty or so years. But the increase is to be ascribed entirely to inflation. In *constant* prices—that is, in terms of real purchasing power—defense spending reached a peak in 1972 and then fell persistently, mainly during Republican administrations, to a slightly lower level this year than in 1958. Even with the recently projected increases through 1983, real spending on defense then will be only a bit greater than in the low-level year of 1958.

The modesty of American investment in defense is even more striking when considering the military proportion of gross national product. In 1962 and again in 1967, approximately 9 percent of GNP went into defense spending. That percentage has fallen steadily and now has been cut in half.

Finally, the defense component of the federal budget has been cut in half. About 50 percent of federal outlays were in defense twenty years ago; now, the proportion is only 23 percent. But our historian falsely asserts that the proportion is one-third, which, astoundingly, makes possible dictation of the entire economy.

Meanwhile, as American real defense spending has been falling, Russian spending has been steadily and rapidly rising. In 1972, Russian spending caught the American, and this year the Russian superiority is some $50 billion, equal to over 40 percent of the American defense budget.

Whether or not it is impossible to have both adequately constrained government and adequately powerful defense,

we certainly can achieve our historian's ideal of a dominating
social-welfare government and military weakness. And the
more dominating that government becomes, the less difference it will make whether we are strong enough to preserve
our national independence.

Tax Loopholes, Income Distribution, and
Tax Payments
(AUGUST 1980)

It is hard to defend the size and much of the configuration
of the federal personal income tax. But it is easy to criticize
it for wrong reasons.

The dimensions of the tax are awesome, and collecting the
tax is an expanding industry. Big Brother now takes an
annual average of about $1000 for every person—including
children and economists. And from the outset, the take has
risen proportionately faster than either population or national
product. During just the last decade, personal income tax
collections rose more than 160 percent, while population was
increasing less than 10 percent and real gross national product was rising some 135 percent.

However, complaints commonly center not on the size or
the rate of increase in income tax collections but on the
supposedly unfair tax benefits—the infamous "loopholes"—
deviously garnered by the filthy rich. It is always savory
grist for the evening news to report the several dozens of
people with adjusted gross income—not to be confused with
taxable income—over $200,000 or $500,000 who in the previous year paid no income tax. From that bit of sensationalism,
it is an easy inference that much income is not taxed and

that the wealthy largely escape taxation while the middle and poor segments of the community foot the bill.

Actually, a large part—some 60 percent—of individual income is *not* taxed. Exemptions in property and sales taxes are much smaller. But very little of the untaxed income—less than 1 percent—is received by persons with income of $200,000 and over. A much greater *proportion* of the income of the wealthy than of the poor is taxed—the loopholes favor the poor and especially the middle level more than the wealthy. And the income of the wealthy is taxed at a much greater marginal *rate.* Taxing bigger proportions of high incomes and taxing them at higher rates ensures that the relatively wealthy pay far more in taxes than their *pro rata* share.

Although the wealthy—however reasonably designated—are not numerous, they pay a very big chunk of the income taxes. Three years ago, taxpayers with adjusted gross income of $50,000 or more made up only about 2 percent of taxpayers, their combined incomes were approximately 10 percent of the total—but they paid almost one-fourth of personal income taxes. While the top 10 percent of income earners paid half of the income taxes, the bottom 25 percent paid only 4 percent.

We could greatly simplify the tax while collecting the *same amount* by cutting the current rate schedule in *half* while eliminating exemptions and applying the tax to total personal income. But, contrary to cultivated mythology, the income tax is highly progressive, and closing loopholes would hurt the lower- and middle-income groups proportionately more than the wealthy. There is little likelihood of change, no matter how economically rational. How many politicians have a taste for benefiting the wealthier few at the expense of the poorer many?

The Hidden Costs of Federal
Loan Guarantees

(DECEMBER 1980)

The billion-dollar bailout of Chrysler Corporation is a conspicuous example of loan guarantees by the federal government. When underwriting the borrowing of firms and other institutions, the government makes no initial expenditure. Instead, borrowers whose credit is guaranteed by the government obtain funds from private lenders in the credit markets. As long as the borrower does not default on the loan, the government does not directly spend a penny for the guarantee. As a result, loan guarantees never explicitly appear in the federal budget.

Does the absence of a budgetary expenditure mean that federal loan guarantees are costless? Hardly. Although they are hidden, the costs of guarantees are real and substantial.

Murray L. Weidenbaum, a noted economist at Washington University and formerly a financial officer of the federal government, has written that loan guarantees do increase federal spending, even when the guarantee is not called by the borrower. By guaranteeing the credit of various potential borrowers, the government increases the total *demand* for credit. This increased credit demand, in turn, raises the level of interest rates for all borrowers, including the federal government itself. Consequently, when the government borrows to finance its impressive deficit, it, too, must pay a higher rate of interest—a rate made higher by the government's guaranteeing the credit of other borrowers.

The federal government's budgetary expenditures are increased, therefore, by its programs of guaranteeing loans; but that increase is nowhere noted as such in the budget.

Even more camouflaged than the fiscal impact is the real

cost to the nation of misuse of resources because of government loan guarantees. That cost arises because loan guarantees do not add to the nation's supply of credit but they do *redirect* where that credit will go. By guaranteeing credit and enabling a particular borrower to obtain funds, the government diverts funds away from other borrowers.

When the government guaranteed loans to Chrysler, it caused more than a billion dollars of funds to go to Chrysler rather than to other borrowers. In the absence of federal loan guarantees, Chrysler would not have succeeded in obtaining those funds. The loans would have gone to other borrowers, who could have used them more productively and would therefore have been more likely to repay them. Thus, government loan guarantees shift scarce supplies of credit from more efficient producers to less productive users —a shift not exquisitely designed to help an economy already characterized by embarrassingly slow growth in productivity.

So, once again, we see the corrosive, debilitating influence of a government which increasingly intrudes upon markets. While the benefits of loan guarantees accrue to specific recipients, the costs are diffused among all of society: Taxpayers pay higher borrowing costs of the government, and would-be borrowers must do without credit they would have obtained in open-market competition.

Politicians can gain the support of the parasitic few who receive the benefits of loan guarantees. But the rest of us bear the hidden costs of those guarantees.

The Budget Is Not a Fine-Tuning Fork

(AUGUST 1980)

As the recession has evolved, the voice of the would-be fiscal manipulator has become more conspicuous. It is never wholly silent. For more than a generation, many economists and politicians have urged an ongoing policy of adjusting tax rates and government spending for purposes of so-called national income stabilization.

The word does spread that there are big problems in such discretionary fiscal stabilization policy and that attempts to use such policy have turned out badly. But the word of wisdom spreads only slowly, as evidenced by current proposals to use tax cuts in order to combat the short-term weakness of the economy.

Many of the problems of fiscal policy are common to any discretionary, *ad hoc* stabilization policy. In trying to pull those levers and twist those knobs to diddle and jiggle the community's expenditures in order to counterbalance other, undesired changes, there are great difficulties in analysis, prescription, and implementation. The difficulties are so great that we are confronted with the sobering probability that we shall do more harm than good.

The first difficulty, of course, is diagnosis. What is the situation now, and where are we headed? It is rarely easy to know just where we are, and no one can know just where we are going and how fast and over what path we will get there. Beginning around the first of 1979, people in high places were telling us, all at the same time, that we might have a recession, that we surely would have a recession, that we already were in a recession—a recession which could be long or short, severe or minor.

Then there is the problem of prescribing what to do. Are

we to increase government spending or reduce tax collections or both? How *big* are to be the spending and/or tax changes? What are to be the *specific* spending projects or the tax reductions? *When* are they to begin and end? What is to be the *combination* of the two policy tools?

After the mighty brains and their computers have diagnosed and prescribed, there are the procedural complexities of carrying out the budgetary program. Count on months of government wrangling and committee hearings. It is an institutional fact that fiscal policy is an unwieldy, clumsy tool, not amenable to delicate, deft manipulation.

After we laboriously get the policy show on the road, we are faced with additional complications. One is the uncertainty of the final impact of the policy. We operate directly, with a considerable margin of error, on *government* spending and taxing. But we operate only indirectly, and with a much larger margin of error, on spending by the *private* sector. The net effect is highly uncertain, not only in size but also in time. Added to the variable lags of diagnosis, prescription, and implementation are those of repercussion.

The government budget is very important. The amount of government spending, what it is spent for, and how it is financed goes far over the long pull to determine how much the economy produces, for what purposes, and in what manner. But we misuse the budget, squandering resources and exacerbating problems, in trying to use government spending and taxing for short-term fine-tuning of the economy.

Swollen Government Spending and a
Sluggish Economy
(JANUARY 1981)

Many are concerned about swollen federal spending in a sluggish economy. If production and employment are to grow more rapidly, they believe, then greater restraints on federal spending must be imposed.

The belief that *less* federal spending will induce more economic growth is at odds with the conventional Keynesian view that *more* federal spending is expansionary. Conventional wisdom would predict that more government spending and a larger deficit would increase total demand, thereby raising production and employment.

The reasoning seems straightforward. Deficit spending means that the government spends more than it receives in taxes. In order to spend more than its tax revenues, the government must borrow either *existing* money from the community at large or *newly created* money from the banking system. In a stagnant economy, the government borrows and spends funds that would otherwise not have been spent, thus raising the aggregate demand for goods and services. A larger demand induces more production, which requires more employment.

But there are at least three reasons why *less* government spending and *smaller* deficits could generate a more productive economy.

First, it is *not* likely that current borrowing by the government in order to finance its deficit will result in appreciably greater total demand. Instead of borrowing nothing but idle money, the government ends up borrowing funds that would otherwise have been spent by others. Some of the massive government spending substitutes—at bloated interest rates

—for business investment in new plant and equipment, investment which is crucial to increases in production and productivity. The chairman of the Federal Reserve Board recently expressed this concern: "The demands by the federal government—the nation's prime borrower but itself insensitive to interest rates—will be met," he noted. "The question is how many other potential borrowers—many with more productive uses of money—are shouldered aside by market pressure."

A second reason why smaller deficits can translate into greater prosperity is that they mean less *inflation.* With smaller deficits to finance, the government will not create as much money. The amount of money would no longer grow more rapidly than the supply of goods on which the money is spent. Diminution of inflation would encourage greater saving and greater investment, hence increasing attainable output.

Finally, reduced government spending makes possible reduced taxation without bloating the budget deficit. And reduced taxation—permitting people more fully to work and save and invest for their own benefit by their own criteria, rather than to feed a parasitic and ravenous Big Brother— contributes to prosperity.

Restraints on federal spending in a politicized world will not be easily achieved. But fiscal sophistication—now long delayed—can provide more resources on better terms for productive purposes, lowered inflation, and reduced burdens on producers and consumers, providing means, stability, and incentives for greater well-being for a freer people.

Unemployment and Government Jobs
(October 1980)

The rationale of so-called public-service employment is simple: In a recession, more jobs are wanted, so use government as "last resort" employer to supplement private-sector demand for labor. The simplicity is deceptive. Predictably, countercyclical government employment has not worked well; further, there is the basic question of whether quick-fix, direct job creation is optimal government strategy.

There is growing skepticism about government jobs as a cure for high unemployment. The skepticism is well founded in both general analysis and particular experience.

One consideration is the time lag between diagnosis of the unemployment situation and implementation of the job program. The lag will be longer, the greater the size of the program and the greater the care in directing the program effectively in genuine job creation. Experience illustrates the likelihood that the economy will have recovered from the recession by the time the job program is fully implemented.

A second reason for a loss of innocence is that government employment programs can be expected to yield only modest increase in employment by government itself. The $9-billion-a-year CETA program, under the Comprehensive Employment and Training Act, has largely *replaced* spending on employment by state and local governments. Not only has there been much "fiscal substitution" of federal spending for other government spending but the spending has commonly been misdirected, even when not fraudulently and subversively administered, supplementing salaries of middle- and upper-level government employees rather than hiring the hard-core unemployed.

Still more fundamentally, even when *government* employment is increased, it does not follow that *total* employment of the economy is correspondingly increased. How does government get the money to spend? From taxes, borrowing existing money, or creating new money. If taxes are increased, private disposable income is reduced, which reduces consumption, and production and thus private employment fall. If government competes for existing funds in the credit markets, private borrowers are to some extent crowded out, and reduced business borrowing and spending result in decreased private production and employment. Finally, if newly created money is borrowed by government from the banking system, inflation will result as spending increases faster than production; the inflation is neither necessary nor sufficient for increasing employment, and it imposes costs, including greater unemployment eventually.

In short, government employment programs are not likely to generate much net government employment, and such gains as there are in government employment will come too late to counter recessions and will be largely offset by reductions in private employment.

Still, government spending is glamorous—it is seeming evidence that government cares about us. The spending will win support from the seeming beneficiaries and from that portion of the community overanxious to do seeming good. So there will continue to be pressure to plunder our own wealth by emphasizing income transfer instead of output, and make-work for the moment instead of investment for the future.

Tax Reductions Without Deficits

(AUGUST 1980)

Government greatly shapes—and typically distorts—the economy. Some of the pernicious effects can be associated with government trying to use its budget as a short-term, fine-tuning device of income stabilization.

Such policy, intended to be stabilizing, is likely to be destabilizing in actual effect. One reason is lags in implementation and repercussion. By the considerable time the budgetary strategy takes effect, circumstances may have changed, so the policy which was possibly appropriate when it was earlier determined is now highly inappropriate in its impact, exacerbating the current problem.

Further, even when we are not done in by lags, we may suffer side effects which outweigh the good aspects of the central policy. Many in this election year want a quick, large cut in taxes in order to stimulate the economy. A reduction in tax rates might have some expansionary effect on private spending and on saving, investing, and productivity. The certainty and the magnitude of such effects would be influenced by how the enlarged budget deficit was financed. And there *would* be an enlarged deficit, for it would require time after the tax reduction to make the adjustments in saving, investing, and producing.

Increasing the budgetary deficit requires increased government borrowing. If already existing money is borrowed from the public, then the money which used to be paid to the government in taxes is now paid to the government in purchase of bonds, and there will be little expansion of saving and investing. Alternatively, if the government borrows newly created money from the banking system, we will increase inflation, which, along with other unhappy consequences, will push people into still higher tax brackets and offset the original tax cut.

So the question becomes: Can we reduce taxes without increasing the budget deficit and its adverse consequences? One notable economist who thinks we can is Martin Feldstein, professor at Harvard and president of the National Bureau of Economic Research.

The key to Professor Feldstein's analysis, presented recently in the *Wall Street Journal,* is that "all important economic decisions are based on expectations. What matters for *current* actions . . . is not the current tax rates but the rates that are *expected.*"

A large *immediate* reduction in tax collections would increase the deficit *now* and probably inflation *now,* while the stimulus to greater output would become effective only over a period of years. So the proposal is to "improve current incentives without any increase in the current deficit by enacting *now* a schedule of *future* tax cuts." These precommitted tax cuts, determined now but becoming operational only after, or gradually over the course of, some five years, would generate changed plans for spending, saving, and investing. The delayed reduction of tax collections will then be financed through a combination of the greater saving and output stimulated by the happy expectations and an accompanying gradual reduction in government spending.

It *is* important to reduce taxes. But there are ways and ways to do it. And it is important, also, that we do it wisely— even if wisdom is rarely as exciting as spectacularly playing to the gallery.

Tax Cuts and "Revitalizing" the Economy
(DECEMBER 1980)

Tax cuts may seem to be *political* panaceas, but they fall far short of being *economic* cure-alls.

New investment in plant and equipment obviously can be important in a sluggish economy, for they help to make our work force more productive. But simply decreasing the taxes that individuals and businesses pay is not likely to spur this additional investment. Even increasing the tax credits businesses receive when making new investments will not guarantee more investment.

A tax cut would not provide the required stimulus, because, by itself, a tax reduction does not lighten the burden of Big Brother on the backs of producers. *Tax collections* can be cut by a sufficient reduction in tax rates, but *government spending* would not thereby be lower. And continued government spending accompanied by reduced government tax receipts would do more to modify the *nature* of the governmental drag on producers than to reduce the *size* of the handicap.

President Carter proposed a tax reduction of $28 billion for next year. But with federal spending unchanged, the already anticipated large deficit would become even more huge. The government must pay its bills. Somehow, the government would have to acquire the $28 billion it would no longer collect as taxes.

There are two ways by which the federal government can acquire funds for deficit spending. Both of these methods directly discourage greater production.

The easiest way is for the government to print more money. This alternative would exacerbate inflation, for it would immediately cause the nation's stock of money to grow faster than the goods on which that money is spent. Bloating prices still more, after fifteen years of absurd, debilitating inflation, would not aid the production of real goods.

The second method is for government to borrow existing funds from people and institutions in the credit markets. Choosing this source of funds, however, means that government would compete more intensively with businesses for credit. The government's increased bidding for scarce credit would drive up interest rates and divert credit from private producers to public parasites. With less credit available and less efficiently used, businesses would make fewer investments—and it is more investment that government supposedly is trying to promote.

If lower taxes were accompanied by reduced government expenditures, the deficit need not increase. There would be less inflation and less crowding in the credit markets as the government's burden on the economy was reduced. Lower taxes *and* lower government spending could then lead to more investment and more production.

While such a policy would do much to stimulate investment and production, it would do little—especially in the short run—to deliver votes from the growing numbers who dispense and receive government largess. Thus does political expediency again preempt sound economic policy.

INFLATION, MONEY, MONETARY POLICY, CREDIT CONTROLS, AND INTEREST RATES

Inflation, Money, and the Fed

(August 1979)

If inflation is not Public Enemy Number One, it will do until another John Dillinger comes along. If prices were to continue to rise at an annual rate of 13 to 14 percent, the price level would double in only five years. Cutting the purchasing power of the dollar in half in that short a period would do more harm to the community than did Dillinger, Machine Gun Kelly, and Bonnie and Clyde combined.

Persistent but erratic inflation, with the rate of increase in the price level bouncing between, say, 6 and 15 percent a year, makes economic activity resemble roulette: Planning becomes more expensive but is largely ineffective; accounting procedures yield misleading results; the tax system imposes unintended burdens; there are shifts in wealth distribution unrelated to productive activity; and international finance is made more mysterious than usual. Some do gain from inflation, as in roulette, but it is a ridiculous way to run an economy.

What causes the price level to rise so rapidly? Some blame inflation on Big Business. Some accuse Big Labor. Others point to the greed of the whole community. And then there are specific problems, such as oil-price gouging by OPEC, wars and rumors of war, and bad harvests.

Such things—market structure, character weaknesses, particular events—sometimes affect individual prices. But they do *not* account for much of the general, large, sustained rise in the price level which we call "inflation."

The price level generally (but not always) is going up, but it has risen at very different rates at different times. Could that mean that the degree of business or labor monopoly varies greatly over a few years, or that greed abruptly increases and then decreases? Of course not. And while wars, harvests, and other events can have temporary impacts on prices, the major long-term movements in the price index are clearly and consistently related to just one thing: major, long-term movements in the *money supply*.

Too much money leads to too much spending, which results in rising prices.

And what determines changes in the amount of money? The money supply is controlled by the Federal Reserve, the governmental "central bank." Both directly and through influencing activities of private, commercial banks, deliberately or unconsciously, the Federal Reserve determines the amount of money. Judging from its peculiar track record, the Fed may typically operate quite unconsciously.

So when you see prices galloping upward, you can be sure that too much money has been pumped into the economy. And that, in turn, is the fault of the Fed. Government has done it to us again.

Inflation: OPEC, God, and the Fed
(NOVEMBER 1980)

President Calvin Coolidge is reported to have said that as more and more people lose their jobs, unemployment results. He might have said also that as things get hotter, temperatures rise. And some—politicians and newspaper reporters—*do* say that as prices increase, we have inflation.

The emphasis is often on *particular* prices, perhaps the prices of oil or agricultural goods: Inflation is imputed primarily to the rise of this or that individual price.

Individual prices do change, sometimes gradually, sometimes abruptly. And since they change by different proportions, they change relative to each other. But do these *individual* price changes—up and sometimes down, fluctuating in different degrees—yield a significant, persistent change in the price *level?* When OPEC raises oil prices or a drought raises farm prices, do we thereby—inevitably and by definition—have inflation?

The price level is a relation between total *spending* on goods and the total *amount* of goods on which the spending is done. If the price level rises, it is because either spending has gone up or the amount of goods has gone down—or both. And total spending is determined basically by the amount of money held by the community.

If OPEC is to maintain higher oil prices, it must reduce production. If our money stock and aggregate spending remain unchanged while the amount of available goods is reduced, the price level will rise. But it is a *one-time* jump in the price level—until OPEC tightens the screws again—*not* a steady, ongoing inflation.

This is the same sort of phenomenon as a once-and-for-all increase in the money stock with given supplies of goods.

Again the increase in spending relative to the amount of things bought will raise prices to a higher plateau. Prices will be higher than they were before the added money, but, after adjustment to that shock, the price level rises no further.

Although OPEC can cause temporary spurts in inflation, we cannot properly blame the cartel and the prices it sets for continuing inflation. In order for a rapid rise in the price level to persist, the amount of spending must be consistently higher than the quantity of goods made available. And *spending* grows faster than the production of goods if the amount of *money* increases faster than production. The Federal Reserve controls the amount of money. When the Fed permits money to increase at 6 or 8 or 10 percent a year while output goes up at only 2 or 3 or 4 percent, of course the price level will rise.

And that is what the Fed tends to do. To add to the community's confusion and frustration, the Fed acts erratically, sometimes even increasing the amount of money too slowly. More typically, the Fed has vacillated between increasing money too rapidly and much too rapidly.

OPEC can make us poorer, as can bad weather, by reducing the amount of goods available. But *inflation* is home-grown. Inflation does not produce more oil or wheat. It produces only more misery, adding the salt of higher prices to the wound of reduced supplies.

"Highs" and "Lows" with Sugar and Money
(SEPTEMBER 1979)

Use of much sugar temporarily suppresses hunger, but it does so by creating a "sugar high." Hunger disappears, and energy surges. But this euphoria is deceptive, for energy quickly diminishes, fatigue follows, and hunger for sugar returns. To relieve the renewed hunger, still more sugar may be eaten, only to be followed by more highs and still further lows. Sugar addiction may occur, and bodily harm can ensue.

There is an analogy in economic activity and policy.

For years, our economy has been operating on "sugar highs" of massive doses of new money. Many have hungered for the expenditure of Treasury funds. A new missile, expansion of social security, a subsidy to education or to a city —all these, and more, have demanded government expenditures. Much of this expenditure is financed not by tax revenues but by creating new dollars. Thus, the new government spending is not a deliberate *shift* from previous spending, substituting new projects for old, but, instead, is simply *added* to the old, ongoing expenditures.

Might this creating of more money increase production? The mere creation of money does not mysteriously broaden our technological knowledge or discover more raw materials. The real, physical aspects of life go on as before—and the only impact of the additional money is on the level of prices. So it is—*if* the community understands what is happening.

But if people are happily fooled by having more money, their "dollar high" leads them to feel optimistic and expansive. Believing that demand for *their* kind of services and products has unexpectedly and uniquely increased, they can be inspired to spend and lend faster, to work harder, and to invest more.

But people are not stupid; they learn. They discover that an increase in the aggregate money stock is all that has basically happened. There has been no peculiar increase for *their* assets, and rising prices are offsetting their larger money incomes. So expansion plans are scrapped, and activity falls back to normal: The artificial "high" has generated a responsive "low."

If people have been similarly fooled in the past, it is harder to fool them again. The "highs" do not now come as easily.

If government wants to stimulate the economy, hyping it to an abnormally frenetic pace, the money dose must be larger than before. The injection necessary to fool people will have to be bigger and bigger in order to make the money increases greater than anticipated.

Unless we *persistently* increase the amount of money at an *increasing* rate, each "high" will give way to a "low." But there are severe physical limits to how much we can increase the rate of output. We soon reach—and, indeed, long ago did reach—a point when money is increasing more rapidly than real output. From that point, further injection of money —like further consumption of sugar—does nothing but harm. We then live no better in terms of real goods; all we accomplish by trying to fool ourselves is the self-inflicted injury of inflation.

Inflation: The Damage Done by the Fed
(AUGUST 1979)

Inflation is not made in heaven. It is made on earth, by certain people. In particular, it is made by people who control the community's amount of money. In this country, those few people operate our "central bank," the Federal Reserve.

For fifteen years, we have lived in an era of persistent, although varying, inflation, with the annual rate of increase in the price level recently in the 12 to 15 percent range. It has been an utterly disgraceful performance—disgraceful because it could have been avoided.

The cause of inflation is not a mystery, known only to a few of us happy geniuses. Major, prolonged increase in prices is caused by major, prolonged increase in the amount of money. A long-continued, high rate of expansion of the money supply has *always* led to an increase in the price level. A substantial inflation has *always* been preceded by a substantial increase in money. And no sustained inflation has *ever* been ended without a prior reduction in the rate of increase in money.

It could hardly be otherwise. Prices rise when spending on goods increases faster than the output of those goods. The rate of output fluctuates, of course, but the long-run trend is for national product to grow at about 4 percent per year. It is easier to produce dollars than to produce real goods. And when the number of dollars grows at 10 or 12 percent, you can be sure that expenditure will go up faster than goods are supplied. Then prices rise. When we flood the market with dollars, the value of the dollar falls. It falls relative to goods in the domestic economy, and it falls relative to other currencies in the foreign exchange market.

All this is fundamental. It is also elementary. And yet government officials in charge of economic management seem to learn but slowly, if at all. One might suppose that the Federal Reserve, of all institutions, surely would appreciate the role of money, for it controls the economy's supply of money. But the Fed somehow finds it convenient to emphasize various other things—interest rates, budget deficits, "special factors"—before even grudging attention is given to money. And, almost incredibly, the 1978 Report of the President's Council of Economic Advisers contains a forty-page chapter on inflation and unemployment which does not use the word "money" and makes only three skimpy allusions to monetary and fiscal policy.

With that wondrous kind of economic analysis and economic policymaking, indeed we should not look to heaven for the cause of inflation. The culprits are to be found in government.

Inflation: A Big Problem with a Straightforward Solution
(AUGUST 1980)

Disease strikes the community, and the untutored savage cowers in the corner. He comprehends neither the phenomenon nor its cause, and thus he cannot prescribe a cure. He is vulnerable to "analysts" who assure him that big problems require solutions of many ingredients.

For fifteen years we have suffered from inflation. Inflation is a monstrous disease, with broad consequences. But problems which are big in size and scope are not necessarily complex in diagnosis and convoluted in correction. Inflation *is* a big problem, but it is manageable—if, unlike the simple, scared savage, we keep our wit and nerve.

Unless the symptoms of the disease are camouflaged by government controls, inflation is manifested in rapidly rising prices. Prices rise because spending on the goods is rising faster than production of the goods: With spending increasing faster than output, it is inevitable that prices will rise. Spending increases so rapidly because money is created too rapidly. And it is the Federal Reserve which permits and induces the creation of money.

Inflations are monetary phenomena; they result from creation of too much money, and they are ended by curtailing the rate of money creation.

But some refuse to acknowledge the monetary nature of inflation. Perhaps they feel that surely a situation as big and bad as inflation must be the result of *many* significant causes; and, further, that many *causes* require many *solutions*. Probably even the kitchen sink is included in some of the surveys of either cause or correction of inflation.

These diversionary, undirected intellectual thrashings do

not come solely from poets and the Federal Reserve. Sometimes these substitutes for analysis are provided by formally designated economists. One economist—well known primarily for association with the Washington, D.C., establishment—speaks of "the [many] ingredients in the recipe" to solve inflation. Another—well known primarily for a type of abstract doodling—calls for a "package" of policies, including wage and price controls: ". . . we need all the anti-inflationary measures there are," he tells us with a straight face, "so that we can avoid tightening any one screw to excess. . . ." Embarrassingly, these people barely nod in passing to proper monetary policy.

In this state of confusion, at best proper policy will be diluted. Oddly, as inflation erratically continues, the one *correct* component of the policy "recipe" or "package"— appropriate monetary management—is commonly the only component which is denounced. If guidelines, controls, subsidies and penalties, restrictions, allocations, jawboning, and various pernicious directives do not contain inflation, they are rarely condemned. Instead, the commonly drawn moral is simply that they were not extensive enough or were not administered with sufficient exuberance. So try them again—do them more and harder. But curtailment of money growth? How quaint, how academic! That sort of thing just isn't done in the best of planning circles!

And so the inflationary disease continues to ravage us— because we tolerate the gamut of futile esoteric prescriptions but scorn the right and obvious one.

Scattergun Attacks on Inflation

(JULY 1980)

Inflation stems from bad monetary management, which results in aggregate spending increasing faster than aggregate output. Inflation can be eliminated only by proper monetary management, increasing the amount of money no faster than production. If it is not seen that inflation is most basically a monetary phenomenon, proper monetary policy is unlikely.

To be sure, the inflation phenomenon can appear terribly complicated. There are prices of inputs and outputs, of domestic and foreign commodities; there are profit rates, wage rates, interest rates, and exchange rates; there is demand-pull and cost-push; there is saving and consumption, productivity and wages; there are wage-price spirals and management-labor conciliations; there are voluntary controls, mandatory controls, and guidelines; there is history and there are anticipations; there are taxes and expenditures; there is big business, little business, and labor unions; there are trade balances and budget balances; there is useful output from productive activity and wasteful output from speculation; there is the private sector and the government sector, along with God and nature.

Evidently, since there are such a welter and variety of actors, indicators, and institutions, some believe that inflation is caused by numerous things and manifested in various ways and, like Gulliver, must be tied down with many strings. So we want Big Brother to intervene here and control there, all the while offering appropriate incantations and exhortations.

Many of the things commonly talked about in connection with inflation—unions, productivity, taxes, and government spending—*are* important in one context or another. But none

has much importance in the context of controlling inflation—
certainly not the importance of the money stock.

An undiscriminating, multifaceted analysis and policy pot-
pourri wastes time and entrenches financial and psychological
bases of further inflation, it exhibits confusion and generates
pervasive uncertainties about governmental competence and
future policies, it results in disarray in the domestic economy
and in our links with the rest of the world economy, and, as
economic difficulties generate political embarrassment, it
inspires still more frenetic experimentation with gimmicks
which are at best ineffectual.

Money and its rate of growth is not the *only* determinant
of the price level and its change. But money *is* the prime
mover, persistently the most critical variable. And it is a
variable—largely in contrast to others—which is subject to
close *policy control.* So if we diffuse our efforts to combat
inflation, we dilute our anti-inflation effect. Worse, when
those fragmented and diverse efforts to kill inflation are
ineffective, there will be some who will then find it convenient to impute the failure to monetary policy, neglected
though it has been.

So first we bumble in our misguided eclectic approach,
and then we misread the bad experience and blame the
policy ingredient which was too little and only grudgingly
used. This is a scenario of failure of will, professional
sophistication, and politics, yielding a failure of economic
policy—a disaster which could have been avoided.

Cause, Consequences, and Cure of Inflation: Psychology and Economics

(DECEMBER 1979)

Some of us have the sense—or jungle instinct—not to flaunt our ignorance. Recently, half a page of a major newspaper was given to literary posturing on the subject of inflation. The ignorance of the writer is easily forgiven; the flaunting and posturing strain one's tolerance.

The author of the essay describes some behavior consequences of inflation. People *do* respond to anticipation of rapidly rising prices by saving less and buying more; time horizons for planning *are* shortened in the face of greater uncertainty, and increasingly attention *is* shifted from real, ongoing productive activity to trying to cope in the short run with an unsettled world.

All this has been said before and better. A dispassionate analyst would couch the phenomenon in terms of individually rational responses to inflation which yield a loss of collective efficiency. The newspaper author prefers to speak distractingly in terms of psychological weakness and social vice. Still, the message that inflation wreaks havoc warrants reiteration.

But while the author melodramatically reviews *consequences* of inflation, there are only superficial and sometimes misleading hints of the *cause* of inflation and a denial that there exists a solution.

We are darkly told that "inflation is a form of instant overindulgence"; by diluting our sense of guilt and willingness to sacrifice, inflation "is pleasure at a price"; and inflation is accelerated by "the unbridled materialism in our society."

Rule number one for the social analyst is to *take people as they are*. They are—among other characteristics—acquisitive and grubby, interested in their own well-being, preferring more rather than less of what they desire. They have been like that since the fiasco in the Garden of Eden. And yet we have not constantly had inflation! *Why* have we had roaring inflation in the last dozen years but not in the 1950s and early 1960s, and not in the 1930s, and not in the boom of the 1920s, and not in the last part of the nineteenth century?

It is unhelpful to contend that inflation "is not an economic problem." Inflation, far from being a mysterious, erratic eruption stemming somehow from Original Sin, *is* decidedly "an economic problem." Specifically, it is primarily a *monetary* phenomenon.

Rising prices are caused by spending increasing faster than output: Prices are bid up because the community wants to buy more at the original, lower prices than is available for purchase. And spending, in turn, is a function basically of the amount of money. When money increases, spending increases; when spending increases faster than output is made available, prices rise.

The necessary and sufficient economic condition for ending inflation is indicated by its economic cause: There must be proper monetary management, confining the rate of increase in the amount of money to no more than the rate of increase in production.

It may be, as the author contends, that economists are not very good at "looking into the human soul." But they know what causes inflation. And they know what is required to cure it. The job might be easier, however, in the absence of silly newspaper essays.

Inflation and Patient Policy
(MARCH 1980)

We are told that inflation is out of control. Does that mean that the knowledge is not sufficient, or that the tools are not available, to eliminate inflation? But we *do* know what causes inflation and how to cure it, and we *do* have the tools required to implement adequate anti-inflation policy. What is out of control is not inflation but, rather, confused and fainthearted policymakers.

Inflation could be gradually ended and a new era of a roughly stable price level inaugurated by adoption of a "monetary rule." The rule would call for a steady, modest rate of increase—around 3 percent a year—in the amount of money. This perennial rate of expansion in the money stock would approximately match the rate of expansion of real production of goods, and the price level would thus remain about unchanged.

Adoption of such a rule by the monetary authorities would not keep the price level absolutely steady; all sorts of events, actions, and anticipations would jiggle the price index in short periods. Well, then, why settle for a second-best of only approximate stability of prices? The reasons for not trying to "fine-tune" the economy are summarized largely by *lags*.

First, there is the *diagnosis* lag, to figure out where we are and are going. We cannot compensate for a shock until we have noted the shock and assessed its repercussions. Of course, even after the lag for observation and meditation, we cannot be *sure* of what tomorrow holds and therefore be *sure* of what we are to try to do with our policy tools. And if we poorly diagnose the problem, we will poorly prescribe the remedy.

Now, suppose we decide that the problem calling for

prescription is inflation. What sort of anti-inflation tactic is best? Most of today's policy proposals sound as though they came from Mortimer Snerd on one of his bad days—nonsense like price and wage ceilings, credit allocation, and gasoline rationing. But imagine that we escape such foolishness and, instead, properly curtail the rate of money creation. How long before we get the desired results? Again there are lags—and variable lags, at that.

After we reduce the rate of money growth, the first impact, probably around six to nine months later, will be on *output* —and thus on *employment*—rather than on the price level. Then it could be another six to twelve months, or even more, before there is appreciable effect on prices. During that year or so, prices would still be going *up* while output and employment were going *down*. That prolonged unhappy combination of events could inspire so much gnashing of teeth that the policy would be impatiently reversed before the intended dampening of prices materialized.

Our problem is not that, in some mysterious sense, inflation is out of control. But to kill inflation, we must first understand what to do—and what not to do. We must suppress the temptation to try to do more stabilizing, and to do it more quickly, than is feasible. And we must screw up our courage to stick with the appropriate policy, which during a transition period of lags will be bitter medicine, but will ultimately restore our health.

On Driving and Monetary Management
(MAY 1980)

Money matters. Money matters much. It seems to follow that monetary policy, monetary management, should receive close and sophisticated attention. Indeed, the community's money supply *should* be well managed. But it isn't.

Only the liberated flower children, living in a commune of barter and food stamps, deny the usefulness of money. Money is oil in the machinery of trade, greatly facilitating commercial communication, the swapping of goods, and the keeping of records.

But the significance of money goes beyond the enormous usefulness of money in reducing the costs of trade. The story of the price level, employment, and production is very largely the story of money. And when we bungle into inflation, unemployment, and reduced output, we irresponsibly weaken the sinews and threaten the very foundations of our national character, wealth, and strength.

Within a setting of an approximately stable price level, market institutions induce and guide people into efficient activity. The efficiency is not only technological and administrative. The efficiency of the open market is *economic:* Innovative technology is effectively administered to use resources in accordance with the revealed preferences of the community. Determining the use of resources through private decisions for individual purposes—as contrasted to decisions of and for Big Brother—is a major characteristic of freedom generally.

But individualistic freedom and economic efficiency are endangered by upsetting the context of a stable price level. With rampant inflation, there is additional market uncertainty and discouragement, we are distracted from genuinely productive activity while trying to cope with rapidly and erratically rising prices, and misconceived policies to control the inflationary monster delay and dilute effective remedies and meanwhile unnecessarily add to our miseries.

What is required to slay the monster is to correct the miserable monetary management which spawned it. If we want a steady level of prices, we require a steady management of money. Steady management of money does *not* mean holding *constant* the amount of money, for *output* will be growing—unless we permit the "small is beautiful" and "era of limits" types to sabotage us.

Over the long pull, output in this productive economy has risen, on the average, at an annual rate close to 4 percent. So the money stock should grow at some 3 to 4 percent. If money grows at about the same rate as production of goods, the price level will approximate stability.

How commonly has the amount of money grown at a rate of 3 to 4 percent? At almost any historical time, money has been permitted by the Federal Reserve to grow either too fast or too slowly. The record of the Fed's monetary management resembles the driving of my wife: except for brief transitional periods, the foot is always pressing too hard on either the accelerator or the brake.

We have paid dearly for the herky-jerky, on-again-off-again tactics of the Fed. We may survive the erratic driving of my wife, but the slow-learning Fed threatens to put the economy and the entire free society into the ditch.

Dopey and the Federal Reserve

(JUNE 1980)

Snow White was intrigued by the perpetual silence of Dopey, one of the seven dwarfs. She asked the other dwarfs if Dopey could talk. She was told that neither Dopey nor anyone else knew if he could talk, for he had never tried!

Snow White might ask also if the Federal Reserve could do a good job in managing the money supply. And there would be much sense in replying that we cannot know, for it has never tried.

Many of us do know that we *must* control the money

supply if we are to control inflation: We *cannot* curtail inflation without appropriately curtailing the amount, or the rate of change in the amount, of money. No one asserts that money is the only thing which affects the price level. But over appreciable periods, money is the prime mover. Creating too much money inevitably will generate inflation, and inflation will *not* persist if the creation of money is properly curtailed.

We know, further, that the Fed *has not* well managed the money supply. We abruptly lurch from creating money too fast to creating money too slowly. The Fed's record of monetary management has been disastrous.

While we *must* control money to control the price level and the Fed *has not* efficiently controlled money, the question remains: *Can* the Fed well enough control money? Has the Fed's record been disgraceful as well as disastrous? It is hardly an exaggeration—if an exaggeration at all—to say that the Fed has never tried to exercise proper monetary control. But the Fed *could* vastly improve its performance—indeed, improve it sufficiently to avoid repetition of historical extremes of inflation and deflation.

Then, why has the Fed done so badly? How can we account for the miserable record?

One possible explanation is simply *incompetence:* Most members of the board of governors of the Fed have been, and are, poor economists. Some of them *have* no theory to use, some even deny that effective theory *exists* or *can* exist, but they participate in decisionmaking which *requires* theory.

A second possibility is that the people running the Fed lack the courage of their analytic convictions, when they have convictions. The good economist not only knows good analytics but *believes* it, has *confidence* in it, and will consistently *use* it.

Third, perhaps some of the Fed's foolishness is accounted for by grubby political purpose and machination, inspired by ideology and personal favoritism and animosity.

A fourth interpretation is that the people running the Fed are indifferent, cavalier, uncaring about the momentous responsibilities with which they are charged and the policies they haphazardly decree.

Finally, some might suspect that they are deliberately, knowingly, calculatingly subversive, actively seeking to do harm.

Of course, there are some thoroughly unlovely people, even enemies, in this largely unfriendly and belligerent world. But we do well to exercise great caution in seeking to interpret events in terms of a "devil" theory. One certainly can find much incompetence, faintheartedness, and petty dogmatism in the history of the Fed. But dishonor and subversion are very different characteristics and tactics. Most of the governors of the Fed have deserved to be fired—but not consigned to hell.

Inflation: Pains of Withdrawal and Pains of Self-Destruction

(NOVEMBER 1979)

According to newspaper polls, inflation is—by a very large margin—the major policy concern of the American public. This overriding concern is well founded. It may be better understood—intuitively and on an immediate, personal basis —by people at large than by government officers, with all the analytical resources available to those officers.

At the current rate of inflation, the price level *doubles* every *five* years. It is unlikely that a free-market economy and a free society in general can long survive such a massive assault. If Karl Marx ever smiles, he must be smiling now.

If friends of freedom have great reason for concern, several elemental questions are apparent: Do we *know how* to stop inflation and then prevent its reoccurrence? Do we well enough comprehend the significance of inflation to *want* very much to control inflation? Do we have the courage and discipline to bear the inevitable *costs* of effective anti-inflation policy?

We do know what causes inflation and how to stop it. We know what to do, not simply in abstract theory but in terms of real procedures through real institutions. The essence of the matter is proper conduct of monetary policy, which is feasible through the Federal Reserve.

There are not many who rejoice in the prospect of persistent, possibly accelerating inflation. And when the wind shifts to the east, we hear occasional lamentations concerning this "Public Enemy Number One" and pietistic dedications to its destruction.

If wishing—or praying—could make it so, doubtless we would rid ourselves of the scourge. But we are now addicted, we are junkies, and curing inflation would entail substantial pain in the form of a temporarily reduced rate of employment and output. Saving ourselves from self-destruction would hurt. Still, the community could stand the short-term pain of withdrawal better than the pain of a habit leading to ultimate disaster. The *community* could take the necessary medicine, even if grudgingly. But will the *government*, including the Federal Reserve, screw up its courage to the sticking point?

There is only severely limited basis for optimism. The recently appointed chairman of the Federal Reserve Board is an able, knowledgeable, and accomplished man. He has emphasized that "monetary discipline" is "essential" to the control of inflation. And in early October [1979] he led the board to wise agreement on focusing policy on the money supply rather than on interest rates.

But the Federal Reserve chairman heads a fainthearted, largely disoriented, and easily confused board. And he cannot prudently show his back to key members of the administration and of the Congress. For many of those worthy people, while praying for deliverance from inflation and loudly excoriating the devil, have proved themselves ready to stick the shiv into anyone who, as a result of pursuing effective anti-inflation policies, endangers their own political careers.

The Strategy of the Fed:
An American Tragedy
(OCTOBER 1979)

What is the basic function of the Federal Reserve, and how should it go about accomplishing its proper purpose?

The Federal Reserve, this nation's central bank, was begun just before World War I. The Fed's own conception of its broad role in the economy has evolved—or wavered—over that long period. Sometimes it has aimed to "accommodate the credit needs of business." In other periods, it has been dedicated primarily to serving the convenience of the United States Treasury.

Many would insist that its fundamental function should be to "stabilize" the economy—promote a setting of full use of resources and avoid significant changes in the price level. Such a stabilized setting would enable the millions of private decisionmakers to concentrate solely on the real economic business of producing and consuming things rather than having to cope with an erratic rate of economic activity and level of prices.

As an agency for economic stabilization, the Fed has a distressing record. Especially over the past fifty years, the Fed has been a well-nigh disastrous failure.

In the formulating and implementing of policy, it is not enough to pronounce general objectives. It is not more operationally useful simply to state that we aim at "full employment and a steady price level" than it is to adopt the rule to "bet only on horses which will win." In light of available options and processes, we must determine which tools to use in working on which variables in order to try to induce the targeted consequences.

The Fed has persistently worked on the wrong variable if it wanted to stabilize the rate of output and the level of prices. It has been mesmerized by *interest rates,* and it should have been operating on the amount of *money.*

Concentrating on interest rates instead of the money supply does not necessarily yield results different in kind—although the degree of control of the Fed over money is greater than over interest rates, and money stands in closer relationship to output and prices than do interest rates. But more is involved. Not only is use of the interest-rate tool less precise and more indirect than use of the money-supply tool, but reliance on manipulation of interest rates is readily perverted.

The Fed's typical concern with interest rates has *not* been to use them for stabilization of output and prices. Instead, the objective has commonly been to *stabilize interest rates themselves.* In particular, the aim has been to keep interest rates lower than true market values.

During inflation, interest rates naturally have been high and rising. In trying to curtail the increase in rates, the Fed increases the amount of money. This does tend to dampen rates temporarily, but eventually the increased amount of money adds to the inflation—and the further rise in prices pulls up interest rates still more. The result of emphasizing the wrong policy indicator—interest rates instead of money supply—is to leave us with higher interest rates, rather than lower, and more inflation, as well.

The Fed either has misconceived its function of stabilization or, in concentrating on interest rates instead of money, it has misconceived how to fulfill its function.

Money and Inflation, Sophistication and Courage

(OCTOBER 1979)

Inflation is an insidious plague. Prices rising at an annual rate of 6 or 8 percent may not seem very important for a short while, but over a decade that magnitude of inflation will *double* the price level.

This rape of the dollar is a disaster for those on relatively fixed incomes, and it greatly complicates business planning and operations, thus reducing the wealth of the entire community. It frustrates individuals, distorts attitudes and incentives, and strains the ties which hold us together in a civil society.

We cannot expect to control inflation unless we know what causes inflation. And many of us do know the essence of the problem and its solution.

What causes inflation is *not* big, bad business. It is *not* lowlife labor. And, contrary to the president, it is *not* the odious OPEC cartel. Neither monopoly at home nor monopoly in the international economy causes an ongoing, rapid rise in the price level.

Inflation is caused by too much spending. Too much spending is caused by creating too much money. And the government—in particular, the Federal Reserve—determines the creation of money. To bring inflation under control, it is necessary and sufficient to bring the money supply under control.

How much spending—and how much money—is too much? Over the past dozen years, spending has increased at an annual rate of nearly 9 percent, basically because of expansion of the amount of money. Of course, real output of goods and services would not expand at that high rate for that long. In fact, output went up at less than 3 percent per year. With spending rising at nearly 9 percent and output at about 3 percent, prices inevitably rose at close to 6 percent. Over the entire period from 1966 through 1978, the amount of money was increased a bit over 100 percent—and the price level went up almost 100 percent.

If the time comes when money persistently is created no faster than goods are produced—typically, some 2 to 4 percent per year—we will then have no significant inflation. With a steady, modest rate of increase in money, roughly matching the rate of increase in real output, the price index would be approximately steady.

Individual prices would still change, of course. Indeed, the efficient working of the market *requires* that individual prices change relative to each other as demands and real costs change. Even the price *level* will do some jiggling, as weather, wars, and rumors shock markets in the short run. But proper management of the money supply would end the era of inflation.

Then why is money not properly managed? It is not that we do not know what to do. But the doing would create pains of slower economic growth during a transition period as we end inflation, and the pained community would then heap great costs on the doers. In an era of self-inflicted shortages, economic sophistication and political courage are the most critical shortages of all.

Credit Controls: Government versus People

(February 1981)

By definition, a world of scarcity is not a world to our liking, for scarcity *means* that we inevitably have less of most things than we should like to have.

We all compete for the products which can be made with our scarce resources. Even if I adjust gracefully to scarcity in general, I rebel against misuse of resources. And I deem it a misuse when the rest of you, in the aggregate, produce a combination of goods different from that preferred by me. Racetracks, cocaine, disco dance halls? I assign values no greater than zero to those things. Why can't the rest of you uncouth types be more like genteel me?

Most of the things we consume are produced, rather than manna from heaven. And much of the production, as well as its purchase, is with credit and borrowed money. One way to mold the economy into closer conformity with my preferences is to apply "credit controls" designed by me.

I might impose limits on installment credit, specifying minimum down payments and lengths of loans. I might vary those specifications according to type of product, favoring stoves and refrigerators over television sets and automobiles. I might prohibit loans to be used to buy stocks and bonds while permitting attractive loans for builders and buyers of houses. I would try—vigorously but not inevitably effectively —to channel resources into *good* goods and activities and away from *bad* goods and activities.

Sounds great, doesn't it, even if procedurally complicated? You would be delighted to have me starve sinful, reckless, frivolous, speculative products and activities and subsidize wholesome, safe, sound, productive uses of resources, wouldn't you? No? You think I have delusions of omniscience? I confuse myself with the marketplace, if not the deity? And yet, Big Brother has sought such power to allocate credit and control the terms of its use—and, in fact, he has sometimes been successful in getting and using such authority to supplant the market.

Presumably, we want more saving so that we will have more investment so that we will be more productive so that we will live better. But credit controls do not increase saving. Instead, they *redirect* saving, crudely discriminating among savers, borrowers, and intermediaries, inefficiently distorting market behavior by superseding private preferences with decisions by government, and wastefully increasing the costs of market operations.

The major problem of controls is not the costs of bureaucratic administration and industry compliance. There is the prior question of what basically is being attempted and how —the specific purposes and the rationale of the tactics. Perhaps even more important, in trying to achieve what is unachievable and should not be attempted in the first place, we are diverted from effective policies and institutions which could attain legitimate goals.

With credit controls, we not only fail to do what would help us prosper best in a stingy world, we impose upon ourselves unnecessary injury and cost. This can make sense only to the subversive and the masochist.

The Silly Futility of Credit Controls
(FEBRUARY 1981)

The infamous Credit Control Act of 1969 empowers the president, through the Federal Reserve, to "regulate and control any or all extension of credit." The Fed can "prohibit or limit extensions of credit under any circumstances the Board deems appropriate," decreeing such credit terms as interest rates to be charged, maturities and sizes of loans, and minimum down payments. It also allows the Fed to establish reserve requirements for specific types of loans and classes of borrowers, with the size of the required reserves serving as an incentive or disincentive for certain kinds of lending.

Last spring [1980], the president, with the acquiescence of the Fed, tinkered with those credit-control powers. Although the controls program actually adopted was only a smidgen of what the president could have done, and it was pursued but briefly, the unforbidden fruit was tasted. And what was tentatively tasted once may be consumed extensively at a later date of even greater panic and confusion.

Credit controls have been rationalized as an anti-inflation tactic and as a device to lower interest rates. In fact, they cannot reduce either the general price level or interest rates. That requires *overall* monetary restraint, and the essence of credit controls is *selection* and *discrimination*, encouraging certain sorts of lending and borrowing while discouraging others. What the nefarious game entails is substitution of bureaucratic priorities for community preferences, with enormous wastes as markets are disrupted and circumscribed and both lenders and borrowers—especially low-income borrowers—are obliged to make costly adjustments to still another set of unhelpful constraints and directions.

Ironically, selective and discriminatory credit controls are not only futile as an expensive tactic against inflation and high interest rates, but, in effect, they are aimed at rational responses of the public to a sorry situation dumped on us by government itself.

It is government, not the public, which—with massive ineptitude and cowardice—has generated inflation. The public has done its best to adapt to an inflationary circumstance. Then government frowns on the resulting "speculation," "overconsumption," and high nominal interest rates. But instead of correcting its own inflationary errors and thereby providing a stable setting in which people will efficiently work and save and consume, Big Brother—with massive ineptitude and cowardice—continues the inflation but takes away some of the community's options of adjustment, including incentives to save.

Only by reducing the growth in the money supply will inflation be cured. And only by restoring justified confidence in the future stable value of the dollar will consumers' spending habits and savings patterns return to normal.

It is commonly said that inflation is Public Enemy Number One. More basically, the number-one enemy is the perpetrator and abettor of inflation—namely, government.

Credit-Card Popguns and the Inflation Dragon

(APRIL 1980)

We are embarked on a new holy war to destroy inflation. This latest crusade is a hodgepodge of largely misdirected and ineffectual tactics. "Credit control" is part of the package. Included among several sorts of credit control is curtailment of extended credit to consumers by credit-card companies, among other lenders.

The appeal of curtailed consumer credit apparently stems in part from feelings of morality and propriety: Permitting individuals to manage their own financial affairs smacks of Sodom and Gomorrah, and it will be pietistically purifying for us to suffer for past sins.

To change the emphasis, jungle instinct suggests that there is something "feverish" about inflation. Perhaps the fever can be abated by cooling the pace of consumer activity.

And what better way to curtail consumption than by limiting use of credit cards?

Behind whatever seeming plausibility of such theological and medical metaphors, there is little substance. Curtailed use of credit cards may make us suffer by increasing costs of transacting business, but it will contribute little to ending inflation.

We can reasonably describe inflation as a large and sustained rise in the price level. The price level rises when aggregate *spending* increases faster than the *output* of goods on which the spending is done. And spending is equal to the *amount* of money multiplied by the *rate,* or *velocity,* at which the dollars are spent. So, with a given flow of production of goods, the increase in the price level can be reduced only by curtailing either the *creation* of dollars or the *velocity* of dollar use.

We cannot expect restrictions on use of credit cards to have significant effect on *velocity* of monetary circulation. If consumer purchases are inhibited, velocity would fall. But increasing velocity is a *consequence* of inflation as well as a *determinant.* If prices were to level out, we could anticipate that velocity would not continue to increase as it has for a third of a century.

How about the effect of credit-card restrictions on the *amount* of money? People will now carry around more currency. They get that currency by drawing it out of banks. Drawing currency out of banks reduces bank reserves. Smaller reserves will mean reduced bank lending and thus reduced money creation—unless the Federal Reserve irresponsibly replenishes those reserves. But if the Fed uncharacteristically follows a responsible policy to supplement the credit-card restrictions, it could follow a responsible anti-inflationary policy without the intrusive, cumbersome restrictions on credit cards.

Similarly, slowing the growth of consumer credit could

reduce demand by consumers for money-creating bank lending to pay those debts—but the Fed could reduce the supply of money even in the absence of such reduced demand for money.

Finally, whatever small contribution the credit-card restrictions may make to curtailment of inflation will be a one-time, once-and-for-all impact. That single-shot effect, for all the pain it causes us, will not kill the inflation dragon. It is not likely even to wound the beast.

The Camouflage of Credit-Card Control
(MAY 1980)

Surely, by now, all of you have done your patriotic duty by cutting up your Visa and MasterCharge credit cards. No? Well, it's the likes of you who are fueling inflation—or so believes the Federal Reserve. How are we to whip inflation if rational, creditworthy citizens are allowed to buy their stereos now, on credit, instead of saving for a year to pay for them with cash?

Recently, the Fed, under pressure from the White House, felt it shrewd to levy controls which will compel banks to *limit* and, to some extent, to *allocate* your credit. And there *is* a sort of shrewdness here: The diversionary counterirritant of credit controls may help to camouflage the failure of the Fed to cure the plague of inflation.

You might think it strange that buying a television set with a credit card will add to inflation when paying with a stack of $20 bills will not. But that is what the Fed purports to think, and that is why you will now have to expend more time and effort to obtain curtailed and allocated finance even when you are willing to pay to get the credit you want for your own freely chosen purposes.

Let's go back to basics and see which is correct—common sense or the Fed.

Inflation is an ongoing, rapid rise in the price level. It results from spending increasing at a faster rate than goods are produced. And spending increases at a fast rate because money is created at a fast rate. So creating too much money is the cause of inflation. Now, where does your purchase of a $500 video recorder fit into the inflationary picture?

At the end of the month, the store which sold the recorder receives $500 from the credit-card bank. If you pay the full credit-card bill, you then have 500 fewer dollars while the store has 500 more, and the total money stock of the community has not changed. Use of the credit card has simply delayed your payment for a few days, and no dollars have been created.

But suppose, alternatively, that you pay only part of the bill—perhaps $200. Then your amount of money is reduced only $200 while the store picks up its $500—the total money stock has risen $300. That appears to be inflationary. But things are not always exactly as they first appear.

For decades, banks have remained loaned up virtually to the maximum, making use of nearly all their reserves. If the bank lends you $300, it will be compelled *not* to lend *others* $300 it otherwise would have loaned. Total loans and total money created will be no larger than they would have been in the absence of your borrowing—*if* bank *reserves* are not created faster than they would have been. And it is the Fed which determines the growth of bank reserves.

Here, then, is the key. What is important with respect to inflation is not the particular *people* who obtain newly created money from banks, nor the particular *uses* of that money. Rather, the critical thing is the *aggregate amount* of newly created money. And the Fed, operating on bank reserves, can control the amount of money.

Why, then, is the Fed divertingly making us suffer ineffectual credit rationing? Good question. But to get the
answer, you require not a midnight economist but a midnight psychiatrist.

The Alleged Misery from High Interest Rates
(January 1980)

Everyone "knows" that interest rates are high these days.
Really? Just what is "high"? Well, look at the marketplace
numbers. The prime rate is over 15 percent; in 1972, it was
less than 5 percent, and in 1977 it was not much over 6
percent. Mortgage rates are about 12 percent, compared to
around 7 percent in 1972 and less than 9 percent in 1976.

Not only are interest rates high by historical standards but
some know also that high rates contribute to inflation. After
all, inflation is a rise in prices, and interest rates are a price,
so one way to combat inflation is to lower rates.

Well, what everyone "knows" can be dangerously wrong.
Interest rates, in fact, are *low*, not high; the rise in recent
years of nominal market rates has been a *consequence*, not
a cause, of inflation; and operating directly on interest rates
in order to lower them will increase inflation and thereby
increase rates.

If you borrow money for a year at 15 percent and prices
rise by 13 percent over that period, your *real* rate of interest
—that is, your rate corrected for inflation—is only 2 percent.
Indeed, it is less than that after taking account of deducti-
bility of interest expenses in calculating income tax. If you
are in the 33-percent marginal tax bracket, your 15-percent
interest obligation is reduced to a net of only 10 percent.

The 13-percent inflation then means you pay a real rate of interest of *minus* 3 percent.

Those seemingly horrendous interest rates are a *result* of inflation, not a cause. The terrible rise in prices in general has pulled up interest rates. There is a close correlation between changes in the nominal marketplace rate of interest and changes in the anticipated rate of inflation. There is nothing surprising in that. Lenders mark up the rates on their loans to offset the effect of inflation anticipated over the loan period. Borrowers understand the game and are willing to pay the bloated rate in the face of corresponding general inflation, which reduces the purchasing power of the dollars which are paid to the lender.

Still, 15 percent is—well—a *big* number, sort of, at least to those of us who are used to interest rates of, say, a civilized 6 percent. How can we reduce interest rates? Easy. Just increase the amount of money. That *does* tend to work for a *short* period. Money is increased by the Federal Reserve buying securities in the open market; increased demand for the securities bids up their prices; and as security prices rise, interest rates go down. However, as the process of money expansion goes on, we thereby add fuel to the inflation. And as prices rise further, interest rates are pulled up still higher. So trying to reduce nominal interest rates by monetary manipulation leaves us with *higher* rates and more inflation, as well.

There is a bit of subtlety in this analysis, but, truly, it is not very complicated. It ought not to be beyond the powers of comprehension of even government officials, monetary authorities, and most others who are overanxious to do good.

Security Prices, Interest Rates, and Inflation
(December 1980)

In mid-November, during the first postelection days, prices of stocks and bonds rose appreciably. A reason commonly given for increases in security prices was purported general "perception of an interest-rate peak."

To be sure, there can be many causes of short-term wiggles in prices of stocks and bonds. When J. P. Morgan was asked for his prediction of stock-market prices, he sagely replied: "They will fluctuate." Still, other things given, anticipated lower interest rates will result in higher security prices.

Interest rates and security prices tend to move in opposite directions, for stocks and bonds are claims to *future* earnings —dividends and interest. How much will buyers pay and sellers require *now* in transferring claims to *future* income? How much must be invested *today* in order to obtain a given income *tomorrow?* Obviously, the answer is implied by the *rate* of return—the interest rate, the discount rate.

If a bond pays $100 each year and the going rate of return on claims of such safety and liquidity is 10 percent, the price will be $1000. One thousand dollars invested in the bond at 10 percent will yield the annual $100 return. Buyers will not pay more than $1000 for the security, and sellers will not accept less than $1000, for in either case the rate of return on the funds would then be smaller than the going, otherwise available 10 percent. But with a *lower* rate of return—say, 5 percent—*more* would have to be invested—$2000—to obtain the $100 return.

Lower interest rates make current investment grow more slowly than do higher interest rates. At *lower* rates, a *bigger* investment is required *now* in order to obtain a given amount of *future* earnings. Lower interest rates increase the *present value* of delayed receipts. The capital markets efficiently reflect today's estimates of the future, with today's decisions incorporating an extended time horizon.

Why might investors suddenly anticipate lower future interest rates—and thus assign higher current prices to long-term assets? Expectations of *interest rates* will be lower if expectations of *inflation* are reduced. Nominal interest rates include an "inflation premium" charged by lenders who must consider the value of the dollars with which they are to be repaid. Less anticipated inflation means smaller inflation premiums. Smaller inflation premiums mean lower interest rates. And lower interest rates are reflected in higher stock and bond prices—and induce more real investment in plant and equipment.

Many grumble about current interest rates being so high—rates which include an enormous inflation premium. Typically, the grumblers also promote policies which directly or indirectly add to inflation. For those of us who are economists but not saints, it is hard to forgive them simply because they know not what they do.

The Fed: Stubborn Faith in False Idols
(NOVEMBER 1980)

In the 1930s, the chairman of the board of the Federal Reserve once cautioned President Roosevelt against putting "undue emphasis" on changes in the amount of money in dealing with the price level and employment. Things have not greatly changed: Rare has been the high officer of the Fed who has unequivocally held to the proposition that money matters much.

One should not infer that members of the Board of the Fed rely heavily on some alternative, largely nonmonetary analysis. A former member has indicated that most colleagues had *no* explicit theory and little of implicit theory, they did not consciously apply *any* theory in voting on policy, and they were much inclined to doubt that any useful theory existed or could be forthcoming. These central bankers, having generally denied the importance of changes in the money stock and rejected monetary and all other analyses, repaired simply to *ad hoc* "reasonableness"—and stabilizing (or deliberately jiggling) interest rates.

The consequences of relying on little more than the instinct of the race have not been invariably happy. During the great inflation of the last decade and a half, increasing pressure from academic and other sources has engendered a degree of Fed sensitivity on money and variations in its amount. There have been instances of suggestion that behavior of the money stock would receive prayerful attention. It is difficult, after all, to ignore completely the close relations between proportionate changes, first, in commercial bank reserve measures and money and, second, in money and the price level.

In October 1979, the Fed announced that it would appreciably modify its policy strategy and procedure, shifting emphasis from interest rates to bank reserves and money. Earlier hopes for rational monetary policy had been disappointed. The hopes of 1979 that the Fed this time understood what it was saying and truly intended to pursue money-stock policy were very high in many circles—despite surly grumblings from Fed spokesmen suggesting that the Fed's monetarist conversion was only partial and grudging, more a matter of reluctant acquiescence than of genuine salvation and rebirth.

Sure enough, thus far the Fed has talked a better game than it has played. From October 1979 through September 1980, the money stock did not rise excessively, but during that year it increased and decreased in highly erratic fashion, with interest rates also gyrating wildly. It is hard to believe that the Fed has tried very hard to implement its own announced new policy centering on the money supply; instead, it has largely continued its pagan worship of the false idol of interest rates.

Some may expect too much from good monetary policy; it is worse to fail to acknowledge the benefits of good policy. Doubtless, in October 1979, some expected too much from the Fed—it is easy to overestimate the sense of the Fed; it is worse to presume that the Fed cannot do better than it has done. At any rate, "monetarism" has been neither established nor disproved over the past year: It has not been tested.

Politics, Inflation, and Interest Rates
(OCTOBER 1980)

A year ago—in October 1979—the chairman of the Federal Reserve Board announced an important change in monetary policy strategy and objective. He indicated that the Fed would pay more attention to controlling money growth in order to subdue inflation and less attention to stabilizing interest rates as an end in itself. This announcement was greeted with general praise and widespread caution—praise, because a slower growing money supply is the only way inflation can be reduced; caution, because pronouncements are cheap to make but expensive to keep, especially in an election year.

The Federal Reserve is supposed to be an independent agency, but it is not immune to political circumstances and pressures. The relatively able members of the board cannot prudently expose the neck or the back to those members of the administration and the Congress whose vision of good economic policy is reelection of themselves or their patrons and whose reelection tactics suggest the subtlety and shrewdness of fighting fire with kerosene.

The president—who has appointed five of the seven current members of the Federal Reserve Board—has now bluntly attacked the Fed for what he terms its "ill-advised . . . strictly monetary approach to making decisions." In a brusque disavowal of the Fed's announced policy, the president said that less emphasis should be given to money growth and more attention to "other factors," presumably the rising interest rates which hover ominously over his reelection campaign.

Despite last year's declaration of the Fed and its recent presidential condemnation, the actions of the Fed belie a dedication to controlling the money supply and thereby reducing inflation. The statements of the Fed have been very different from its actions. And, unhappily, it is the Fed's *statements*, not its *actions*, which the president has attacked.

The Fed has *not* gradually reduced the growth rate of the money stock in order to induce a slow, sustained reduction in the rate of inflation. Instead, the money supply—along with interest rates—has fluctuated widely, falling too abruptly last spring and rising much too rapidly since then. The amount of money is growing far beyond our ability to increase the supply of goods—and, ironically but explicably, the inflation thus irresponsibly generated will pull up interest rates.

Even a president and his secretary of the treasury should be able to comprehend that, as inflation continues, interest rates will remain high. As lenders increasingly doubt the Fed's resolve to control money and inflation, they will increase the inflation premiums they add to interest rates in order to compensate for the ever-cheapening of the dollars which they are later repaid.

Attacks on the Federal Reserve's already weak will to moderate the growth of money can only delay the containment of inflation and make the chore more painful. Meanwhile, nominal interest rates will remain high. But votes may be obtained by condemning the only policy that would eventually control inflation and thereby squeeze the inflation premium out of interest rates.

A *Primer on Inflation*

(O c t o b e r   1 9 8 0)

Suppose you had the ear of the president for just a couple of minutes on the causes and cure of inflation. What would you try to convey? Perhaps something like the following points.

1. The source of inflation is to be found in ourselves (including conspicuously the Federal Reserve), not in our stars —and not in OPEC or monopolistic business or big labor or consumer greed or a diluted work ethic.

2. The level of money prices is a relationship between money expenditure and output. Whatever increases spending or reduces output contributes to inflation.

3. Expenditure is determined by the amount of money and how fast it is spent. Output is affected by a host of things—resources, technology, institutional constraints and incentives. While money can be increased at a rate approaching the speed of light, output increases at a pace resembling that of a tortoise, and velocity of monetary circulation turns heavily on anticipations.

4. In all this, money is strategic: It is subject to policy control which is relatively prompt and precise—even if monetary repercussions are delayed; and many of the other

variables—those pertaining to anticipations and incentives —are partial functions of monetary policy, actual and perceived. Fiscal policy can complicate, but not supersede, monetary policy in the context of inflation control. Government spending and taxing are more important with respect to long-term considerations of productivity and the size and nature of the public sector than to the immediate problem of inflation.

5. Stability and coherence of policy—and thus predictability of market parameters and credibility of monetary authorities—are more important than the particular method of measuring the amount of money.

6. Forget interest rates as either a policy target or a policy variable. If we manage money well, interest rates— and other particular prices—will take care of themselves. Trying to manipulate interest rates will preclude good monetary management.

7. The correlations of money supply with price level and with national output are significant, but repercussions of changes in money develop with lags—variable lags, at that. Patience is required—and the political calendar leaves insufficient time between elections for full market adjustments.

8. Because of adjustment lags, stemming partly from institutional factors (including long-term contracts) and partly from market information being neither costless nor instantly attainable, curtailing monetary growth will reduce the rate of *output* before reducing the rate of price increase.

9. Cutting the rate of money growth "too" abruptly imposes such sharp injury on the community as to endanger perseverance with anti-inflation policy. Cutting money growth "too" slowly not only prolongs softness of the economy but also extends the period of inflation, leaving us with a resulting higher price plateau.

Destroying inflation, Mr. President, requires comprehension and wisdom. It requires also courage and will.

Inflation, Gas Rationing, and Snake Oil

(MARCH 1980)

Many people have been saying peculiar things about alleged benefits of rationing gasoline by use of coupons distributed by government. At least some of them should realize that they are peddling snake oil when they support gas rationing.

Just what is such rationing supposed to accomplish (other than greatly increasing the government bureaucracy)? Evidently, just about everything except cure Uncle Louie's rheumatism. One of the alleged gains from rationing is reduction of inflation.

Inflation typically is considered to be a large, persistent rate of increase in the price level. More generally, inflation is a reduction in the value, or the usefulness, of the dollar.

Now, how would gas rationing reduce, or correct, inflation? The answer may seem straightforward. For rationing is part of a price-control package. There would be no point in requiring buyers of gas to present coupons, along with money, unless there were a shortage of gas—that is, unless people in the aggregate wanted to buy more gas than was available. And there would be such a shortage of gas only if the money price of gas were pegged by government below the free-market level, which would balance demand with supply.

So first we impose an artificial price ceiling. That inevitably creates a shortage. Then we ration the short supply among the competing demanders by a system of coupons. Each coupon would entitle the person to buy a unit of gas at the pegged money price, with the total amount of coupons equal to the total supply of gas.

So what is wrong with that? The gas is distributed through the community at a money price below the level a free market would have generated. A great deal is wrong with that system—and with the analysis which supports it—but, remember, here we are concerned with just the inflation aspect.

First, the price-control/gas-rationing scheme would not produce more gas. On the contrary, over the long pull, at least, it would reduce the available amount. Buying the same or a smaller amount of gas at a lower price reduces money expenditure on gas, of course. But what do people do with that money they now do not spend on gas? Sit on it? Not likely. They will spend it on other things or they will directly or indirectly lend it to others who will spend it on other things. The increased demand for other things will bid up other prices. So the control/rationing scheme for gas would change *relative* prices, with gas prices pushed down and other prices going up, but the price *level*—which is what inflation is about—would not be diminished.

Then why not do the same thing with *all* prices? Put ceilings on *everything* and require ration coupons for distributing everything because there will be a shortage of everything? That idiocy, along with generating other absurd consequences, would diminish the usefulness of the dollar. For no longer could money alone buy *anything:* you would have to pay ration coupons along with money. And reducing the value of money, we should recall, is, by definition, inflation.

Promoting gas rationing as an anti-inflation policy makes even snake-oil selling look good in comparison.

TV's Inflation and the True Story
(SEPTEMBER 1980)

Many rely primarily on television for the news of the day. Thus, they usually learn about inflation from dulcet-voiced and trusted TV reporters. But what they learn about inflation is always inadequate, commonly inaccurate, and uncritically progovernment even when government is the real villain of the story.

Evidence of this misdirection and bias was recently presented in the *Wall Street Journal* by Tom Bethell. Mr. Bethell's examination of every "CBS Evening News" story about inflation during 1978 and 1979 is discouraging—especially when his research reveals that NBC and ABC do no better in reporting inflation news.

TV news stories exhibited nearly total neglect of the one factor responsible for persisting, rapid increases in the price level: excessive money creation by and through the federal government. By continuing to increase the nation's stock of money faster than producers can increase the supply of goods and services on which that money is spent, the government inevitably causes inflation. However, in only 6 percent of all of CBS's reporting on inflation was there even a hint that money had a role in inflation.

What, then, does television news blame for inflation? The implication in most reports was that price increases were the cause of inflation. That analytic profundity is analogous to saying that one's high temperature is the cause of one's fever! As the fever *is* the high temperature, price increases *are* the inflation. The *fact* of inflation is remarkably confused with its *cause*.

This confusion helps to engender a sophomoric bias in television's inflation reporting. By blaming price increases for inflation, television news makes businesses look like grubby subversives. After all, if rising oil or food prices are the cause of inflation, then the solution of the problem is simply to order businesses to keep their prices lower—and thereby also stop profiting excessively. While TV news strongly implies that greedy businesses seeking unearned profits are to blame for inflation, government is generally absolved—an absolution that is the logical outcome of the failure to acknowledge government's role in creating inflation by creating too much money.

Uncritical acceptance by network sophisticates of government press releases about inflation is sobering. This acceptance is surprising as well as disconcerting when one reflects on TV's adversary role in other areas, as manifested during Vietnam and Watergate. The doubt and skepticism which have characterized "investigative" news reporting has generally been replaced by faith in Big Brother—along with hostility toward business—when it comes to presenting news about inflation. As a result, Americans have received distorted, erroneous, biased reports about inflation—a disease which likely will be eradicated only when its real cause, and thus its only cure, is generally appreciated.

Inflation and Garbage

(AUGUST 1980)

Inflation is caused by too much spending relative to available goods. Excessive spending is caused by creating too much money. The correction of inflation is reduction of the growth of money—and thereby of spending—to a rate closely comparable to the growth of commodity production.

But many—politicians, radical activists, social philos-

ophers, even occasional purported economists—profess to
see the world differently. For them, inflation is a phenomenon
largely, if not entirely, disassociated from money. For them,
the sources of inflation are to be found about anyplace other
than the obvious—in government budgets, the balance of
international payments, low productivity, business and labor
monopolization, specific commodity shortages, or, when
all other explanations fail, business greed and consumer
irresponsibility.

Why this analytic myopia and astigmatism?

One conspicuous possibility is *incompetence*. Never under-
estimate the power of inadequate faith in good theory and
stubborn reliance on bad theory.

Associated with incompetence is the *shotgun tactic*. If you
do not sufficiently comprehend a problem to give a clean,
coherent prescription, then advocate *many* things, most of
which will do either no good or actual harm but a few of
which may inexplicably help.

A third possible explanation is a combination of *ideology,
political strategy,* and *sociology.* Those rejecting the monetary explanation of inflation and its cure characteristically
want to be "involved," to wield power. They have a predilec-
tion for bureaucratic command and constraint, for the heavy,
autonomous hand of the state. They prefer *ad hoc* fiscalism
to impersonal monetarism, particularly monetarism applied
by a stable rule. They sometimes find it convenient blithely
to ascribe much inflation to naughtiness in "the corporate
sector," and thus policy supposedly aimed at inflation can
serve also to revamp the private-property, free-contract
structure of the economy. Indeed, inflation is perceived not
essentially as a definable and manageable *economic* problem, certainly not an economic problem amenable to general monetary policy, but a pervading, amorphous *social*
problem, calling for suspension of traditional market rules
and procedures in favor of discretionary political controls.
Lack of coherent theory leads to reliance on inspired "in-

sight"; reliance on inspiration leads to reliance on directly administered control instead of market process, socialistic direction instead of equilibrating mechanism.

Finally, we find *minimization of, and surrender to, inflation*. While monetary changes are conceded to have impact over the long run, that period is deemed too long for policy purposes. Monetary policy, it is claimed, is ineffective in the short run, and, to the extent it slowly becomes effective, it results in unacceptable costs in unemployment and reduced output. So relax and enjoy permanent inflation, an abiding disease less painful than its cure.

The confusions we have reviewed cannot be lightly dismissed as poetry. They are garbage. And if we swallow such swill, we will deserve our resulting miserable fate.

GLOBAL THINKING: TRADE, FINANCE, AND DEVELOPMENT

Trade If You Must—But Stay Away from Foreigners
(July 1979)

Despite romantic notions of the shrewd but honest "Yankee trader," many have doubts about international trade—at least, about imports. Whatever may be the attractiveness of domestic trade, we'd best beware trade with foreigners, who are wily rather than shrewd, devious rather than honest, and who commonly have beady little eyes, set too close together.

The misgivings seem to be supported by the recent United States balance of trade. Beginning in the 1870s—a century ago—Americans consistently sold more goods and services to the rest of the world than they bought. We have had an "export surplus"—until the last few years. And this "import balance" has been substantial. The goods-and-services import balance is commonly, but misleadingly, called an "unfavorable" balance or a "deficit."

Who gains and whose loses in a trade? It *is* true—isn't it?—that what is gained by one trader has to be lost by the other. From where else could the gain come?

No, the gain of the one trader does *not* come out of the hide of the other. If that were the case, why would the loser have participated in this uncoerced exchange?

But how can Charlie and Linus swap assets so that *both* are made better off? There are *mutual* gains when *each* trader prefers to have the things he buys than the things he must sell. Charlie prefers, or puts a greater value on, the goods he *imports* than the goods he *exports* in order to pay for what he buys. But the same is true of Linus. Charlie and Linus are not twins in their preferences. With different tastes and different inventories, they attach different values to goods. And each considers himself to be better off, on balance, by obtaining his imports for the export price he is obliged to pay.

But wait. Are we saying that a person is made better off by what he *imports* (that is, by what he *acquires*) and that *exports* are a price to be paid, a cost to be borne? Precisely. The gains from trade emanate from *imports;* exports are a *drain* of wealth; and the *more* we get per unit of exports, the better.

So we currently have an import balance of goods and services, as we did throughout our first century, a period of great economic growth. When we have an import balance, we obtain, for our own consumption and investment, more of the current output of the rest of the world than they get from us. Faced with scarcity, wouldn't it be nice to have *free* imports, exporting nothing at all to pay for what the rest of the world contributes to our standard of living!

Normally, it seems obvious that a buyer gains from what he *gets*, not from what he gives up—and the *lower* the price he must pay for what he gets, the greater is his gain. But in the realm of international economics, in which we deal with those wily, devious, beady-eyed foreigners, some oddly prefer less to more of good things and to pay higher prices than lower.

Free Trade: A Good First Approximation

(JANUARY 1980)

Everyone does it, but few can adequately explain why. That is true of a number of activities. The reference here is to *exchange,* including *international* trade.

The prospect of mutual gains to the parties in an exchange is a major motivation of economic activity, and the conclusion that mutual gains are typically *possible* lies at the crux of economic theory.

When bargaining units put different relative values on things they possess, there is a range of exchange ratios, or prices, within which trade will benefit *each* unit. Each is made better off by giving up some of what it values relatively little in exchange for things it values relatively highly.

Appropriate *specialization in production* increases the total of goods available for trade and consumption. A producing unit is to specialize in those commodities in which it is *relatively* most efficient, in which it has a *comparative* advantage.

International trade, based on comparative advantage, increases world production and frees nations from the restriction of consuming only their own particular outputs.

But economists do not assert unequivocally that free trade is the only rational commercial policy. Free trade can, indeed, contribute to efficiency in use of the world's resources. But a particular nation in the world economy, like an individual producer in the domestic economy, *may*—under certain circumstances and especially in the short run—gain by appropriate trade restrictions.

Many arguments, of varying degrees of respectability, have been offered in defense of trade barriers. We may temporarily support "infant" industries or protect producers against foreign "pauper" labor. Or supposedly we may improve the terms of trade, stimulate national income, and strengthen the balance of payments.

Still, there are good reasons for hesitancy in advocating barriers to trade even when theory suggests that they might sometimes be appropriate according to certain criteria.

First, there are complex problems in determining when the prerequisite conditions for imposing restrictions actually *exist*, in choosing the most appropriate *mode* of restriction, in determining and administering the optimum *degree* of restriction, and in maintaining *flexibility* to modify the program as conditions change.

Second, the conclusions of abstract and sophisticated analysis may be abused by those poorly equipped and little inclined to appreciate the limitations of the analysis. And they may ignore the possibility that the desired results of curtailed trade can be obtained by preferable alternative methods.

Finally, policies of trade restriction which could yield certain advantages if followed by only the one country may be partially or wholly offset by retaliation. Commercial warfare tends to nullify relative gains among countries and to make every nation absolutely worse off.

In foreign economic policy, as in domestic, the proper presumption favors freedom, mutual advantage, and competitive efficiency. The burden of proof is on those who advocate restrictive, exploitative, and monopolistic deviations. While theory does not yield an unqualified case for free trade, the bias of economists against trade interferences is both powerful and well justified.

Trade and Society: Two and a Half Cheers for Free Trade

(SEPTEMBER 1979)

Trade is the heart of market activity. And the theory of mutually beneficial exchange is a fundamental element of economic analytics. But economists sometimes claim too much for trade theory and too little for trade itself.

Why would there ever be uncoerced exchange unless each participant judged himself to benefit from the trade? Each *does* benefit. In his own estimation, each considers himself better off as a result of the swap. This is possible because preferences differ, and each trader puts a higher value on the things he buys than on the things he sells.

If each participant considers himself a net gainer, it would seem that wholly unrestricted trade is a good thing. In actuality, there are many restrictions—even outright prohibitions—on trade. Most of the restrictions pertain to specified goods—pornography, drugs, weapons, professional services by unlicensed personnel.

To note the *existence* of limitations on trade is not to condone the limitations, of course. Perhaps the community is wrong to limit or ban mutually agreed exchanges, at least between competent adults. College students tend to be enthusiastic free-traders, even (or especially) when naughty pictures or cocaine are among the traded goods. But even the Liberated Generation is willing to curtail contracts between the Department of Defense and the university's nuclear labs.

Few people, if any, are perfectly pure free-traders, admitting absolutely no exceptions to the free-trade rule. And it behooves economists to be modest: To *account* for trade is *not* the same as proving that all restrictions on trade are unambiguously bad by universally accepted criteria.

But we are hardly required stubbornly to assert a wholly unqualified rule of free exchange. Especially when trade may have appreciable repercussions on "third" parties, there must be delimiting "rules of the game."

Within an arrangement of uniform rules and wide options, exchange plays a key social role. It is, in fact, much of the glue which holds the individualistic community together.

People pursue their various personal interests through mutually beneficial trade. They need not be closely acquainted with each other, much less like each other. Indeed, they may bargain against each other in order to obtain maximum personal benefit from the deal. Still, both *do* gain: Each *does* contribute to the well-being of the other. In a world of acquisitive strife stemming from scarcity, mutually beneficial trade coordinates much of our self-centered activity and helps us to live with one another.

It is wise to eschew dogmatic defense of free trade. But the burden of proof should be on those who propose restrictions of exchange. For trade is conducive not only to economic efficiency but to community survival.

Change and Social Welfare: Protection and Production

(February 1980)

Things happen. Some changes help to increase the total of available goods. But even productive changes may leave *some* people worse off. The total pie of output is made larger, but it is sliced in such a way that some are hurt.

Indeed, it seems well-nigh inevitable that any occurrence —an invention, a discovery of resources, a shift in demand, a government policy—will injure some even while benefiting others. Can we compare the losses with the gains so as to determine if aggregate "social welfare" has increased?

Removing import barriers, for example, will help consumers, producers who use imported materials, and, indirectly, our exporters. But it will mean more competition for certain other domestic producers. Since some are hurt, is the policy of freer trade good?

It surely will not do to say that *no* new resources should be used and no shift in resources should be allowed if anyone is thereby harmed. We cannot freeze the economy in its present state throughout the rest of eternity. But are the ongoing changes good or bad, on balance? We cannot decide just by counting noses. Perhaps all the rest of you are benefited by some development, but I am hurt. I deny that your gains are more important than my loss just because you insensitive, uncultivated clods outnumber me.

If there *will* be changes and those changes cannot be evaluated simply by comparing *numbers* of gainers and losers, how can we decide if social welfare has been increased?

Might winners *compensate* losers fully and still end with a net gain? If the change leaves no one worse off, because losers are compensated, and also leaves winners with some of their gain, perhaps social welfare has been increased. Or, if compensation is not actually made, how about giving those who would lose by the change a chance to *bribe* those who would win to forgo the change? But if the bribe would have to be greater than the loss, then the losers are better off to hold still for the change.

In their more esoteric moments, economists like to talk about such compensatory and bribery principles. But pure logic may not adequately represent real-world implementation. Problems of *determining* and *administering* a program of relief for victims of tariff cuts are immense. What are to be the criteria by which to distinguish the firms and workers eligible for compensation? How great is to be the compensation? What is to be the form of the compensation, given over what period?

In addition to questions of calculation and dispensation, there is a prior question of *why* there should be compensation uniquely for this particular case of economic adjustment. Market adjustments are being constantly made in numerous circumstances—including adjustments when tariffs are *raised*. It is not feasible that *everyone* be *wholly* compensated for all possible costs of adjustment.

Perhaps the community would be better off not to fret so much about compensations for changes and to devote its efforts more fully to producing. In a stingy world, schemes of protective compensation are a poor substitute for processes of efficient production.

Imports, Employment, and Efficiency

(NOVEMBER 1980)

Buy American, we are told, for that will protect the employment of United States workers. American consumers—selfishly concerned with their own individual well-being—have not readily followed this advice, as evidenced by large imports of automobiles, clothes, steel, television sets, and other goods. Domestic businesses and workers who increasingly compete with these imports have sought protection by the federal government.

Import restrictions will, indeed, protect *some* domestic employment. If fewer Japanese automobiles can be sold here, then more domestically manufactured cars will be produced—employment in the United States auto industry will be higher.

But there are also negative effects on United States employment which are less visible. By restricting imports, we reduce the number of dollars foreigners earn. With fewer dollars to spend on our exports, such as wheat and computers, foreigners would buy fewer of those goods from us. So production and employment would contract in American export industries and the suppliers of those industries.

While this reduced employment is diffused among many industries which sell some of their output abroad, protected employment is conspicuously concentrated in the specific industries directly sheltered from foreign competition. To the extent that foreign nations retaliate with their own increased restrictions on our sale of goods to them, our loss of employment in export industries would be compounded.

But so-called full employment is not everything. People can have jobs in which they produce far below their potential usefulness. In a world of scarcity, mere helter-skelter busywork is not good enough. Are resources used to maximum effect technologically and to maximum value economically? Operations of free people in open markets allocate resources efficiently.

The very purpose of interferences with competitive market allocation is to use resources in ways which are *not* efficient by community criteria. When the state can be used for protection against competition, private advantage can be gained at the expense of the economy at large.

Industries which require governmental shelter for survival are inefficient in comparison not only with similar foreign industries but with domestic producers in general. For in the absence of restrictions on imports, resources in inefficient import-competing industries would be induced to shift to other production. By market standards, too many people and too much capital are kept in protected industries. They would be used more valuably if they relocated—a relocation which is restricted and delayed by government distorting market signals and diluting market incentives.

By inducing resources to stay where they are less efficient, import restrictions reduce our national output. They subsidize inefficiency. They thereby make us less wealthy and less strong—all in the name of promoting employment. But it is not necessary to trade off efficiency for employment. The real choice—which should not be hard to make—is between efficient employment and inefficient employment.

Foreign Trade and Cold War

(JANUARY 1980)

We are chilled by the winds of returning Cold War. The arena of battle includes foreign trade.

Ideally, each community in the world economy specializes production in accordance with its comparative advantage and then trades. Each thus "maximizes" desired output, and together they achieve an "optimum" distribution of their combined production. The comparative-advantage principle does not assume injury to be imposed upon one's trading partner; indeed, it is of the essence of normal exchange that *both* parties gain. By contrast, a policy of cold war does make infliction of injury, at least in a relative sense, a goal of national policy.

Recent events have reminded us that there can be considerations of power which intertwine the *political* element with the *economic*.

Aside from allowing unrestricted trade with the enemy bloc, two initial alternatives are apparent—namely, *eliminate* such trade or *restrict* such trade.

Presumably implicit in the argument to abolish trade is

desire to avoid *absolute* increase in the strength of the enemy. There may be a "peril point," where the enemy attains a critical level of power, and trade would help them attain that level. This is a dismal basis for policy, for we may expect the enemy's absolute strength to increase over time, even in the absence of trade.

If trade is allowed, we may desire that restricted level of commerce which would maximize our *relative* strength: Trade beyond that level presumably would increase the total gain of each party, but would increase the enemy's gain more.

This approach of limited, rather than eliminated, trade is probably more appealing. But there are difficulties. How does one *measure* power and gains of power? Then, to what extent is maximizing "power profit" a matter of the *nature* of trade—"strategic" versus "nonstrategic"—rather than the *quantity* and *terms* of trade?

When we move beyond dispassionate analysis of alternatives into the realm of implementation of trade warfare, there are additional sobering considerations.

Using commercial policy for power objectives involves Machiavellian manipulation largely foreign to the traditions and aptitudes of the civilized world. Not only is our heavy-handed enemy less constrained than we in psychology, cultural heritage, and governmental organization, but the opposing alliance systems are very different. NATO consists of one superpower—although accounting for less than 40 percent of the group's aggregate gross national product—and fourteen other nations, democratic and highly independent; the Warsaw Pact is seven authoritarian countries, thoroughly dominated by the world's other superpower.

The problem is not one of size or income; the population of NATO is half again that of the Warsaw Pact members, and the ratio of GNP approaches two to one. We have vastly greater overall economic strength.

But are we tough enough? Do we sufficiently hunger for survival as a free people, and sufficiently comprehend our position, obligations, and options, to bear the costs of effective confrontation with a ruthless foe? And will we have the discipline and sophistication to preserve our free society while engaging in a protracted street brawl?

Chicken Little and the Fall of the Dollar

(JULY 1979)

Over the past two years [beginning late 1976] there has been much beating of the breast over the international "fall of the dollar." Such concern would be better reserved for the fall of the sky—or at least of Skylab.

The foreign exchange market is, indeed, a market, where things are bought and sold at a price. The things bought and sold are the world's moneys—dollars, yen, francs—and the price is the exchange rate. If the market is permitted by the Big Brothers of the world to operate freely, with people buying and selling in their own interests, the market is readily *cleared;* no one is frustrated by shortages or surpluses.

In a free market, prices can change; the market is then telling us something about relative values. If prices are *not* permitted to move, the market cannot clear for long, for the world itself *will* continue to change. And a market not permitted to adjust to changing circumstances must be *managed* by law and decree, with arbitrary and discriminatory controls, restrictions, and interventions, administered by the heavy bureaucratic hand.

Unfortunately, the foreign exchange market, like many others, has not escaped the price controllers. The exchange-rate peggers had their way—generating a lamentable series of international monetary crises—for a quarter of a century after World War II, until the early 1970s.

For over six years, exchange rates have enjoyed a modified, or "dirty," float. No longer have they been firmly pegged for indefinite periods, but they *have* been subjected to considerable government manipulation.

During the last two years of this muddled situation, what has happened to the dollar is not exclusively a loss of purchasing power in the international market but also realignment of its individual values: Overall, the dollar has depreciated only moderately, going down substantially in terms of some currencies but up in terms of others.

Where there *has* been an increase in dollar demand for foreign currencies relative to supply of foreign currencies seeking dollars, it has reflected, most basically, growing and reasonable fears, here and abroad, that American inflation will not be adequately curtailed.

Finally, changes in exchange rates benefit some as they injure others: American imports from Japan have been made more expensive, while exports to Japan have been helped; Canadian goods now cost us less, while our exports to Canada are disadvantaged—and United States trade with Canada is as large as our trade with Japan, France, England, and West Germany, combined.

There may be legitimate alternatives to a system of freely floating exchange rates, but the abominable arrangement of indefinitely pegging rates in the absence of an international adjustment mechanism is *not* one of them, nor is the camouflaged tactic of exchange-market intervention by government. And yet, there are those who, astonishingly enough, hunger and thirst to return to the discredited arrangement of rate pegging.

Money, Exchange Rates, Prices, and International Payments

(JANUARY 1980)

Since late 1976, the international value of the dollar has fallen. The fall has not been as dramatic as some have supposed, and the dollar has not fallen in terms of every foreign currency. Still, the average price of the dollar has declined.

During these same years, we have experienced also much inflation, and our balance of international payments has been in deficit. These are not wholly isolated experiences; they did not occur simultaneously by coincidence. There has been a common prime mover affecting the exchange rate, the price level, and the international accounts. Fortunately, this causal variable is subject to adequately precise policy control. That variable is the *money stock*.

The amount of money dominates monetary expenditure, and monetary expenditure dominates the rate of inflation and the condition of the balance of payments as well as the foreign exchange value of the domestic currency. The *money stock*—changes in its magnitude and in its rate of change, anticipations of its changes, and marketplace assessments of the consequences of possible changes—is the most fundamental variable in price level, balance of payments, and exchange-rate analysis and policy.

Exchange rates, let it not be forgotten, are prices; prices which are free to fluctuate are equilibrium-inducing variables in the market; it is advisable to permit such variables to vary.

When prices vary, they are reflecting realities of the market. When the dollar falls persistently and appreciably, we are being told that there is excess money growth—an excess of dollars *created* over dollars *demanded* to be held—and that the excess money growth in this country exceeds the growth of excess money supply abroad. The problem is exacerbated when the rate of excess money growth is not only generally *great* but is characterized also by high *variance*, resulting from stop-and-go, herky-jerky policies of the Federal Reserve.

But do not blame the thermometer for recording the temperature. If the actual value of the dollar falls, we compound our problems by pegging exchange rates and preventing the market price from reflecting reality. Even if we were happily to peg rates at equilibrium levels initially, we could not expect the market-clearing rates to persist forever. In a changing world, adjustment will be a never-ending pursuit of a moving equilibrium. And a market not allowed to equilibrate itself will erratically flounder and ultimately founder through the discretion and decree of overpowerful bureaucrats.

Our proper policy course seems clear: First, implement a stabilizing *"monetary rule"* of a sustained, modest rate of money growth, and, second, set *exchange rates* entirely free to float in equilibrating accordance with the market. The "monetary rule" of a stable, small rate of monetary expansion would put our *domestic* financial house in order; and freely fluctuating exchange rates would be an efficient market-clearing link between the dollar and *other* currencies.

Proper management of the money stock, along with maintenance of a free foreign exchange market, would end the era of inflation and end our concern with the balance of payments. And there is a way to manage money properly— if only we find the will.

Gold, Stabilization Policy, and Exchange Rates
(JUNE 1980)

For several years, there have been no good ol' international monetary crises, which disgraced the world economy for a quarter of a century after World War II. But we have not eliminated equally disgraceful domestic crises.

International financial problems and adjustment are not wholly divorced from domestic problems and adjustment. Indeed, they generally are closely intertwined, with recurring crises in both, or with adjustment in one area obtained at the cost of instability in the other, or—in an ideal which should be attainable—with effective equilibration in both.

During the regime of the International Monetary Fund from the late 1940s until 1973, most of the major economies were committed to pegging exchange rates while also rejecting changes in national income and price levels. But these are the major variables of international adjustment. So there was no mechanism of adjustment, and we were begging for recurring crises. We got what we begged for.

With shifting demands, changing technologies and sources of supply, and different rates of income growth, there will be continuous occasion for economic adjustment. But if no adjustment variables are permitted to vary, the strains must be repressed and camouflaged rather than relieved. The repression and camouflaging include exchange controls, import quotas, and other restrictions on commerce. It should be apparent even to the International Monetary Fund that that is no way to organize the world economy.

The IMF is still with us. But for over seven years [since early 1973], most exchange rates have been partially free to adjust in accordance with market forces. Floating exchange rates have greatly relieved the international financial strains, even though we have had only a "dirty" float of managed flexibility. And there have been considerable swings in exchange rates, as monetary and fiscal authorities around the world have typically done badly in trying to stabilize their respective economies.

All this has rejuvenated a bit of interest in the gold standard. It is proposed to reestablish a firm link between gold and national currencies, and thus to stabilize rates among the various currencies. This kind of arrangement was in its heyday for a generation just prior to World War I.

The gold-standard proposal warrants respectful consideration—in contrast to the disreputable IMF arrangement. Under both the gold standard and the IMF, exchange rates are stabilized. But the gold standard is a genuine *system* of international finance, for it embodies an adjustment mechanism, and the jerry-built IMF arrangement does not.

Still, the gold standard fails to provide for international and domestic balance simultaneously. The stable exchange rates of the gold standard are maintained through accommodation of domestic incomes and prices. The gold tail wags the economy dog.

Closer to the ideal would be freely fluctuating exchange rates combined with appropriate monetary management to maintain a noninflationary but prospering domestic economy. Such a combination is feasible. But if the monetary authorities and legislators continue to be too stupid or too cowardly to do their duty, then the second-best gold standard will look increasingly attractive.

Coping with Risk

(AUGUST 1980)

Under the best of circumstances, the world is a changing place. Many of the major, widely pervasive changes which shape the basic economic context in which we live are largely beyond our immediate control. Preferences and demands shift, sources of supply dwindle or increase, agricultural output is affected by erratic weather fluctuations, technology develops, attitudes evolve, international events—wars, embargoes, alliances, inflations—abruptly shock us.

There is no point in whimpering over the inherent uncertainty of a world subject to changes we cannot preclude by decree. The tide *will* come in, even if we command it to stay out. But it is not inevitable that we periodically get our feet wet. People have, and can further develop, some powers of comprehension, foresight, and prediction. To the limited extent we can understand and anticipate, we have opportunity for marginal control and adaptation—if we permit ourselves to do so.

Given the unavoidable fact that we are in a world of scarcity and of change, the issue is one of how best, how efficiently, to adjust and make do. Are we to adjust through devices of central decree, relying on the wisdom and good grace of Big Brother and his bureaucratic legions, or are we to adjust as individuals in an open society, as free men in free markets?

Consider the foreign exchange market. If foreign exchange rates are left free to fluctuate, they will, as will any price in a free market. By reflecting the market reality of changing demands and costs, the fluctuating rates continuously clear the market. But for most of the period since World War II, rates were artificially pegged for indefinitely prolonged periods. Inevitably, pegged rates created the unending chaos of shortages and surpluses.

Advocates of pegged rates point to the advantages of stability and its predictability. Fixed rates between currencies supposedly comfort people and facilitate planning, thereby encouraging international trade and investment. But the world, be it remembered, is one of change. Imposing stability on a selected variable means that some sort of adjustment will be required elsewhere. Living with uncleared foreign exchange markets led to exchange controls and quotas and other ham-handed restrictions. So traders and investors, instead of efficiently coping with impersonal *market* variables, had to wrestle with the erratic decrees of a necessarily fallible and predictably bumbling bureaucracy. Trade and investment were hardly encouraged by the resulting confusion and frustration.

The lesson has been made manifest again and again in numerous contexts. We must somehow cope with risk in any case. People are sufficiently shrewd and concerned with their own individual well-being to adjust well to market changes. The market informs us of preferences and alternatives. When it is suppressed and supplanted by price controllers and allocators and dispensers of permits, efficiency is lost, and freedom is diluted. No one gains from such foolishness— except Big Brother.

Economic Development, Saving, and Foreign Aid

(SEPTEMBER 1979)

There are no buttons to push which will overnight—or over a decade—transform a poor nation into a wealthy one. If there were, no nation would long remain poor.

The crux of economic development is a substantial and persistent rate of increase in *per capita* income, perhaps with the proviso that the increased output of the community be widely dispersed.

The ever-enlarging flow of goods which provides economic betterment is not manna from heaven, nor is it produced from an unlimited supply of resources. The basic fact of scarcity thus calls for productive efficiency. And efficiency, in turn, calls for devoting some resources to capital goods— equipment, factories, dams, harbors, roads, schools.

For economic development, there must be capital accumulation from invested savings—although development requires much in addition to capital.

There are two domestic sources of capital. One, some resources now producing for current consumption may *shift* into production of capital goods. Second, *total* output of the economy may increase, with the additional output (or some of it) channeled into capital production. In either case, *total output is greater than consumption*. The excess of output over consumption requires saving and constitutes investment.

Whether we accumulate capital through cutting consumption with a given output or through holding consumption constant while increasing output, there must be a gap of output over consumption. The creation of this gap involves saving; and saving frees resources for capital formation. Saving makes productive investment *possible*. Whether the saved resources are then wisely used is another matter.

But suppose that a country consumes all of its own output. Could it not then build up capital with *gifts or borrowing from abroad?* Yes, but that does not change the basic prerequisite of capital accumulation. For with international gifts and loans added to home resources, we now must require that consumption be less than the *whole* of the nation's available resources, foreign plus domestic. Foreign aid and investment will not contribute to capital accumulation if the country uses the foreign resources simply for greater consumption.

Loans and gifts from abroad make *possible* capital accumulation without curtailing consumption. But, alternatively, they make possible additional consumption. It is essential that consumption not rise by the amount of the acquired foreign resources.

The moral is clear: Although assistance from abroad can help a country grow, it does *not* relieve the country from the chore of saving out of total resources available. For the would-be developing country, foreign aid does *not* make possible escape from the discipline of saving. Growing countries must do their own saving.

Foreign Aid and the Requirements of Economic Development

(JANUARY 1980)

Since World War II, the United States and other nations have channeled tens of billions of dollars into economic aid to "underdeveloped" countries. Motivations and objectives of aid have included humanitarianism, political stability abroad, military security for the free world, and economic gain for both giver and recipient.

Aid is not the only, and not even the most important, requirement for growth of Third World countries. A major reason why aid alone is not sufficient is that "capital" alone is not enough for economic development.

One usually thinks of aid initially in financial terms. By giving dollars to country Alpha, the Alphians can buy materials, machinery, and consumption goods. The aid is generally given in money, but the flow of money is converted into a "real" flow of goods and services. Thus, outside aid can supplement domestic saving and give the Alphian economy command over additional resources. But to make effective use of available resources, there are "social" and "political" and "psychological" prerequisites.

Are there enough literate and energetic workers? Are there enough experienced, imaginative, and motivated entrepreneurs? Are there adequate incentives for efficient work and risky investment? Is the government sufficiently "stable" to maintain order and to enforce the rules of property rights? Are the mores and philosophy of the community cordial to "growth" activities? Can population increase be kept under control?

There are significant differences in the degree to which economies effectively seek out and exploit economic opportunities. Attitudes toward wealth differ in different places and times. Even though there is latent interest in increasing productivity, incentives are lacking or are misdirected by a constraining government and its bureaucracy. While a desire for higher living standards is well-nigh universal, the effort necessary to produce much beyond bare subsistence sometimes appears too great, especially for people in a depressing climate and afflicted with disease and malnutrition.

Progressive economies require a spirit of adventure that is inconspicuous among some peoples. To make marked economic advance, there must be substantial freedom from convention and taboo.

Attitudes toward the sacred cow, the kind of work women do, the kind of work whole castes may do, birth control, and willingness to trade with strangers have an important effect on the rate of growth. Development requires risk-takers, and some can hardly afford to take risks; the wealthy farmer can experiment, but the bare-subsistence farmer must stick to established, even though backward, techniques. And no one will risk much in conventional, legal commercial activity when most of any resulting gain will be expropriated by Big Brother.

Everyone wants to be better off in some sense, and nearly everyone wants to be better off in a material sense. But communities differ in their success in coping with a world of scarcity. The reasons for the differences are several. They include massive ignorance, debilitating attitudes and habits, and stultifying institutions. The greatest of these—because it engenders the others—is the yoke of suppressing institutions.

"New International Economic Order": Old Political Machination
(SEPTEMBER 1979)

There has been an escalating confrontation between wealthy and poor nations—between the largely industrialized countries of the Northern Hemisphere and the underdeveloped and sometimes undeveloping nations of the Southern. The confrontation is of the utmost seriousness, although it is widely ignored in this country.

Much of the international debate and many of the proposals by the Third World have been associated over the past five years with a vague notion of a "New International Economic Order"—so called, although few details of the New International Economic Order are *new*, the motivation and thrust are at least as *political* as they are economic, and it all smacks more of discretionary, tactical *machination* than of coherent, efficient order.

The New International Economic Order proposal has supported primarily not creation of wealth but international redistribution of wealth (on a *governmental* rather than *individual* level)—the redistribution being justified as retribution for past sins by wealthy nations. It has promoted also shoring up of autocratic political establishments more than creation of mechanisms for economic reform and development. Lobbyists have advocated a more equal (and thus, allegedly, more equitable) slicing of the world's output pie, even if that would entail a reduction in the size of the pie, and replacement of the efficient market with political manipulation through a United Nations bureaucracy.

There have been partially successful pressures to establish discriminatory trade practices, providing subsidies for exports from the less developed countries. And there have been such policy objectives as raising and stabilizing Third World export earnings, cancellation of their international debts or at least delay of repayments, and aid which is automatic and unconditional.

More basically worrisome than the grab bag of proposals of special arrangements for New Order countries are the premises and orientation lying behind them. The difficulties of such countries, it is aggressively contended, stem solely from oppression and exploitation by advanced countries; discussion is couched in terms of poor countries' rights and wealthy countries' obligations; there is little appreciation of the significance of either the price system or of secure property rights; the essence of the solution is wealth transfer, not wealth production; the means for achieving the solution is to be political direction, focused in the United Nations, not market inducement and allocation. And the demands become more strident as considerations of economic rationality and efficiency evaporate from the discussion.

Such issues may seem esoteric. But it is not shrewd to ignore them. The problems of international poverty and power are massive, the debate is not becoming more coherent, and the conflict poses increasing dangers to world wealth and peace.

The Lessons of Hong Kong

(NOVEMBER 1980)

Hong Kong, the only remaining Western colony of significance, provides an improbably intriguing and possibly
instructive story.

Hong Kong is 5 million people crowded onto a few bar-
ren rocks. The land is not only severely limited relative to
the rapidly growing population, but is of very low quality.
All oil and raw materials and even most water is imported.
No outside development aid is received. Yet this veritable
beehive has prospered since World War II, with real incomes
rising rapidly to a level second in Asia only to Japan, and
it is a formidable international competitor, giving rise to
foreign barriers against its exports.

How to account for this spectacular development into a
major industrial trading and financial center? The answer in
general seems clear: The astounding productivity stems
from aptitudes and attitudes, with public policies and social
institutions giving reign to the one and shaping the other,
providing both opportunities and incentives to people to
improve their conditions.

Running counter to conventional advice from international agencies, national governments, and academic economists, Hong Kong has *not* indulged in active government
development planning, in price-fixing, in trade or capital
controls, or in subsidies and special concessions to either
domestic or foreign producers. It *has* followed policies of
low taxation, minimal government involvement in commercial life, and generally the sale of specific government services at market values—although there are subsidized housing
and cash supplements to the really poor, along with com-

pulsory primary education and extensive public health services.

Some detailed implications for economic development have been drawn by an eminent English economist, Peter Bauer.

One, existence of bountiful *natural resources* is neither necessary nor sufficient for development. There are many instances of growth with few resources—not only Hong Kong but the Low Countries, Switzerland, and Japan. On the other hand, resources have not been effectively used by the American Indians and most of today's Third World.

Two, *population increase* is not an insurmountable barrier to development—the options and motivations of people are more important than their numbers.

Three, economic performance owes much more to the quality of people and their institutional circumstances than to their formal education.

Four, there are misdirecting and stultifying fables disseminated by many development advisers, including the following: ". . . poverty must be self-perpetuating; . . . balance-of-payments difficulties are inevitable in economic advance from poverty; and . . . comprehensive planning and foreign aid are indispensable or even sufficient for economic progress."

In general, Professor Bauer concludes: "The decisive role in economics of personal aptitudes and motivations, social mores and appropriate political arrangements, is the outstanding lesson of Hong Kong. . . . Physical or financial resources are much less important, or even insignificant, compared to personal and social factors and . . . firm but limited government."

Population, Breast-Feeding, and
Dastardly Merchants
(DECEMBER 1979)

Population and its rate of increase greatly affect the standard of living. Over prolonged periods, national *output* does well to grow by 4 percent per year. With high population growth, per-capita income cannot grow much, if at all. Some countries, with population rising at 3 or even 3.5 percent, must run fast, in terms of output, just to stay in the same place.

One of the specific—and most complex—considerations in all this is breast-feeding of infants.

Breast-feeding provides good food for the child; it also provides a considerable degree of temporary protection against new pregnancy of the mother. In so-called Third World countries, where population and health problems are most acute, there has been a *decline* in breast-feeding; for various reasons, fewer mothers breast-feed, with a shorter average period of nursing for those who do.

Since breast-feeding seems both to enhance infant health and to depress the rate of population increase, it would appear that breast-feeding is to be encouraged and that anything which discourages nursing is undesirable. The matter is not that simple.

First, there are alternatives to, and thus costs of, breast-feeding. Breast-feeding requires time, along with the mother's presence and her own caloric intake; it can greatly restrict other activities, including outside work; it can diminish usage of nutritious supplementary commercial foods; and it may reduce use of more reliable, even if expensive, methods of contraception.

A critical question, whch cannot now be given a definitive

answer, is the net effect of breast-feeding on population. To
the extent that breast-feeding biologically reduces the probability of pregnancy, it helps to *reduce* population growth;
but if it also reduces child mortality, it tends to *increase*
population. If breast-feeding is supplemented by commercial infant food, mortality is *reduced*; if breast-feeding is
replaced by commercial food, mortality is *increased*. Prohibiting commercial food—as some have urged—prolongs
breast-feeding, which can *diminish* pregnancy; but curtailing commercial food reduces reliance on modern means of
contraception, which can *increase* pregnancy.

Finally, the *cause* of the decline in breast-feeding also is
uncertain. To what extent is it to be imputed to improved
employment opportunities for women? Or to increased availability of contraceptives? Or to greater supply of commercial infant foods?

Some, with misplaced certainty and misdirected zeal,
insist that the decline of breast-feeding is a catastrophe
and that it has been plotted by evil people seeking their own
gain. They either reject or do not consider the possibility that
mothers rationally adjust behavior in light of such changing
social and economic circumstances as greater employment
opportunities for women and increased availability of contraceptives. Purportedly, they seek to help consumers by
reducing the options of consumers.

Those anxious for a cause must find nefarious plots and
dastardly deeds—and, of course, nothing is more nefarious
and dastardly than people of commerce providing information and alternatives to the community. After all, there is the
risk that if the community likes the alternatives enough to
buy them, the sellers might make a profit!